All But My Life

To Sherry
with friendship -
Gerda 2. ~~~~

Above and left: the pictures of her parents and brother that the author carried in her shoe during the years she was in the hands of the Nazis. *Bottom left*: Lt. Kurt Klein in 1945. *Below*: the author a few months after her liberation.

All But My Life

by

GERDA WEISSMANN KLEIN

HILL AND WANG · NEW YORK
A DIVISION OF FARRAR, STRAUS AND GIROUX

I dedicate this book
—to the memory of my children's grandparents
Julius and Helene Weissmann
Ludwig and Alice Klein
—to the men of the Fifth U.S. Infantry Division
who fought for the ideals I believe in
and
—to my husband with all my love.

G. W. K.

ACKNOWLEDGMENTS

I WOULD LIKE TO SHARE MY JOY AND FULFILLMENT, ON SEEING my book go into print, with the many friends who gave me encouragement.

I should like to mention with special gratitude Mr. Sloan Wilson, who saw this book in its first draft, and whose enthusiasm gave me the courage to show it to the publisher.

My warm thanks to Sarah Stone who typed the manuscript tirelessly for a period of three years, and to Irene Goldberg, Rita Scharf, and Kate Sterman, who all helped with the typing.

PREFACE

As I FINISH THE LAST CHAPTER OF MY BOOK, I FEEL AT PEACE, at last. I have discharged a burden, and paid a debt to many nameless heroes, resting in their unmarked graves. For I am haunted by the thought that I might be the only one left to tell their story.

Happy in my new life, I have penned the last sentence of the past. I have written my story, with tears and with love, in the hope that my children, safely asleep in their cribs, should not awake from a nightmare and find it to be reality.

Part One

Chapter I

THERE IS A WATCH LYING ON THE GREEN CARPET OF THE LIVING room of my childhood. The hands seem to stand motionless at 9:10, freezing time when it happened. There would be a past only, the future uncertain, time had stopped for the present. Morning—9:10. That is all I am able to grasp. The hands of the watch are cruel. Slowly they blur into its face.

I lift my eyes to the window. Everything looks unfamiliar, as in a dream. Several motorcycles roar down the street. The cyclists wear green-gray uniforms and I hear voices. First a few, and then many, shouting something that is impossible and unreal. "Heil Hitler! Heil Hitler!" And the watch says 9:10. I did not know then that an invisible curtain had parted and that I walked on an unseen stage to play a part in a tragedy that was to last six years.

It was September 3, 1939, Sunday morning. We had spent a sleepless night in the damp, chilly basement of our house while the shells and bombs fell. At one point in the evening when Papa, Mama, my brother Arthur, then nineteen, were huddled in bewildered silence, my cat Schmutzi began to meow outside in the garden and Arthur stepped outside to let her in. He had come back with a bullet hole in his trousers.

"A bullet?"

"There is shooting from the roofs, the Germans are coming!"

Then, in the early gray of the morning we heard the loud rumbling of enemy tanks. Our troops were retreating from the border to Krakow, where they would make their stand. Their faces were haggard, drawn, and unshaven, and in their eyes there was panic and defeat. They had seen the enemy, had tried and failed. It had all happened so fast. Two days before, on Friday morning, the first of September, the drone of a great many German planes had brought most of the people of our little town into the streets. The radio was blasting the news that the Germans had crossed our frontier at Cieszyn and that we were at war! Hastily, roadblocks had been erected. Hysteria swept over the people and large numbers left town that day.

I had never seen Bielitz, my home town, frightened. It had always been so safe and secure. Nestled at the foot of the Beskide mountain range, the high peaks had seemed to shelter the gay, sparkling little town from intruders. Bielitz was charming and not without reason was it called "Little Vienna." Having been part of the Austro-Hungarian Empire before 1919, it still retained the flavor of that era. Almost all of Bielitz' inhabitants were bilingual; Polish as well as German was spoken in the stores. In the center of the city, among carefully tended flower beds, stood its small but excellent theater, and next to it the Schloss, the castle of the Sulkowskys, the nobility closely linked to the Imperial Hapsburgs.

Nothing in my lifetime had ever disturbed the tranquility of Bielitz. Only now, when I saw people deserting it, did I realize how close, dangerously close we were to the Czechoslovakian frontier; only twenty-odd miles separated us from Cieszyn.

There had been talk of war for many weeks, of course, but since mid-August our family had been preoccupied with Papa's illness. Mama and I had been away in Krynica, a summer resort, from early June until the middle of August. Papa and Arthur had been unable to accompany us, and we returned when we received a telegram from Papa, suggesting we come home because of the gravity of the international situation. It had been somewhat of a shock to see how ill Papa looked when he met us at the station. His right arm was bothering him and Mama, alarmed, had called the doctor. The doctor diagnosed the illness as a mild heart attack and Papa was put to bed immediately.

The following day two specialists were summoned to Papa's bedside. That same day we received a cable from Mama's

4

brother Leo, who was in Turkey. It read: "Poland's last hour has come. Dangerous for Jews to remain. Your visas waiting at Warsaw embassy. Urge you to come immediately."

Mama stuck the cable in her apron pocket, saying, "Papa is ill, that is our prime concern."

Papa was to be spared excitement and worry at all costs, and visitors were cautioned not to mention the possibility of war to him. Mama little realized the fate we all might have been spared had she not concealed the truth from Papa. Yet on Friday morning, September 1, when German planes roared through the sky, Papa, who had been ill for two weeks, came face to face with reality. It was a tense day. I spent most of it in my parents' bedroom and instinctively stayed close to Papa.

As that first day drew to a close, nobody touched supper, no one seemed to want to go to sleep. Mama sat in a chair near Papa's bed, Arthur and I watched from the window. Horses and wagons loaded with refugees continued to roll toward the East. Here and there a rocket, like blood spouting from the wounded earth, shot into the evening sky, bathing the valley in a grotesque red. I looked at my parents. Papa appeared strange, almost lifeless. The yellow flowers on Mama's black housecoat seemed to be burning. Outside, the mountain tops were ablaze for a moment, then they resounded with a thunderous blast that made the glass in the windows rattle like teeth in a skeleton's head. Everything was burning now. I looked at Mama again. Her soft, wavy, blue-black hair clung to her face. Her large, dark eyes seemed bottomless against her pale skin. Her mobile mouth was still and alien. The red glow was reflected in each of our faces. It made hers seem strange and unfamiliar. There was Mama, burning with the strange fire of destruction, and in the street the horses and wagons, the carts and bicycles were rolling toward the un-known. There was a man carrying a goat on his back, ap-parently the only possession he had. On the corner several mothers were clutching their infants to their breasts, and near them an old peasant woman crossed herself. It was as if the world had come to an end in that strange red light. Then, all of a sudden, Papa spoke to me.

5

"Go, call the family and find out what they are doing."

I went downstairs. I sat down next to the phone with a long list of numbers. I started at the top and worked to the bottom, but there were no answers. The telephones kept ringing and ringing. I pictured the homes that I knew so well, and with each ring a familiar object or piece of furniture seemed to tumble to the floor.

I became panicky. It seemed as though we were alone in a world of the dead. I went back upstairs. My parents and Arthur apparently had been talking. They stopped abruptly.

"Nobody answered, isn't that right?" Papa asked. I could not speak. I nodded. There was no longer any pretense. Papa motioned me to sit down on his bed. He embraced me with his left arm.

"Children," he said, "the time has come when I have to say what I hoped I would never have to say. I remember as if it were yesterday the cries of the wounded and the pale faces of the dead from the last war. I didn't think it possible that the world would come to this again. You believed I could always find a solution for everything. Yet I have failed you. I feel you children should go. Mama just told me that Mr. and Mrs. Ebersohn have asked to take you with them to look for refuge in the interior of Poland. I am sick when you most need my strength. I want you to go, children. I command you to go!" His voice had assumed a tone of authority that I had never heard before. I saw Arthur look up startled at the mention of his girl friend's parents. More than ever he looked like Mama, but somehow he reminded me of Papa as he stood there tall, erect, and determined.

Almost without hesitation, he said, "No! We are going to stay together."

My parents' eyes met. I had a feeling there was relief and pride in their faces.

"I hoped you would say that," Papa said brokenly, "not for my sake, but because I hate to cast out my children to complete uncertainty. I believe that God will keep us together and under the roof of our house."

He dropped back exhausted on his pillows. The effort had

6

been too much for him, and sudden stillness fell over the room. Strangely, all sound ceased outside as well and we noted that the sky was no longer red.

When I awoke the next morning everything was as peaceful as ever. The sun shone so brightly in my room. The fall flowers in our garden were in full bloom. The trees were laden with fruit. In my room everything was as it had always been, and what's more, even Papa was out of bed. His arm was in a sling, but he was up, and it seemed so wonderful I was sure the night before had all been a nightmare. No, not quite, because in my parents' faces I could read something that hadn't been there yesterday.

When we met downstairs for breakfast everybody seemed cheerful. Papa was joking. Mama joined in this seemingly carefree banter. The maid had left to be with her relatives. Papa jokingly asked me whether I wanted the job. Nobody mentioned the war. I walked to the radio and turned it on. There was a sharp click, but no sound. I tried the phone, the lights, but all electricity was off. In a way that was good. There was no contact with the outside world. It was a wonderful, peaceful Saturday. But evening brought fury to the end of that last peaceful day. Sporadic shooting started from the rooftops, an attempt at delaying the enemy while our army retreated to Krakow. We looked for shelter in our cellar and sat there through the night. Toward morning the shooting stopped altogether and the vehicles of the Polish army ceased to roll. We came up from the cellar for a cup of tea in the living room. At I sat down on the couch near the window I could see the people outside in an obviously gay and festive mood, talking and laughing, carrying flowers, and everywhere the clicking of cameras.

"Mama, look," Arthur said. "Do you suppose—?" and he broke in the middle of the sentence, not daring to say what seemed impossible.

"No," Mama answered, and then Arthur pulled his watch out of his pocket, the roar of a motorcycle broke the stillness of our home, and his watch fell to the floor. It was 9:10 A.M.

I looked out again. A swastika was flying from the house across the street. My God! They seemed prepared. All but us, they knew.

A big truck filled with German soldiers was parked across the street. Our neighbors were serving them wine and cakes, and screaming as though drunk with joy, "Heil Hitler! Long live the Führer! We thank thee for our liberation!"

I couldn't understand it. I didn't seem to be able to grasp the reality of what had happened. What are those people doing? The same people I had known all my life. They have betrayed us.

The breakfast tea turned cold on the table. Papa and Mama looked down at the floor. Their faces were blank. Papa seemed so old, so gray. He had changed so much.

I smelled something burning. A hot coal from the big green tile oven had fallen through the grill onto the carpet. I remembered a similar accident a year or two before and Mama had been terribly upset. Afterward she had turned the carpet so that the burned spot was under the couch. This time I wanted to shout a warning, but my throat froze when I saw my parents staring at that coal. They saw the carpet burn slowly, but they didn't seem to care. Finally, Papa got up and with his shoe carelessly shoved the coal back to the grill. Nobody spoke.

I looked out the window and there was Trude, a girl I had known since childhood. She and her grandmother lived rent-free in a two-room apartment in our basement in return for laundry service. Now I saw her carrying flowers from our garden, white roses of which we had been so proud because they bloomed out of season. She handed them to a soldier, breaking her tongue with the unfamiliar German, "Heil Hitler!" The soldier reached for the flowers, but somebody offered him some schnapps. He took the glass instead, the flowers tumbled to the dusty road, the boots of the soldiers trampled on them. I started sobbing, crying, releasing all my emotions and anxieties in that outburst. Arthur jumped over to me, put his hand over my mouth. "Are you crazy? Do you want to give us away?" But I did not hear him. The tears felt so good. He finally slapped me. "Think of Papa's life. If they hear you crying—" I couldn't stop. He pulled me down from the couch, dragged me over the carpet, and up the stairs with Mama holding my mouth. They put me to bed, where I cried into the pillow until, exhausted, I fell asleep.

Early in the afternoon the drunken, jubilant mob was still celebrating its "liberation" and hoarsely shouting "Heil Hitler." Papa and Mama smiled. Their smiles seemed more painful to me than my screams and tears, and I learned at that moment that I must not always cry when I wanted. I realized that we were outsiders, strangers in our own home, at the mercy of those who until then had been our friends. Although I was only fifteen I had a strong feeling, more instinct than reason, that our lives were no longer our own, but lay in the hands of a deadly enemy.

Mama tried to maintain the pattern of our life, even on that fateful Sunday. She prepared dinner and we sat down as usual, but no one could eat and when the food was cleared away we sat in silence. Arthur got out books about the war of 1914 and looked up data about its development, but Papa said, "This is a different war. This one cannot possibly last four years. Four weeks, perhaps four months at most."

Early in the evening, when the shouting of the drunken mob had died away, there was a knock at the door and a whispered, "Mrs. Weissmann." It was our neighbor Mrs. Bergmann, the mother of my friend Escia. She looked pale and shaken as she relayed the news that during the afternoon several Jews had been rounded up in the streets, locked in the Temple, and the Temple set on fire.

"Men had better stay out of sight," she whispered.

Papa and Arthur exchanged glances. Mama's eyes widened and she pressed her lips together. But Mrs. Bergmann told us too that England and France had declared war on Germany that morning. She stayed only a few minutes. When she rose to leave, Mama saw her to the door and I followed them. Before they opened the door Mrs. Bergmann and Mama listened a while, then finally Mrs. Bergmann turned the knob and through a tiny opening glanced up and down the street before she slipped out.

9

We sat a while longer in silence, none of us wanting to go to bed. That was the first evening in my life that I saw Mama without needlework in her hands. She just sat and stared into the fire. After a while she got up, outwardly calm and regal, and said, "Go to bed, children. We all will need rest and strength."

Her words climaxed the first day under German rule.

The next morning, I was in the kitchen with Mama when Mrs. Rösche, one of the neighbors, came in with another woman and asked for our Polish flag.

"The flag?" Mama asked. "What for?"

"To make a German one, of course. It's really simple. You leave the red stripe as it is, cut a circle out of the white, and put a black swastika on it."

Mama grew pale. At first she looked for our flag in places where she knew she wouldn't find it. Finally she brought it forth, knowing that she would have to sooner or later. Mrs. Rösche asked if Mama happened to have some black ribbon. She said she didn't. The other neighbor produced a piece. She told us it was good ribbon—that it would last for many years!

Those two neighbors spent all morning sewing a Nazi flag to hang from our house. Why they did it, I'll never know. Perhaps they felt that we would be inviting trouble not to display the flag.

When the flag was finished, they asked, "Where's Arthur? He is big and strong. He could hang the flag."

Mama sent me to call him. I found him in his room, lying in listless apathy. When I told him what was asked of him, he shouted,

"Are you all out of your minds? Never! Never! I won't do it. Tell them that I am gone, tell them that I am dead, tell them anything!"

And so Mrs. Rösche and the other woman struggled to fasten the flag through the little hole in the roof. I couldn't bring myself to look out of the window for days, but when I did, there was the blood-red symbol of the tragedy that had engulfed us.

Chapter 2

IT TOOK THE GERMANS EIGHTEEN DAYS, EIGHTEEN SHORT DAYS, to conquer Poland. No hope was left that our troops could send the enemy reeling back. Krakow fell, then Warsaw, and the Germans still advanced without opposition. We waited now only for the liberation that would come from France or Russia, or, as a few optimists dared hope, from England or America. Many stories were circulated about the brutal methods which the Nazis employed in the East. Some Jews were coming back from areas overrun by the Germans. After what they had witnessed they felt it was safer to return to their homes. Some came back to find their houses empty, most of their valuables gone, others to find their homes occupied by former maids who graciously permitted the owners to spend a night or two in an attic or basement, perhaps let them take some of their clothes, and sped them on their way.

Having been permitted to stay in the comfort of our own home, we did not have to worry, for the time being at least, about shelter. Papa's next concern was his business. He was part owner of a factory that processed furs. Often he spoke of wanting to go to the factory to see what had happened to it, yet he knew as we all did that this would be too dangerous. We heard tales of people who went to their stores or factories only to find SS troops or the Gestapo there. They never returned. Bielitz was primarily a textile center, with an international reputation for the fine fabrics it produced. The standard of living was higher than almost anywhere else in Poland because of the large number of skilled mill workers. There were warehouses all over town filled with fabrics. In the wake of the Wehrmacht, German officials appeared and requisitioned them all.

We lived in the outskirts of Bielitz in a large, comfortable house that was over a hundred years old. Although the upstairs had been remodeled when my grandparents were married, there were still uncovered beams in the kitchen ceiling, a wide hearth, cracked stone front steps, old-fashioned windows with latches, and, in place of central heating, large tile ovens in the rooms. I loved my home because it had so many mysterious nooks, a cold earthen floor in the cellar (which I pretended was a dungeon), a rambling attic through which the wind howled, and best of all, a large garden and orchard. Part of it ran along the side of the house and joined a courtyard where there were several shacks in which we stored wood and kept chickens. Behind the house was the real garden, running along a slope, for all of Bielitz was scattered over the foothills of the Beskide mountains. Our garden had well over a hundred fruit trees, some of them very old, countless berry bushes, and a garden house surrounded by lilacs. At the edge of the garden ran a tiny brook. This was the home I had known and loved all my life.

It was not long after the whole population had been forced to register with the police that Jews received notices to turn in all gold, automobiles, bicycles, radios, even fountain pens. At first it did not seem to matter, because we were still at home, but life soon became more and more difficult. One always had to keep vigil at the window, and when a car stopped in front of the house, or the dreaded green uniform approached the front door, Papa and Arthur would hide in a closet.

At first they refused to be intimidated. Papa protested over and over again, "I didn't do anything to anybody. I am not afraid."

But Mama would just look at him, and that was enough. He would hide until we would sound the all-clear. Many times we heard of instances when German soldiers came to a house for information, and if a man happened to open the door, took him along; frequently that was the last the family ever saw of him. We seldom sat down to a meal without interruptions of some kind. We became tense. We learned to distinguish the noise of the hateful boots at great distances.

About the beginning of October there was a timid knock at the door. It was not the ominous thump of the Gestapo, but a hesitant, tired signal. It is strange how many feelings a knock can express, if you listen carefully. It was my father's sister Anna with her daughter Miriam, who was my age.

Aunt Anna embraced my father, and cried, "My brother, my brother, how I thank God that He kept you for me. I am alone."

Between sobs she told us her tragic story. Two days before the Germans entered Bielitz, she, her husband, and two children had boarded the train in an attempt to reach Warsaw. Day and night the trains had been attacked. She told us how the engine had run out of water, and how the passengers had formed a human chain to pass along cups, bottles, and pails, filled with water for it while the dead and dying lay all about them. There were nights when they had crouched beneath their seats, bombs and bullets flying over their heads. During one such attack Aunt Anna had fainted and her husband went to get some water to revive her. While he was gone a bomb fell. When she regained consciousness someone told Aunt Anna he had been torn to shreds. He never came back. Finally the locomotive was hit, and the train went no farther. Aunt Anna and her children got off and wandered on foot toward the East. It was a hot, oppressive night, she recalled. The moon was bright, and they saw what seemed like thousands upon thousands of shooting stars. They and others who were with them took it as a good omen, and went on through a sandy little desert near Kielce. They moved steadily through the night toward a forest, counting on it to be their salvation after the heat, but there they met a closed line of German guns and troops. What they had mistaken for shooting stars had been German paratroopers. Now they had their first direct experience with the Nazi methods. First, the men were segregated from the women. Thus, just after having lost her husband, Aunt Anna saw her nineteen-year-old son taken away. The men were lined up, and every tenth one was shot. The rest were marched toward the forest. Aunt Anna ran toward the scene of the massacre to find her son. A few bursts from a machine gun quieted the moanings and cries of agony, and then the footsteps of the disappearing German column echoed away in the hot wind.

Soon there was nothing left, until the voice of fifteen-year-old Miriam beside her cried gently, "But Mama, I want to live."

On foot, by horse and buggy, and by car, they came back to Bielitz. First Aunt Anna went to her home, but found a German family living there. She passed the houses of friends and relatives but found them empty. She had hardly dared to hope that we would still be at home. Finding my father gave her new hope. They had no clothing, except the garments they wore during their flight. They had no food, no money. Everything was lost. They stayed with us, of course.

The next morning, another hesitant knock was heard at the door. It didn't seem possible when Aunt Anna saw her son on the threshold! She could hardly believe it was true. Such happiness is rarely experienced in the ordinary span of life. Yet it was David, haggard and hungry, but alive. He told us his part of the story. When he was taken into the woods, his group stumbled onto a small company of Polish soldiers who had been hiding. During the confusion and shooting, he had climbed a tree which still had a lot of leaves, and hid there until the Germans led their prisoners deeper into the woods. A short while later uncounted shots took the lives of many. David waited in his secret roost until nightfall, and then started his journey back, walking mainly by night, resting or sleeping in wooded areas or stables by day, until he reached our home.

Days passed like a dream, like an illness with no end in sight. We lived looking forward from one day to the next, glad when a night had passed and the Gestapo hadn't knocked at our door.

A great change came over Arthur. He grew restless and tense. Books, which normally occupied him day and night, lay untouched. He would not leave his room. He didn't shave.

14

He didn't dress. He hardly touched his food, and I doubt if he slept.

One morning, when the war was almost six weeks old, Arthur announced at breakfast that he wanted to go to the center of town. We all knew that this was a dangerous venture. My parents realized that Arthur wanted to find out whether Gisa, his girl friend, had come back from the interior of Poland, whither she and her parents had fled the day of the invasion. They raised no objection to his going, told him to use his own judgment. He shaved and left, saying only, "I am going now."

Papa and Mama watched from behind the curtains as he went down the street. They trembled and caught each other's hands when they saw him pass a German soldier. They breathed easier when the soldier paid no attention to him. We waited anxiously, wondering how long it would take Arthur to come back, making allowance in case Gisa should have returned. I saw Papa swallow pills twice during that interminable wait. I watched Mama half-heartedly start several chores. We did not speak about Arthur or his mission but were painfully aware that each minute might spell tragedy for him.

Finally, after what seemed an eternity, we saw him coming slowly toward the house. He went up to his room without speaking.

I went up to see him a few minutes later. Gisa's picture was on his night-table. She was a lovely girl with big dark eyes and blond hair. She smiled in that picture, but as I stood looking at it her smile suddenly seemed sad.

I had learned not to ask questions, so I stood quietly until Arthur spoke as if to himself.

"The dog lies dead in front of her house."

"Rolf?" I asked.

He nodded.

"I wonder," he said after a while, "whether he died from hunger, or was killed, or whether he followed Gisa and her family, and lost them along the way and came back to die."

Chapter 3

In mid-October a notice came in the mail ordering men from sixteen to fifty to register. We were just sitting down to lunch when it came. Mama's eyes widened as she let her glance travel from Papa to Arthur. Her lips tightened as if suppressing a cry. Papa began to pull at his mustache with his healthy hand. Arthur and David looked at each other, then lowered their eyes and pretended to be preoccupied with their food. Aunt Anna was putting salad on Miriam's plate. Her hand quivered, the lettuce spilled. And I could think only one strange thought: that I had not realized how pleasant luncheon had been the day before.

Finally Arthur said quietly, "I have heard about it. I know what happens. Young men are taken deep into Poland to rebuild what was destroyed by the bombs." There was a quiver in his voice.

Mama, Papa, and my Aunt Anna were pale as David added, "We will leave the day after tomorrow."

So they had known, but had remained silent. I was surprised that Mama did not cry. She merely paced the floor, her lips pressed together. Papa's arm hung heavy in its sling. Aunt Anna said nothing.

Later that afternoon I went up to Arthur's room. He was looking through his books, from time to time glancing out into the garden, where the first autumn wind was whining through the trees. Leaves were piling up on the grass. The day seemed exceedingly short.

Neither of us talked much. Arthur tried several times to start a conversation but when we tried to joke our words seemed stilted, unreal. Finally, we fell silent.

I didn't know my parents any more. I didn't know my

16

brother. I had never seen them silent. I would have preferred that everybody cried, that my parents cried, that the walls of the house cried, that it should rain and thunder. But this deadly silence was worst of all. The silence forced itself into my being, filled me with fright and wonder.

When Arthur and David went to register the following morning I accompanied them. Boys and men, many of whom we knew, stood in line, registered, got numbers.

One of the boys, a classmate of Arthur's, told us that after registering, many boys from other towns were taken to camp and killed.

"Nonsense," Arthur said to the boy, "what foolishness people try to invent."

On the way home, we paused where the Temple used to stand. There was a mass of charred wood and bricks and scattered glass. Only one pillar stood whole and proud, strong in the autumn wind. We crawled over the debris, not caring if anyone saw us or not.

Arthur picked up a couple of pieces of glass and handed me one. He put a strong arm around me and said, "Look at that pillar. It is safe. We have to have faith. Never forget it, Gerda."

I lost that little piece of glass somewhere in the woods of Czechoslovakia, many years later, but I never forgot my brother's words.

Aunt Anna, David, and Miriam had left earlier to spend the night with a family in the apartment house where they had lived before the war. The family had been fortunate enough to remain in the building and had spoken to the people who now occupied Aunt Anna's apartment, hoping that when they would see David leaving they might give him some of his belongings to take along. Aunt Anna thought she might try this, but promised to be back in the morning.

So we went home that sad day, October 18, 1939. We went to Arthur's room. I sat down in a chair near the window and watched him. He sat at his desk, cleaning out drawer after drawer. Some papers he read and put back carefully.

I was proud of my brother, although at times I resented girls who sought my friendship because they wanted to meet him. I often saw their envious glances when I was with him and was used to the question afterward: "Who was that dark, handsome boy with you?" I was always glad and proud to say, "My brother." For Arthur had something open and likable about him, and he had a frank, flashing smile that no one could resist. He made friends easily, old people and young alike. His wit and intelligence matched his appearance. Whatever he did, he did extremely well. He had received a master's degree in chemistry that June. In another year he would have earned his doctor's degree. He wrote for a prominent publication, *The Literary Guide*. Just for the fun of it, he once started painting. One of his first pictures won a prize. I admired him. I often envied him. I remember him best sitting at his desk that last afternoon, looking through the mementos of his youth.

Finally Mama called us for dinner. It was as it had been all those years, those wonderful years of our childhood, when we played in our warm room, the autumn wind howling in the garden, the fire crackling in the dining room, all of us going there to share our delicious warm meal. But this was to be the last supper we would ever have together.

Arthur carried the burden of conversation that night. Lingering over our tea, I could see my parents' desperate wish to prolong this evening as much as possible.

Finally Papa said, "You had better get to bed early tonight."

That was the closest reference to the parting in the morning.

I couldn't sleep that night. The wind was still whining in the branches of the trees. Somewhere in the distance a dog barked pitifully. I tiptoed to Arthur's room. He was sound asleep. I remember sitting carefully at the foot of his bed, looking into the darkness, and there I fell asleep. The next thing I remember was Arthur's voice, "Please, Papa, let her sleep. She is still a child."

I wasn't sleeping, I heard it all. I got up and ran down to the kitchen. It was still dark outside.

Mama was busying herself with breakfast. She told me to put on my coat and gave me some money to try to get some rolls for Arthur. I was to find Zeloski. Zeloski had been our

18

gardener and general handyman. Now he worked for a bakery and delivered rolls and bread in a huge basket.

It was pitch black outside, and a fine cold rain was falling. There was a light in Arthur's window. He apparently hadn't finished his last-minute packing. And there was a light downstairs in the kitchen. The rest of the house was dark, and so were all the houses on the street, except for a few lights in kitchen windows.

Then I spotted Zeloski coming down the street. I ran to him. He was hard of hearing. I pulled his sleeve.

"Zeloski," I said, "I want some rolls for Arthur. He is going away, you know."

"He is going away?" he asked, stupefied. Zeloski had always adored Arthur. Whatever Arthur did was right in Zeloski's eyes. Whenever Arthur and his friends trampled on flowers and broke bushes while playing Indian, Zeloski always found a way to shift the blame from Arthur, even if it meant putting it on me.

He gave me some rolls, and I gave him the money.

"Too bad," he said, "the boy was so bright."

Shaking his old head, he started shuffling on his way.

"What do you mean 'He was'?" I shouted at him.

"You won't see him again," he said.

I started shaking his arm.

"Zeloski, are you crazy? You are an old fool."

Some of the rolls spilled from his basket. He shook his head sadly.

"I hate you!" I screamed at him, and kicked some of his rolls toward the gutter. Then I ran toward the house.

Papa, Mama, and Arthur were sitting at the table. I put the rolls in the bread basket. Mama poured Arthur's cocoa. I sat down at my place. I don't recall what they were talking about, but when Papa looked around, I felt that he was taking in the picture of all of us at the table. He wanted to say something but his voice broke. With an abrupt movement, such as I had not seen since he had become ill, he got up and ran out. Mama indicated with her eyes that I should follow him, and

19

she continued talking to Arthur, who appeared to ignore the incident.

The scene in the hall upstairs was heartbreaking. Papa stood close to the door of Arthur's room looking in where his clothing was carelessly thrown around. He leaned against the wall, his healthy arm held over his eyes. Thus bent, he hardly seemed the six-foot man who had used to walk so erect. How gray his brown hair had turned. Then I saw big tears running down his cheeks.

It was the first time in my life that I had seen my father cry. He was crying without a sound. Until then, my big strong father had been the ultimate power, granting or denying everything in my life. Now he was as helpless as I.

An overwhelming feeling of pity and pain swept over me. I embraced Papa. The touch of my arms made him shiver, and a suppressed and terrible sobbing cry rose from his throat, a cry which I will never forget, which had no resemblance to the human voice; it sounded rather like the cry of an animal when it has been stabbed and is dying. I was to hear that cry later, many times, when people were being killed.

"Oh, Papa, Papa!"

He motioned me away.

I went back down to the kitchen. Mama was buttering a roll for Arthur, and they were talking. After a while Papa came in, and Arthur looked at the clock. It was getting close to six. Oh my God, how fast the time had gone! There would be another ten minutes before he would have to go. Then we would have to say good-by; there was nothing now to prevent it from happening. The minutes stretched to eternity. I had a desire to get it over with as soon as possible.

Finally Arthur got up. He put on a short jacket over a navy-blue sweater, and lifted his knapsack, then set it down and walked over to Papa. He opened his mouth to say something, but then remained silent.

Papa rose slowly. First he raised his healthy arm, and then, with incredible effort, he moved his half-paralyzed right arm in a crude embrace. It was almost a miracle that he could bend that arm. We knew it caused him pain almost beyond

20

endurance. He put his left hand on Arthur's black hair, then with a quick motion, his right hand. It was for us children a familiar and comforting gesture.

How pale his hands were now, but they did not tremble. Papa's glassy eyes looked up. Then he pulled Arthur toward him. His lips pressed Arthur's forehead.

"God be with you, my son!" He took Arthur's shoulders, and pushed him toward Mama's embrace. Her small, white, fine hands rested a moment on his head, but she was smiling. I never saw her look so strong.

Arthur lifted both her hands to his lips, and returned her smile with one of his gayest, saying, "Maminka," which he used to call her when he was a very small boy.

Mama said quietly, "It is an easy good-by, my child, because I know you will be back soon." Still smiling, she kissed his forehead.

Then, with a quick, almost relieved gesture, Arthur turned to me, lifted me up, kissed me on both cheeks, and said gaily, "It will be a pleasure not to have you always trotting behind me."

That broke the tension. I caught his arm, and stood on tiptoe, trying to swallow my tears. He stooped down to me and whispered quickly, "Be strong, they will need you."

Then he quickly ran down the steps to the sidewalk.

We all followed. We wanted to go with him to the station, but he turned around.

"Please," he said, "do me one favor. I don't want anyone to come."

No, he didn't want us to see how he was going to be locked up in a cattle car under the whips of the Nazis. He started walking very fast down the street. It was just getting light. Then he slowed down. He stopped. I knew he wanted to turn around and to see the picture of his family in front of his house and wave a last good-by, but he didn't. He hesitated a moment, but didn't turn around. Instead he started to walk faster and faster toward the unknown.

Chapter 4

PAPA TOUCHED MAMA'S ARM SOFTLY FOR A MOMENT AFTER Arthur was out of sight. I followed them back into the house. Nobody spoke. Papa and Mama found it difficult to be together that day.

Papa withdrew to the Bible. Aunt Anna, when she returned, went into her room and closed the door. Mama put on a coat and shawl over her head and went out. I followed her to the cemetery, a few minutes' walk from our house. It was on a hill fenced in by a high brick wall. Some parts were very old with tombstones dating back to 1700. Mama walked slowly along the gravel path, her steps quickening as we approached the section where our family was buried. Black marble tombstones with faded inscriptions rose from behind the shrubbery. I saw one fresh inscription gleaming in gold: "Julie Mückenbrunn." That was the grave of my mother's mother. She had died a year and a half before. I saw Mama put her head on the stone, as she must have put her head against her mother's breast many times as a child. Completely engrossed, she muttered, "My child . . . my child . . . oh mother!" and started to cry bitterly. I could not catch all she said. It was a strange, quiet soliloquy, yet I felt that a voice was screaming within her, "Oh God, bring him back to me."

Then Mama stood upright and addressed the stone in a different manner.

"You are lucky, mother. If only I could be certain that someday my children would be standing on my grave."

When we reached home, I went straight to my room. There was no use to try to make conversation. Everyone had the desire to keep to himself.

Idly, I started looking through a photograph album. I came across pictures that had been taken during the past summer.

I lay down on my bed, looked up at the blue ceiling, and made a wonderful game of remembering the past, using these fragments to weave dreams for the future. No present existed. It was a wonderful escape. For instance, there was Krynica, where Mama and I had gone in the summer. It was an elegant summer resort, about three hundred kilometers southeast of Bielitz. I recaptured the thrill, the excitement of the preparations, the dressmakers, the fittings, and finally the journey. I remembered it all so well. I had loved Krynica from the start. Our hotel faced the Carpathian mountains on one side, beautifully landscaped gardens on the other. There was a wonderful swimming pool, tennis courts. If only Mama hadn't insisted on going to the promenade concert every afternoon, which meant being properly attired with hat and stockings. How I hated it! I remembered too the open-air concert we attended the day before we left. It was a lovely August afternoon, white benches, lovely flowers, happy people, deeply tanned men and women in colorful summer frocks. I was so proud of Mama. She looked beautiful in a navy and white print dress and wide-brimmed white hat. The orchestra played Viennese waltzes. She always smiled at those waltzes. They brought back her girlhood, for once at a ball in Vienna she was chosen Waltz Queen.

Suddenly, a slim young man ran up to the pavilion, pushed the startled conductor aside, and called out:

"Are all you people crazy? Are you unaware of what's happening this very hour?" Pointing toward the silent mountain peaks where Poland's frontier met German-occupied Czechoslovakia, he continued, "From up there disaster is coming at any minute. There is going to be a war, and you are sitting here dressed up, listening to pretty music. Go home, take up arms. Let us stand against the enemy!"

His white shirt was open at his neck, his sandy hair fell on his forehead, his hands were restless, his voice possessed a strange quality of power and conviction. Soon the police arrived and the young man was taken away.

"A maniac," the people muttered. "He will be locked up for disturbing the peace." But most everyone left the concert.

Mama had thought that we should go back to Bielitz at once but I urged her to stay on for another week as we had originally planned. Mama was still undecided when in the morning the telegram from Papa arrived saying that he wanted us to come home. We packed hastily and left on the next train.

As we passed close to the Czech border I wondered fleetingly if there would really be a war. The forests were green and looked so peaceful, the wheat stood ripe and rich in the fields, and peasant children waved to the swiftly moving train. But as we stopped at larger stations the thought of war came back again. Baggage was piled high on platforms, crates and trunks marked "Warszawa" in large letters could be seen everywhere.

In the early evening we arrived in Bielitz. Papa and Arthur met us at the station. At the sight of them my uneasiness vanished, although I noticed that Papa did not look well. He said his arm was bothering him. Mama was alarmed.

"You look so pale, Julius," she said.

"No," he answered, "it is you who are so tanned."

The house was cool, and I experienced the wonderful feeling of being home again.

Was it the day after our homecoming, or several days later, that Mama summoned the doctor for Papa and that he was put to bed? But I did not want to think of Papa's illness now, or of the coming of the Germans, or of Arthur's going away. How much easier to think of all that had happened before the war, of my school, a private girls' high school run by sisters of Notre Dame, where we were required to wear demure navy-blue uniforms with light blue piping, brown rayon stockings, and simple shoes. Only during the summer vacation could we wear the clothes we wanted. Yet the austere uniforms did not bother us in the least. They only made our summer clothes seem brighter, more desirable.

These thoughts were a wonderful escape from the present. Comfortingly, the past was unwinding before me, my wonderful childhood, safe and sheltered, too sheltered perhaps for what the years ahead were to bring, but full of lovely memories from which to draw strength.

Days passed and stretched into a week without news from Arthur. Nobody had heard from any of the boys. Daily I went to the Kultusgemeinde, the Jewish Community Center, to find if word had been received from anybody. During the second week after Arthur's departure, when I had come home with yet another negative answer, Mama told me that Papa was resting and that Mr. Pipersberg was with him. That immediately put me into a better mood for I adored Mr. Pipersberg. He was of medium height, had wavy gray hair, a small, clipped mustache, friendly, sparkling blue eyes, and an infectious smile. He was Papa's close friend and business associate. He was a widower with married children, so he now devoted himself to the factory. Charming and intelligent, he had traveled all over the world, knew many amusing stories, and always had one to suit any occasion. He spent much of his time in our house and on holidays always brought us lovely gifts.

Mama told me to go upstairs and announce that lunch was ready. Papa and Mr. Pipersberg were engaged in a serious talk when I entered, discussing the risks involved in going to the plant. It was too dangerous, they realized, and finally they decided that neither of them should attempt it for a while.

The afternoon passed pleasantly. When Mr. Pipersberg got ready to leave, I decided that I would go with him part way and see Ilse, one of my friends. It was less dangerous for a girl of my age to venture into the streets than for a man. Ilse Kleinzähler was one of my best friends. Her father had gone with the same transport as Arthur, and she, her mother, and her four-year-old sister, Kitty, had gone to live with her grandparents. Unfortunately, the grandparents lived on the other side of town and we did not see each other as often as I should have liked.

As we left the house, Mr. Pipersberg said, "I am going to the factory."

"I thought you decided against it," I said.

"Oh, I am not going inside," Mr. Pipersberg replied, "I just want to pass by."

25

"In that case I will go with you. I can go to Ilse's house from there."

He hesitated. "I don't know if you should."

"You know they wouldn't do anything to me," I said, and that settled it.

It was a cold, dark day; a slight frost was already on the autumn leaves. I wondered how the factory would look, having heard that the trees surrounding it had been felled by the Polish Home Guard in a vain attempt to stop the German advance. After half an hour's brisk walking we began to see it. I was shocked by the sight of the barren gray walls. Four buildings, forming a rectangle with a courtyard in the center, stood grim and forbidding in those unfamiliar surroundings.

We did not dare approach the main gate but turned off just before we came to the paved road leading to it and went to a small side entrance. However, it was locked so we walked around the building to find another entrance. As we turned a corner we came to a dead stop. From where we stood we saw huge trucks parked within the gates. Heaps of costly pelts were being loaded onto them. I felt Mr. Pipersberg's hand tightening around my arm. The accumulation of years of work was being carried off.

Instinctively, I looked toward the windows of my father's office. Then I heard a strange laugh from Mr. Pipersberg. Trembling, he pointed to a large red sign with bold white letters:

Dogs and Jews Not Allowed to Enter

"I am glad your father is not here," he said, "I am so glad. There is no use going in." He slowly turned away, a pathetic picture. "You had better go home. Run fast. I want to be alone."

Without a backward glance I hurried home. I had lost all desire to visit Ilse.

At home I avoided my parents and silently went up to my room. Again I lapsed into daydreaming about the past. All at once I realized that Mr. Pipersberg reminded me strongly of the young man in Krynica who had created the disturbance

26

at the open-air concert. Mr. Pipersberg must have looked like him when he was young.

Lost in thought, I suddenly became aware that my doorknob was turning slowly. I jumped up from my couch to throw open the door. There stood Mr. Pipersberg, his face gray as ashes. His overcoat was gone, his jacket was spotted and crumpled. I led him to my bed, and he lay down.

"What happened to you?" I asked.

He put his finger to his lips and motioned me to be quiet. "Don't tell anybody. Get some warm water and cotton, if you can."

When I returned he had removed his jacket. His shirt, flecked with blood, was clinging to his body. As I helped him remove it, I saw him bite his lip. There were wounds on his back and chest. His left eye was bloodshot, turning blue.

He was silent as I dressed his wounds, then he spoke, as if to himself. "I couldn't stand it. I had to go in, and then they asked who I was. None of the workers wanted to tell them, so I said I was the owner. 'You are a Jew, aren't you?' and so they beat me. Some of the workers moved as if to interfere, but they were afraid and they finally turned away. I barely made it to your house.

"Don't tell Papa," he warned me. "Let me spend the night here."

I brought him tea and a sandwich. He sipped the tea, but couldn't eat. "Is there any news from Arthur?" he asked. When I replied that there was none, he shook his head and closed his eyes.

That night I went to Arthur's room for the first time since he had left. Everything was untouched, just as he had left it. My mother had not even made the bed. There was still the faint imprint of his head in the pillow. I curled up at the foot of his bed, so as not to disturb it.

Next morning I woke early and tiptoed to my room, wondering if Mr. Pipersberg would want some hot coffee. He was gone. My blankets were neatly folded. The only evidence of what had happened the evening before were the wads of bloody cotton in my wastebasket.

Chapter 5

DAYS PASSED. IT WAS NOW THE BEGINNING OF NOVEMBER. DAILY I went to the Kultusgemeinde but still there was no news from Arthur. There were, however, many rumors circulating that new transports were being formed; some even had it that all Jews were to be deported.

Bielitz had been incorporated into the German Reich by this time, along with all other territories which had belonged to the Austro-Hungarian Empire before the First World War. The part of Poland not officially incorporated into Greater Germany was commonly referred to as the *Gouvernement.* Bielitz was only some thirty kilometers west of the dividing line that ran through Auschwitz (Oswiecim), which later became the most horrible extermination camp in all Europe. As a result of the rumors, many of our relatives and friends started to leave for the *Gouvernement,* believing that the restrictions imposed on them in Bielitz would not apply there.

Aunt Anna had decided to go to Czortkow, her home until she had moved to Bielitz some years before the war. It was deep in Poland and was now occupied by the Russians but she hoped that once she was in the *Gouvernement* she might be able to go through to Czortkow, where she still owned real estate. She urged us to join her.

"You still have some belongings and valuables that you can take along," she said. "Besides, I am sure that Arthur and David are in the *Gouvernement.*" She pleaded with Papa but without avail.

"I can't keep you from going," Papa said, "but we are staying. I can't work with my arm, we have almost no money, but here we will manage somehow. Helene was born here, the children were born here, and I have lived in Bielitz for more

28

than twenty years. After all, we have friends here. We are staying."

So Aunt Anna and her daughter Miriam left. For a while we had letters from them, but in December, 1940, our letters came back stamped in red: MOVED WITHOUT LEAVING FORWARDING ADDRESS. We never learned what happened to them, except that they never reached Czortkow.

Several days after Aunt Anna left, shortly before noon on a bitter cold day, a woman we knew came to tell us that she had heard the Gestapo was making the rounds looking for Mr. Pipersberg.

"Try to find him," she said to my father, "and tell him to hide."

Such warnings were not ignored. We knew that Mr. Pipersberg would probably be in the home of his former secretary, not far from the factory. From a window in her house, he could watch it in comparative safety.

"I had better go," I said.

It was icy. The snow was blown by a strong wind. There was hardly a road to follow. I saw a horse-drawn sleigh with two peasants inside wrapped in blankets. I asked them to give me a lift, which they did. The tired old horse painfully pulled the creaking sled. I was half-frozen before I reached the little house.

Mr. Pipersberg was there. He was about to eat but when he saw me, he jumped up from the table. When I explained why I had come he told me to return home quickly, then he ran out of the house to find a place to hide.

I hadn't gone a hundred yards when I saw a big black car with uniformed men pulling up to the house. They went in. I started to run. After a few minutes the car passed me again, speeding back. Suddenly, the magnitude of what I had just done struck me. I could visualize the Gestapo questioning Mr. Pipersberg's secretary. How could the frightened woman avoid telling them that the daughter of his best friend had been there? I reproached myself bitterly for not having stopped the car to admit that I had warned Mr. Pipersberg, that I alone was responsible, that my parents had known nothing about it. But it was too late.

I pictured my homecoming, finding my parents gone. Perhaps I had saved Mr. Pipersberg, but endangered my parents! Breathless, hoping against hope, I ran. My parents were home. The relief of seeing them was so great that I did not immediately notice how excited they were. I started to tell them everything, but Papa just numbly shook his head. I knew then that something else had disturbed him. He soon told me what it was. Word had just come about the transport that had taken Arthur away. For eight days the boys had been locked in cattle cars, taken to the *Gouvernement,* and turned loose in the woods. Then the SS troops had beat and shot them at random. Those who were able to ran away. Thirty-six prisoners were said to have been killed. Someone brought this news to the wife of a man who had escaped.

We heard nothing direct about Arthur. Perhaps in defense, a belief was born in me. "Arthur is living," I kept saying to myself. "He must be." But now my parents' worry suddenly turned to me. If Mr. Pipersberg were not to be found, the Gestapo might look for us. We spent a terrible, anxious night. Something snapped in my mother's mind. She kept mumbling over and over, "Arthur, Arthur, where are you?" She was beyond fear for herself.

I could not sleep, I could not lie down. I sat at the window of my bedroom and watched night fade into morning. The Gestapo did not come.

Two weeks passed. Then one day, late in November, the mailman stopped. He delivered a printed card ordering all Jews to report on Monday, December 2, 1939, at six o'clock in the morning, to an armory on Hermann Goering Strasse. Each person was allowed twenty pounds of clothing. All valuable objects, money, and keys to all closets, clearly tagged to indicate to which lock they belonged, should be put on a table in the front hall of each house. Violators of this order would be punished by death.

There it was! We were to leave our home. That well-known silence again engulfed us, broken only later that night when

Mama resumed her cry of "Arthur, Arthur!"

In the morning a man stopped by to say that we could sell some of our things. Papa did not want to leave Mama's side, so he told me to sell everything. Word spread quickly and the people of Bielitz came to our house and to others to buy. They brought carts to our door, dragged the furniture out, and loaded it. Our home was being torn apart and all I could do was to stand by and watch.

One man gathered all our silver and flatware into a bushel basket, added a few crystal bowls, and handed me a couple of dirty, crumpled notes in exchange. I wondered where he had gotten them. Another person picked up a glass from the set which Arthur and I had given our parents on their twentieth wedding anniversary the previous April. It was a liqueur and wine set, beautifully engraved. He held the glass by its slender stem for a moment, then let it fall to the floor. It broke into a hundred pieces.

"I want that set," he said to me, "but I can't offer you much since a glass is missing," and he pointed to the pieces on the floor.

I watched the shelves of the library emptied. Someone took the owl from a bookcase. It was a ceramic bird, claws resting on two books, the Bible and Aristotle. Its eyes were electric bulbs. Arthur had often read by its light. To me the bird had always seemed alive. As a man carried it away, its eyes were glassy and cold.

Someone whisked away the dining-room tablecloth, the one Mama had worked on for over a year. It was all handwork, with a silver fringe.

In place of the familiar paintings, there were light-colored patches on the wall.

The sanctity of our home was gone, the chain of tradition broken, the shrine built by love and affection desecrated . . . and there I stood with a few pieces of paper money—dirty, crumpled, greasy bills—and a handful of coins. Shame burned in my hand. I closed my eyes and turned to go upstairs and give the money to Papa.

Papa's arm was heavy in its sling. Mama's breakdown was

complete; finally she fell asleep from sheer exhaustion. The day after tomorrow we were to leave our home. What could we do for Mama? She was constantly calling for Arthur.

I had terrible visions of what might have happened to him. Had he died of hunger and thirst in the cattle car? Had they beaten him, or had he run into the forest, only to die of cold? Did a bullet hit him and kill him instantly, or did he have to suffer? Is he in the forest of the East, or in the waters of the San? His clothes are surely cold and wet. Are his eyes open or closed? These pictures kept haunting my mind. Did it really happen to him? If not, why did he not write or send a message? He must be alive, I kept saying to myself, and then I saw his face in the dark, motionless, surrounded by icy water. Mama was calling him again and again. That night I felt so close to death that I wanted it desperately. It seemed an easy solution, a quick way out. We had heard of a family who committed suicide together. I half-wished my parents had suggested it.

I was standing at my window, my forehead against the cold glass. It was late and I hadn't gone to bed. It seemed almost a luxury to die, to go to sleep and never wake up again. Then I felt Papa's hand on my shoulder. I didn't turn. He put his hand on the nape of my neck and turned me forcibly toward him. He looked steadily at me and then answered my thoughts.

"Whatever you are thinking now is wrong. It is cowardly."

I couldn't deny it. He lifted my chin up and looked at me firmly again.

"Promise me that no matter what happens you will never do it."

I couldn't speak.

"I want your promise now," he said.

"I promise you, Papa," and in the years to come, when death seemed the only solution, I remembered that promise as my most sacred vow.

The next morning good news came. We would not have to go to the armory. The transport was postponed. We could stay in our home. But Mama was no better. She slept most of that day and the next.

Chapter 6

SHORTLY BEFORE CHRISTMAS IT SNOWED HARD FOR SEVERAL days. Normally, I would have been out on my skis, sliding over the hills; this year I had not even thought about skis.

Two days before Christmas a thaw set in. The sun shone brightly and the snow melted rapidly. The streets were dirty. In the afternoon a German policeman knocked at the door. His shouting, at first unintelligible, turned out to be an order directing us to move to the basement, where Trude had lived. Papa, Mama, and I hastily started to bundle our things together and move some furniture into the hall.

"Faster, faster," shouted the policeman in a rasping voice, and Papa, poor Papa, struggled to lift the pieces with his lame arm. Going downstairs, I passed Trude. She was already taking her things upstairs.

"I am glad," she said, without malice or sarcasm, "that we are having a nice place for Christmas." She simply stated it as a matter of fact. It seemed the most natural thing to her.

I felt rage rising in me; I might have hit her but Mama was behind me, pushing me down the stairs.

The basement was flooded, the walls were damp, and the electricity had been cut off. Mama went up to the attic and found an old kerosene lamp that hadn't been used since the First World War. I watched her polish it and clean the chimney with a soft cloth. She then lit the wick. It smoldered but finally burned, smoking a bit. Mama replaced the chimney in its socket, and turned the wick up. The old lamp threw a soft light around the table, toward the mildewed walls, toward a few familiar furnishings. We were in our home still, yet I felt that we were far away.

On Christmas Eve, as on all Christmas Eves as long as I

could remember, I went to see Niania. Niania was the only person who had come to see us regularly and who didn't seem afraid of what the Germans would say or do. Her position in our household was unique. Niania Brenza was an old Austrian, still loyal to the long-dead Emperor Franz Josef. Reflecting the period when our region had been part of the Austro-Hungarian Empire, she spoke only German. Niania's life had been a hard one. She had lost her husband when she was quite young, and had brought up her four children by herself. Her only son, a lawyer, married shortly before World War I, enlisted in the Austrian Army at the outbreak of the war, and was killed in action. He never saw the daughter his wife bore him. Mrs. Brenza's daughter-in-law had taken a job as housekeeper not too far away from us and Mrs. Brenza had brought up the child, Irma.

Niania often told me about the events that led to her coming to our house. It was in April, 1924, that a fire destroyed the house she lived in, including all her possessions. Niania knew my grandparents slightly and, the day after the fire, came to ask my grandmother for some clothes. She came, she told me, wearing an old postman's jacket which had belonged to her late husband, the only item of warm clothing that had not been destroyed by the fire. My grandmother had an idea.

"My daughter Helene," she said, referring to my mother, "is expecting a baby soon; we are looking for someone to take care of it."

So Niania, then fifty years old, and Irma, age seven, moved into our house. At the outset it was to be only until Mama was stronger but as it turned out Niania stayed in our house for the next thirteen years, until two years before the war.

Once during those years Niania had taken a room a few houses away from us with her daughter-in-law and Irma but for the most part Niania lived with us and Irma grew up in our house.

Niania took care of me from the day I was born. She taught me to sit up, she taught me my first steps and my first word, "Papa," after that, "Niania." I called her that always. We all relied on her, we confided in her. She seemed to be in charge of everything. Best of all, she knew so many wonderful stories. It was not until Irma, her grandchild, married that Niania finally left our house for her own, nearby. She was then sixty-three. Every morning in warm weather she waited at her open window as I went to school to toss me an apple or a piece of candy. On cold days she would stand in the doorway, wrapped in the huge brown and green checked shawl on which I had so often fallen asleep in her arms. There she stood, waiting to inspect whether I wore my warm underwear and woolen mittens. And on long winter evenings I would go to see her and sample her delicious potato pancakes. It was then that she would dip into her seemingly inexhaustible stores of exciting, mysterious stories.

Although the Germans had summoned her to the police station and warned her not to enter our house, Niania came and went as before. None of the neighbors reported her, possibly because she was so old or perhaps because they realized how closely our lives were linked. Niania brought us the things Jews couldn't buy: sugar, jam, sweets, an occasional egg. When we protested that she was depriving herself she would look at me and say,

"The child has to eat, she is growing; my life is almost over."

That was my Niania, a proud and simple woman; her spirit shone brightly in that world of betrayal.

I went to see Niania on Christmas Eve. Christmas in her house seemed pretty much as it had always been. The tree, the same ornaments, the smell of fresh pine, and little, thoughtfully wrapped presents for us. Only the presents were different. In former years Niania had usually given me books or toys. For Mama she would have some handwork—a crocheted vanity set or embroidered cushion. This year she had woolen mittens and sweets for me, for Mama a glass of jam and a pound of sugar. The gift I took to Niania was very different indeed. Instead of clothing and the usual basket with fruit and wine, this year we had nothing to give but a pale green Chinese vase on which two dragons served as handles. After I had opened her gifts, Niania offered me cookies; they were the same as always but somehow they tasted different.

From her window I could see our garden. Snow was falling again and the garden house seemed to me like a gingerbread house with spun sugar thickly covering the roof.

After Christmas our rations were cut severely and on each ration card was stamped the word JEW. Our rations were less than half the rations of non-Jews. Our coal ration turned out to be even more meager but with only two rooms to heat, and by wearing heavy clothes indoors, we managed to keep warm. With the new year came the order to wear white armbands with a blue star on which the word JEW was inscribed. Shortly thereafter, we were instructed to wear a yellow star with black inscription; the new colors would be more distinguishable against the snow.

Concern and doubt about Arthur never left us and then, just after New Year, a letter came from Gisa, addressed to him. How he had waited for news from her! It said that she and her family were living in Krakow and that they had lost everything. She went on to say that her father was very ill. I replied immediately and informed her that Arthur was no longer at home. A few days later another letter came from her, containing wonderful news; she had heard about Arthur from another source. He was in Russia, and safe. Now we waited eagerly for more letters. We thought that soon she would have direct news and forward a letter from him.

One cold day early in February, Peter, a friend of Arthur's, arrived from Krakow. Krakow was about eighty kilometers from Bielitz. It was possible at times to obtain a travel permit and Peter had managed it. Gisa had told him to see us and bring us the latest news about Arthur. The reason, he explained, that Arthur had not written directly, was that mail was being held up by the censor. So Arthur had sent news to Gisa by means of someone who had returned from Russian-occupied territory.

Peter stayed for dinner and it was a wonderful evening. Mama and Papa seemed younger and happier, and questioned the poor boy for more and more news. In the end, he probably invented some to make them happier.

36

When he started to take his leave, I walked up the stairs with him to the door. Outside the icy wind was howling.

I turned my happy face toward him to say good-by, and told him laughingly, "Oh please, tell me just one more thing about Arthur."

He didn't answer.

I thought at first that he hadn't heard me above the howling of the wind, so I repeated my question.

He grasped me by both shoulders, looked into my eyes, and whispered fiercely, "Gisa doesn't know anything about Arthur. She is trying to make your parents feel better. Oh, why did I tell you! No, please," he continued, "it isn't quite so. There are some rumors. There may be a foundation—"

He left me standing out in the snow, dazed. Shattered hopes were worse than no hope at all.

When I returned to the basement, Mama and Papa were talking. They were so happy I decided not to tell them what Peter had told me.

I spent a tense night waiting for morning—waiting to see Niania. Although I had sometimes kept secrets from Papa and Mama, I never kept any from Niania. But when morning came I decided that I was not even going to tell Niania about it. I was tempted to confide in her, yet somehow I could not get myself to do it. The secret about Arthur was mine and mine alone.

I don't think my silence was due to a noble desire to spare my parents the painful truth. Probably it was the typical behavior of a teen-ager, always willing to dramatize, to play the martyr. The feeling of sparing them disappointment and pain gave me new confidence and strength.

Letters kept coming from Gisa and always they contained indirect news about Arthur. Then, in March, a cablegram came from Mama's brother Leo, in Istanbul, Turkey. It read: "Got Arthur's letter. He is well."

Our joy soared high, but then I remembered that I had written him that we had no news from Arthur, and that we were worried. I somehow felt that he might have made up the cablegram to calm our fears. On the other hand, I felt that he would not take such a grave responsibility upon himself. I tried to enjoy the news but I couldn't do it fully.

That evening while Mama was busy preparing supper Papa called me to him. "Sit down, Gerda, there is something troubling you. Won't you tell me what it is?"

"Nothing, nothing, Papa," I insisted.

He looked at me firmly as if reading an open book. "It is about Arthur," he said, "and it started the night Peter was here. Now tell me what it is."

I was at the point of telling him when suddenly, without my knowing why, different words formed on my lips.

"Yes, Papa," I began, "it started the night when Peter was here." I spoke slowly, deliberately. "When I heard him talk about Arthur being free from our troubles I couldn't help but envy him."

I toyed with my hair as I spoke. "I miss going to school so much and doing all the things I used to. I know that I should be ashamed that I begrudge Arthur his freedom, but I cannot help it."

"Well, so that's it." Papa sighed. "I was afraid that Peter might have told you something he did not tell us."

I was trembling inwardly but my story had worked wonderfully. I had a rare feeling of pleasure. I felt like an actress in a great scene.

Next morning Papa went up to the attic where he unearthed some textbooks that Mama had used when she attended Austrian schools.

"You were quite right," he said to me, "in what you told me last night. I should have thought of your schooling before. I intend to teach you all I can."

We had studied and read Polish in school and I had also studied French and Latin, but my first language was German. I had grown up speaking it, although I had never learned to read and write it. Papa now set out to teach me this part of it.

He proved a fine teacher. I learned far more than I would have at school. When I told my friend Ilse about my studies, she wanted to be included. She came as often as she could and Papa taught both of us. I often felt that up to now I had not really known Papa. In the many months that we worked together he revealed his dreams and his frustrations.

Papa came from a town on the Austro-Hungarian border. His parents had wanted him to become a rabbi. He told me how the sunlight falling into his room at home had distracted him from studying the Talmud and brought forth a longing to see the spring flowers blooming in the meadows.

"I had to get outdoors," he said. "Can you understand that?"

Finally he had gone to Vienna and worked his way through medical school.

"Medicine brought me closer to life and death," he reflected. "I loved talking to people, and I wanted to heal their bodies." Then, as if ashamed of what he had said, he added, "But never underestimate the teachings of the Torah and the wisdom of the Ten Commandments. In them you can find a whole way of life, ethics, and the basis of human actions. They were written thousands of years ago, yet they are the foundations of every law in the world."

Papa was about to get his degree when the First World War came. He joined the medical branch of the Austrian army and was one of the first to go to the front. He operated and amputated day and night.

"No, medicine was not ideal," he said. "I couldn't detach myself from death and suffering. Medicine was not my true vocation after all.

"I met your mother during the war," Papa continued. "We were married right after it ended. I didn't go back to medical school. Mama did not urge me to. In the joy of the war's end it was easy to give it up."

Papa was puffing on his pipe. There was silence. He did not continue, but I sensed what was on his mind. I knew he had some regrets about not having become a physician after all.

Papa taught me a lot. Mathematics, chemistry, medicine— whatever he could draw from his vast store of knowledge. And so we spent long hours together.

Toward the end of March Papa and I were working in our basement kitchen—Mama had gone to visit an ill friend. We paused in our discussion to listen to the mailman pass our front door and were about to resume when Mrs. Prozna, a neighbor, knocked at the door. She produced a gray envelope.

"Mr. Weissmann," she said, "this letter really belongs to you. I don't know why Arthur addressed it to me." There was a second of stunned silence. Then Papa tore the envelope out of Mrs. Prozna's hand, and there it was—Arthur's handwriting!

Papa didn't stop to open the envelope, he just kissed the startled woman's hands. He couldn't talk. Neither could I. Then Papa opened the letter and started to read. His hands trembled, his head shook, his eyes were so moist and heavy that he had to pause to wipe them. But what wonderful news! Both Arthur and David were safe in Russia. Even more miraculous, on their first night in Lwow, as they walked the streets looking for food and shelter, they had met Uncle Aaron, David's father, who was believed dead! David's father was already trying to bring Aunt Anna and Miriam to Russia.

Upon reading the letter we noticed that the first page was addressed to Mrs. Prozna. Arthur wrote that he didn't know if we were still at home, and therefore was addressing the letter to her in the hope that she might be able to give it or send it to us.

Also in the letter was a message just for me, a few lines in which Arthur wrote, "I know that you are as brave as you promised me to be." Those words, in my brother's hand, seemed at that moment to compensate for all my grief and worries.

When Mama returned, she clutched the letter and stood at the window praying before reading it. Papa, Mama, and I sat together all that afternoon, rereading the letter again and again. For the first time in those many weeks we talked about what had constantly been on our minds—Arthur.

I felt a renewed impulse to tell my parents about my conversation with Peter. It was hard not to do so and receive credit for keeping the secret. But I felt, too, that I ought not to tell even now, for perhaps my parents would never trust me again.

Chapter 7

ARTHUR'S LETTERS CAME FREQUENTLY THAT SPRING. THEY WERE something to look forward to although he always wrote with restraint, knowing well that many prying eyes would read his letters before they reached us. He was well and had found work in a chemical laboratory in Russian-occupied Lwow, which was about 350 kilometers from Bielitz. He told us that he would try to send us money, and sure enough, shortly afterward it came. Mama cried, but whether from happiness or sorrow I couldn't tell.

I was hard at work on my studies and within two to three months was able to read and write German, having mastered the peculiarly angular script that had seemed so confusing at first.

Jews left Bielitz for the *Gouvernement* in ever-increasing numbers. Before the war, Bielitz had a population of about eight thousand Jews. By the spring of 1940 there were hardly more than three hundred, and among them almost no young people. Young men like Arthur had left with the transports and few girls remained as the months passed. Among my friends, there were only Ruth Singer, who lived with her widowed mother, Gretel and Herta Teichner, who also had only their mother and grandmother, Mary Reichman whom I seldom saw for she had to care for her ill father, Rita Schanzer, whose two brothers had gone with a transport, and Ilse Kleinzähler and Escia Bergmann. Rita's father, an officer in the Polish army, was reported missing in action. Ilse was my closest friend. Of all these girls only Escia and I had both our parents with us.

Gradually our money dwindled to nothing. With food to

buy we found ourselves facing a grave problem. It was Mama who solved it. She had always done beautiful work with her hands; her knitting and embroidering had been admired by friends, relatives, and neighbors. Now she had an inspiration. Needlework was much in demand but yarn was scarce. We overcame that by unraveling old sweaters and shawls and working endless evenings by the flickering light of the oil lamp, and when oil became more tightly rationed, by candlelight.

We did some beautiful work. Having helped Arthur with his chemistry I knew how to dye wool and cotton. We made sweaters, dresses, and bonnets and let people know that we had lovely things to sell. Soon we had quite a reputation. We had more orders than we could fill. There was only one catch. People paid us between eight and ten marks for a sweater, a fair price when a pound of bread cost about twenty pfennigs. But now we could only buy bread on the black market, and for about thirty marks a loaf, so we had to knit three sweaters —a week's work—in order to earn enough for one loaf.

Then Mama decided to ask people to pay us in food instead of in money. This was a wonderful improvement for us.

When a particular sweater had to be finished in a hurry our knitting needles clicked from morning until night and often till dawn. And as we worked, Papa would smoke his pipe and read aloud to us.

Papa kept close account of our expenses. Watching him work with his crippled arm, I remembered how he had used to sit at his ebony desk checking monthly accounts. How straight he had always sat, how handsome he had looked! Above his desk had hung the picture of "The Black Madonna" by Dorné. We had the painting still; rolled and well wrapped, it was hidden under Papa's bed against the day when we might have to sell it for food. And here sat Papa, pale and sallow, at a kitchen table, in a frayed old suit, with pots and pans hanging close over his head since there were no cupboards to put them in.

I could not contain my fears.

"Papa," I asked, regretting it as soon as I had spoken. "Papa, how much money do we have? How long can it last?"

He looked at me. "Don't you worry." He smiled, and somehow it was as it had been before, and I was relieved.

Our work provided us with food and there was always a tomorrow to look forward to which might bring liberation—or a letter from Arthur, or spring.

That May eighth I was sixteen. What a lovely sunny morning it was! The buttercups were out, and there were violets down in the moist part of the garden near the pond, along with lilies-of-the-valley. On the afternoon of my birthday a warm, scented rain, so typical of May, fell. But best of all, a letter from Arthur arrived: a letter meant for my birthday came exactly on the day! His picture was enclosed. It showed him wearing a new suit. He looked older, more mature, but also strange, and it was not only the little mustache he wore that made him look different. I was so happy, I kissed the picture and danced with it. Then I went out to the garden and threw myself on the wet grass and cried and cried. I didn't know why I was crying, except that it wasn't from happiness. It wasn't so much the war, it wasn't my parents, it wasn't even Arthur being away, or the situation we found ourselves in. Those tears were for myself. I felt deprived of my share of life. In the awakening of spring I felt a great longing for laughter and for dancing. I felt cheated, and I was crying because I felt sorry for myself. I felt restless and dreadfully alone.

A few days later a sign was put up in our garden—ONLY GERMANS ALLOWED.

Not being able to go into our garden was very cruel, especially to Papa, who in the summer, when his heart bothered him most, needed the fresh air and a chance to walk in the open without fearing arrest. I found a substitute. I visited my friend Escia. Escia's parents supervised the cemetery. When the war came, they had moved into a couple of rooms adjoining the chapel. I went to visit her as often as I could and we used to stroll through the cemetery. We tended some of the graves, especially those of soldiers and children. I had known so many, how old they had been, where they had come from, something of their lives. Escia and I spent many undisturbed hours amid beautiful flowers. The dead became our friends.

And so, shut off from a world of reality which was a time of triumph for our enemy, we lived in fear and in hope. Fear was a monotonous part of our daily life. The progress of the war seemed of secondary importance. I simply could not accept the countless Allied reverses as reality. Only vaguely did I feel that they had to be, that the Germans must reach a peak before inevitably going downhill. When the Wehrmacht marched victoriously into Denmark and Norway Papa sadly shook his head. "Can nobody stop them?" he asked.

"It will be as it was with Napoleon," Mama remarked, resting the knitting in her lap. Then both fell silent.

I looked from Papa to Mama. They are getting old, I thought. They don't seem to understand that all this is strategy, that everything is planned to seal Hitler's doom. To this idea I clung, and it gave me hope in the hours when I should have despaired.

When German troops were reported in Paris, when France fell, we were stunned. Papa sat reading without turning the page, his eyes fixed into emptiness, his lips quivering under the graying mustache. "Papa," I whispered, cuddling closer to him, afraid. "Papa, it will be over soon, won't it, Papa?" The pale fingers of his healthy hand touched my forehead and traveled down my cheek in the old caress. His eyes were unseeing, filmy. He whispered huskily, "With God's help it will."

The room was oppressively hot for Mama had shut the windows to cut off the sound of the jubilant voices emanating from our neighbors' radios. We sat in silence into the night, not bothering to light the lamp.

There was only one ironic consolation in the German victories. For the time being they were too busy to bother us much.

The summer wore on. Arthur's letters came frequently and seemed the only reality in our gray existence. He was working in a factory that made preserves, thus putting to use his training in chemistry, and we reasoned happily that he could not possibly be hungry in such a place. There were several letters from Aunt Anna too. She was in the *Gouvernement* but had as yet been unable to move on to her destination, the town of her birth. It was not as easy as she had thought to get a travel permit from the Russian authorities.

In September we got a long-awaited message from Mr. Pipersberg. The news was indirect. We gathered from it that he was hiding under an assumed name in the *Gouvernement*. We knew that there were people who obtained "Aryan" papers and hid with farmers in villages. Papa was happier that day than I had seen him in a long time. We did not know that this was to be the last message from Mr. Pipersberg. That same fall, letters ceased to come from Aunt Anna as well.

It was a year now since the war had started. Who would have thought that it would last a whole year? Although the hours stretched endlessly on bleak afternoons, from twilight into long, long evenings of monotonous sameness, somehow the weeks seemed short as they melted into months and seasons.

The new year was approaching. It had been a victorious year for the Germans. Their rations were doubled and as an added holiday bonus they also got coffee, tea, chocolate, and fruit. Thus they celebrated the conquests that had made them masters of Europe. On New Year's Eve I asked my parents if I could stay up until midnight to see the new year come in. I had never before stayed up for the beginning of a year and I wanted "to see the year of our liberation from its very first minute," as I put it to Papa and Mama. Much to my surprise, Papa and Mama agreed instantly. We sat around the table idly, neither Mama nor I knitting. It seemed luxurious just to sit and have the wick in the kerosene lamp turned up higher than usual, throwing the circle of light wider while the lamp consumed precious fuel. I felt rich and somehow grown up. "It's midnight!" Papa announced presently, and the words which followed were drowned out by the pealing of church bells in the frosty night. I felt a mounting excitement, I had witnessed a moment of history. The year of 1940 was gone. The new year was certain to bring the end of the war. "Mama," I said, "I wish I were a year older. Next year at this time, we will celebrate with Arthur. We will have a big party." "The biggest party ever," Mama said, smiling. And for the first time in my life I was able to bid Mama and Papa "Good night" and "Good morning" all at the same time.

The winter continued cold and stormy. I rarely saw my friends and eagerly looked toward spring. Spring came late, at first hesitantly, then rich and lush, and within us, under the gray layers of fear, anticipation turned into almost certain knowledge that something was bound to happen soon, that the war would come to a speedy end.

Then it came, early on a Saturday morning. Through our open windows, from every direction we heard radios blasting the now familiar fanfares which always preceded announcements of victory. We heard voices charged with excitement without being able to catch the words; we thought we could make out Goebbels' hoarse exhortations. Something big had happened, we all felt it. That afternoon, Ilse came and told us what it was. Neutrality with Russia had been violated; German troops had crossed the frontier. Upstairs, the radio was still booming announcements of victory after victory. The part of Poland that had been occupied by Russia—where Arthur was—was rapidly falling under the German heel. Again there would be murder and persecution.

I tried to motion Ilse to silence. I did not want her to go into more details in front of my parents, but then I realized that they must find out sooner or later. They stayed numb and speechless. Arthur was in Lwow—or Lemberg, as the Germans now called it. Would we ever hear from him again?

It was that night, or perhaps several nights later, that I awoke with a positive feeling that something was awry. Every nerve alert, I jumped out of bed and lit a candle. It was in the early hours, perhaps about 3 A.M. Instinctively I looked over toward Mama and Papa. One glance, and I saw that Papa and Mama were lying in their beds, lifeless!

Without hesitation I got vinegar and started brushing their

temples. I repeated over and over, without alarm, without fear, "Papa, Mama. . . ."

Mama's eyelids finally flickered.

"Was I ill?" she murmured in astonishment.

I could hear that Papa's breathing was growing slower and weaker. Terror seized me but I remembered the pills that Dr. Reach had given him. I quickly found the bottle, but I could not get the cork out. After a few moments of fruitless fumbling, in sheer desperation I bit off the top of glass, took out two small pills, and tried to push them into Papa's mouth. His teeth were clamped tight. I screamed, and somehow forced them into his mouth. Mama was asleep again. After a few seconds Papa opened his eyes. He coughed and turned over. I managed to make him swallow some water and he fell asleep. His breathing became stronger, more steady. Now I trembled, releasing my fright and excitement. I could not return to bed. Standing at the small cellar window, I watched the dawn.

There was nothing I could do. Nothing. The only physician who was allowed to treat Jews, Dr. Reach, himself a Jew, lived a twenty minutes' walk away. I could not go out because of the curfew; the streets were patrolled. There were no phones for Jews. As I waited, my thoughts wandered to Arthur. I missed him at that hour more than ever. I needed his strength.

I went back to bed, and mercifully sleep came.

I woke late, Mama calling me for breakfast. Papa was up as always. I tried to remember, wondering if I had had a nightmare. Looking at Papa, I knew that I hadn't. His face was drawn and he had an unhealthy pallor. He had suffered a heart attack in the night, before I wakened, and when Mama woke, her strength had failed her and she fainted. Looking back now over the many years, I wish they had died together that night, peacefully, in their beds, but together. . . .

As I started to eat breakfast, I felt my lips and gums hurting me. Looking into a mirror, I saw a small cut inside my mouth. The glass had cut me without my realizing it. I am glad that the scar will be with me as long as I live.

That noon a letter came from Arthur that must have been

in the mail before the German attack. He sent another picture and enclosed a single dried rose. Nothing could have been more beautiful to Mama. She stuck it in a vase and looked at it often, touching it gently.

From that day on and for many days to come I placed all my hope in religion. I found a new source of strength. Night after night I said my prayers ten and twenty times. I tried to inflict punishment on myself. When my parents were asleep I would get out of bed, crouch on the floor, and sleep there, next to the cold, moist wall. Often I denied myself nourishment because I was sure Arthur was not eating. My lessons with Papa became irregular and I did not study. Papa did not insist; I was sure that his mind was not on teaching either. Periodically, I gave up my favorite pastime—reading. Often I would not hear when spoken to. For the first time in my life I felt I understood people who retire to convents and monasteries, who torture their bodies in humble poverty to attain eternal salvation. Papa tried to talk to me but usually I would burst into tears. After a while he gave up.

One day, at Ilse's house, I met Ulla. Ulla was a girl in her middle twenties. She had black hair parted in the center, a prominent nose, and beautiful green eyes hidden behind thick glasses. To me Ulla was beautiful. She represented everything I ever wanted to be. Ulla's father was a professor and she had studied in England. She had a Ph.D. in English literature. I was fascinated with her and asked her countless questions about England. Worship must have shown on my face. She seemed pleased, and asked: "Would you like me to give you English lessons?" Would I! Elated, I hurried home. Papa and Mama were glad to see me once again bubbling with excitement, although Papa was a bit worried about the possible danger connected with studying English, since it was forbidden by the Germans. "But, Papa, imagine the surprise Arthur will have when he gets home and I speak English to him"—Arthur had studied English for several years and spoke it quite well. There was a shadow of a smile on Papa's lips. He patted my head. "All right," he said.

With zest I threw myself into my studies. Twice a week I

went to Ulla's, carrying a shopping bag with a few potatoes covering my English grammar.

One hot day in July I was on my way to Ulla's, wearing a white dress, too short, too childish for my age, and pinned to it the star of David with the word JEW. My hair had grown long, and I wore it in braids. As I passed the municipal swimming pool I could hear the gay music of the small orchestra inside. Surrounded by exquisitely kept lawns and flower beds, it was the most modern and beautiful pool in Poland. How many happy days we had all spent there.

Through the gates I heard the playful voices of the bathers. I saw colorful beach balls thrown high in the air. I heard the delicious gurgle of fresh water. Feeling hot and sticky, I was full of envy and resentment at being denied all this. My long-sleeved dress and the potatoes seemed unusually burdensome.

Suddenly I felt a heavy hand on my shoulder and heard, "What do you want here?" barked at me.

It was a policeman.

"Nothing," I murmured, "nothing," and I began to move along.

His eyes fell on my shopping bag.

"What's in there?" he asked.

"Just potatoes," I replied.

He turned the bag upside down. The potatoes rolled into the gutter and out fell the book with its incriminating title.

"Ah, that's it!" he exclaimed with obvious relish. "Come to the police station. Learning English will be the last pleasure of your life!"

I followed him meekly. What else could I do? I reproached myself bitterly, and felt a paralyzing fear, for I knew it was not uncommon to be condemned to death for violations of rules no worse than the one I had broken. My parents would probably be held responsible for what I had done.

In a few hours they would become worried waiting for me. Papa would pace the floor and Mama would finally run over to Ulla's, only to learn that I had not been there. Then she would rush home, hoping that I had arrived in the meantime. Then she would hurry over to see Escia and ask if I had been

49

there, and she would continue her vigil until nightfall. I couldn't think beyond that.

I wanted to plead with the policeman to let me go, but I couldn't talk. There were tears in my eyes.

The music and the laughter of the bathers faded into the distance. The sun seemed to have ceased to shine. All of a sudden I felt cold, and I started to tremble.

When we got to the station house, the policeman took me into a room where an older man with a shiny bald head sat at a wide desk. The bald man had been writing, but he stopped and looked up when the policeman pointed to me, and with obvious pride described his discovery of my crime. When he finished the officer behind the desk barked at me, "Do you realize what you have done?"

I simply nodded.

He picked up my book and glanced through it. The passing minutes seemed an eternity.

The policeman sat down and smoked a cigarette, quite satisfied with himself.

The officer laid down my book. Then he looked at the policeman and said, "This is a terrible crime. It is almost espionage to learn English while we are at war with England. The punishment will be meted out accordingly."

There was a lump in my throat. I wanted to say so many things, to plead, but I was unable to speak.

"I have to give it a few minutes' thought," he announced. Then, turning to the policeman, he thanked him for his good work and sent him back to his patrol.

As soon as the policeman left, the bald officer turned to me. His voice softened to a more human tone.

"Now run home as fast as you can," he said, "and forget your English."

For a moment I couldn't believe my good fortune and I stood as though nailed to the floor.

"What are you waiting for?" he snapped.

I wanted to thank him, but words would not come. At that moment I did on impulse what I had been taught to do as a child, when meeting a distinguished person. I curtsied. I curtsied low and ran out.

I ran home as fast as I could. I experienced inexpressible joy on seeing my parents again, seeing again the basement room that we called home. But I couldn't tell my parents what had happened. The next day I announced that I was fed up with English lessons and that I would start them again "after the war."

They didn't question me, for which I was grateful. They made no comment. Perhaps they were relieved at my decision, knowing the risk I had been running.

I have often thought about that officer, and wondered why he let me go. Was he really kind? Did he have a daughter my own age? I wish I knew. I met many hundreds of Germans in the years that followed, but only two, and he was the first, who behaved as though they were human!

After the all too brief weeks with Ulla I again fell into a state of apathy. I could not read, slept little, and cried a lot.

It was the beginning of September, 1941, almost two years to the day since the German motorcycles had sped through the streets of our town, when Ilse stormed excitedly into the house to tell me of a boys' camp that had been formed by the SS. Ilse always had the news first, since she lived near the Kultusgemeinde, the Jewish Community Center, where all the news circulated. Ilse and her mother had visited the camp the previous day and she told me that there were thirty Jewish boys in it. "It really is not bad at all," Ilse informed me. "You know, you think of a camp in terms of all the stories you hear."

Ilse asked me to visit the camp with her the following day. I declined.

That evening Papa said to me, "I am surprised at you. Why don't you want to go? Do you realize Arthur might be in a camp like that and how glad he would be if someone would visit him?"

That did it.

Together with her mother, Ilse and I went late the next afternoon to the camp. It was only a short distance from

Bielitz and could easily be reached from our house by a short-cut which led over meadows and several small brooks.

The camp—a converted factory—was a big square four-story building with a yard in the center. An old German guard stood at the entrance and when we told him what we wanted he let us in.

Mrs. Kleinzähler, Ilse's mother, knew one of the boys and started talking to him. I felt quite lost. I walked over to a window, pretending to look out, but I was curious to see the boys. I had seen few Jewish boys since the transport had left.

Their room was big, one side of it occupied by a row of bunks. There were family photographs tacked to the wall over the bunks. An oblong table stood in the center of the room and a few of the boys were eating.

I felt so self-conscious, I did not know what to do with myself. Ilse stood in a far corner with her mother and I did not have the courage to cross the room. I felt that everyone would watch me.

Suddenly a tall man of perhaps thirty with a Red Cross band around his arm, either a doctor or male nurse, approached me, introduced himself, and asked whether I was from Bielitz. He told me that he had lived here for several years. We discovered that we had quite a number of friends in common.

As we talked I became uncomfortably conscious of a man watching me from a nearby bunk and intermittently writing. He would write a couple of lines, then look at me, write, then look again.

He was slim, wore a navy-blue shirt and gray slacks. He had a tan, lean face, a prominent nose, a cynical mouth, and a determined chin. When he looked up, his eyes behind his horn-rimmed glasses were steel gray, searching, and seemingly cold. His hair was dark and wavy. What struck me most forcibly were his fingers. They were long and nervous. I felt uneasy under his searching eyes.

The man to whom I was talking told me that antique furniture, paintings, and other valuables from the homes of Jews who had been liquidated were stored in the factory.

Here they were repaired and refinished, if necessary, and then sent to furnish the apartments of German officers.

"We have quite a collection of paintings," he said. "Would you care to see them?"

"I would love to," I replied.

We went up two flights. He opened a heavy door and we entered the storeroom. In the fading afternoon light I saw beautiful paintings, vases, inlaid tables, marble-topped consoles, Chinese curios, pianos, tapestries, treasures from many homes. They were covered with dust.

I fancied that I had seen some of the things before—in the houses of friends.

As I was admiring an inlaid table my companion was called away. I wandered alone among the furniture until I came to a corner of the room, where, behind a piano, I saw a life-size portrait of a beautiful girl holding a torch. Her hair was hanging about her shoulders, her eyes shone with a strange power of hope and conviction. She was so incredibly beautiful that I gasped. I had never seen hope, power, and determination thus expressed. The faint light coming through the dusty windows illuminated the canvas to perfection.

"Isn't it beautiful?" said a voice behind me.

"I wonder who put her there," I said without turning around. I was carried away by my emotions.

"I did." The voice was nearer now.

I turned around, and there he stood, the stranger with the penetrating gray eyes. I was annoyed that he was there, and yet pleased that he understood what I meant.

"What would you call her?" he asked.

"Hope," I said without hesitation.

"Or Wisdom," he added. "Come, I will show you something."

He led me to the other end of the storeroom. In a corner stood an easel, a canvas on it with a half-finished painting.

"Do you paint?" I guessed.

"A little," he answered. "Stand there, as you did in front of the picture," he ordered.

I started to laugh.

He took my hand and pressed it firmly.

"You are going to sit for me," he commanded with a determination that I disliked.

"No," I said, just as determined, and started down the stairs. Ilse and her mother were ready to leave. We said our good-bys, and I turned to the imperious artist.

"I hope you can keep the picture in its hiding place for a long time."

"Our picture," he replied.

I felt like fighting with him, but restrained myself.

"I will take you home," he said, turning to Mrs. Kleinzähler and Ilse. As we left the building he turned to me and said, "By the way, we were not properly introduced."

His name was Abek Feigenblatt. I wanted to know more about him, yet I was afraid to ask. I was curiously disturbed, annoyed and yet pleased. He must be around thirty, I thought, practically an old man. Just then he asked how old I was.

"Sixteen," I said, but corrected myself. "Almost seventeen."

He smiled. "Well, I will see you soon," he said.

"Perhaps." I was not too encouraging.

"I know I will," was his confident reply as he waved good-by.

Nervous, excited, and feeling foolish, I turned and entered our house.

Chapter 8

THE FOLLOWING SUNDAY PAPA DECIDED THAT HE WOULD GO WITH me to the cemetery. It was the only place where Jews could freely enjoy nature. Until that Sunday Papa and Mama had shown no desire to visit it, even though their parents were buried there. But Papa had been confined to the house so much he longed to see green trees and breathe fresh air.

We visited the old section of the cemetery that I liked best. It had not been tended for years and a thick, untrimmed hedge ran all around it. Many of the stones, we noted, were sinking deep into the earth. Papa read the barely legible Hebrew inscriptions, and translated them for me.

Suddenly we heard somebody approaching. Looking up, I saw Abek. After I had introduced him to Papa he said that he had met Escia strolling along one of the paths and she had told him that Papa and I were nearby.

"I wanted to see you," he said simply. I felt Papa's swift questioning glance, but he did not say anything.

When Abek learned that we had been reading the inscriptions on the stones he addressed Papa in fluent Hebrew. This seemed the right moment for me to get away.

"I am sure that you and Papa will get along fine without me. I want to see Ilse anyway," I said, and ran as fast as I could.

After an hour or so, I saw Papa and Abek coming down the path leading to Escia's home, talking with great animation. Papa was glad to find someone he could talk to about the study of Hebrew.

"Just imagine," he told me, "Abek has a book that I have wanted to read for a long time. Now I can finally get it."

"I am very glad," I said unenthusiastically, "but I think we ought to go home. Mama will be waiting."

Papa looked at me curiously. I usually urged him to stay out longer. He spent too much of his time in the damp cellar room.

"Let us go home then," he agreed.

"I'll see you very soon," Abek said in farewell.

We walked home in silence.

Papa told Mama of the encounter with Abek, and how glad he was to have found another Hebrew scholar. I was knitting, and tried not to pay any attention.

While Mama was fixing supper, Papa called me to his side. "I want to talk to you about Abek," he said quietly.

"What about him?" I feigned indifference.

"I am convinced that the boy cares a lot for you."

"Papa, you are talking silly. I don't even know him." I started to walk away.

"Wait just one minute," he said, "Abek is a fine boy. I could see it during the short time that I spent with him. The fact that you hardly mentioned him is proof enough that you may care for him. I only ask one thing of you: whatever life may bring, try not to make any decisions during this horrible war. Grow up slowly. Enjoy life. I want to see you laughing more than anything else. You have already cried enough in your young life."

Several days later, when Abek came and brought Papa the book he had promised, I made it my business not to remain at home.

Papa was quite annoyed that I did not return until late, and he told me that Abek had asked about me several times. He had even offered to fetch me from Ilse's house, where I had gone, but Papa had persuaded him to stay.

The news from the Eastern front was disheartening, and there were no letters from Arthur. This time we all knew much better how to conceal our concern.

My girl friends in Bielitz had heard from their brothers. Gisa, in Krakow, wrote again and again, this time not kindling our hopes, but expecting comfort from us.

One bright morning early in October the mailman handed me two letters, one from a friend living in the *Gouvernement,* the other, a square white envelope without a return address, addressed in black ink in unfamiliar writing.

As I opened this one the black ink seemed to be transformed into a rainbow of colors. Scribbled on a tiny sheet, in Arthur's handwriting, were a few words telling that he was well and working and that he would write more as soon as the mail could go through normal channels again. Someone apparently had taken that note into the *Gouvernement,* and a stranger had transmitted it to us from there.

Papa's and Mama's eyes glittered with tears of joy. It was. the second time Arthur had escaped the murderous Germans.

That afternoon Abek came. In my happiness I was kind to him and a different relationship developed. From then on he came almost daily. Inasmuch as he worked outside the camp, restoring paintings and hanging them in German homes, he came and went unchallenged. He seemed to enjoy more privileges than anybody else in camp, perhaps because he painted portraits for the guards.

He brought me books, and we had many discussions. Often, after having talked to me for several hours, he would return to camp, only to write me a lengthy letter.

Life had new meaning, and became more and more interesting. Abek no longer assumed the superior air with me that he employed in talking to others, but unconsciously fell into the role of older brother. He was six years older than I, but this difference in age, which at first had seemed greater to me, became less and less important. My parents were glad about Abek's coming. Papa had someone to talk to, and they knew it was very good for me to have a friend.

Toward the end of October we received our first direct letter from Arthur since the Germans had attacked Russia. It was not much different from his earlier brief note. He was working in a chemical plant and was well. Though he assured us that we were not to worry about him, I thought I detected a reference to hardship.

November came with lots of snow and frost and we had to face the prospect of a bleak, heatless winter with little food. One morning Ilse arrived, completely out of breath. After she recovered she told us that a policeman had seen her beautiful piano and had ordered her to turn it over to him. With tears in her eyes she said, "Please come home with me, Gerda. I want to play it for the last time."

Since Jews were not allowed on busses, we had an hour's walk in a bitter wind. After the ordeal Ilse's house was a haven of warmth. Her grandparents and mother anxiously inquired about my parents. Ilse's little sister Kitty, a sweet child with large dark eyes and piquant, pointed face, cuddled on my lap and asked to be told stories, until finally Mrs. Kleinzähler called her away. The grownups left the room and I stayed alone with Ilse. She sat down at the piano; I settled into the deep wine-colored couch and listened to her playing.

The snowy wind was howling at the windows and by four o'clock it began to grow dark. Ilse did not turn on the light. She kept on playing without pause; first, gay waltzes, then stormy polonaises, Chopin's "Funeral March," lilting dance melodies. Her choices reflected our many moods. When the street lamps across the road were lighted, their dim light fell on Ilse and created a grotesque shadow of her on the polished wood of the piano. She was now completely absorbed, giving herself entirely to her music.

Away from her piano Ilse was shy and withdrawn; only through her music was she able to express herself openly. Her music seemed to ask over and over again that painful "Why?" that our hearts kept asking; and that "Why?" she asked with bluish lips three and a half years later in another darkness in a wet, cold meadow as she died in my arms, having barely turned eighteen.

The door opened slowly. I was not conscious of Abek's entering. Without saying a word he sat next to me. Ilse continued her playing. He put my hand in his and kept it there. I tried gently to withdraw it but when I saw his eyes I stopped. With both hands he held my trembling fingers. Then I felt his warm breath and his quivering lips upon my hands. First very gently, then with growing passion, he kissed each finger and each nail. I looked at him, but he didn't seem to see me. Finally Ilse stopped playing, rose from the piano, and turned on a lamp. I was glad for the break and jumped up and went to her. For a moment nobody spoke. Then Ilse offered us tea. I said I would prefer to go home before my parents began worrying about me. Then I asked Abek how he had known where I was. He told me he had been to my home and my parents had told him. He offered to take me back again. I replied that it wasn't necessary. Besides, although I didn't tell him so, I didn't like to be with him on the streets. I always felt his humiliation when we met German soldiers and he had to take his hat off and step down from the sidewalk to let them pass. Abek, possibly because he sensed my feeling, suggested we take a new route home, along a road just being built. Since there were no sidewalks in yet there would be little traffic, and almost no likelihood of meeting Germans. After saying good-by to Ilse, off we went.

The wind had stopped. It was snowing gently. Abek started to tell me about his family. They lived in Sosnowitz, about forty-five kilometers north of Bielitz. His parents were very old. He had six sisters and three brothers, all much older than he. His religious training had been orthodox, and he had rejected it without finding peace in his more liberal outlook. He had never been more talkative. All at once he interrupted himself and in his mocking, ironical way he quoted the final words of a famous Hebrew poem written by an orthodox Jew turned reformed, who, like Abek, had never quite found himself in his new environment: "And even if I wear the silken shirt and assume modern manners, happy and full of joy I will never be!" And that was the portrait of Abek's soul. The chains of the ghettos bound him and the bitterness and the ironical smile were a mask to hide his self-consciousness. At that moment I pitied him even though both of us were now bound by the same chains. His childhood had been different from mine. I had known a happiness and freedom that he had never known.

He continued, "For you religion is something wonderful.

It's a port in a troubled sea. It's a clean, pure feeling. You believe and still you are free, but for me—"

He didn't have to say it. I knew now how he felt.

We reached home and I said I had better go in.

"But," he said, "there is so much yet I want to tell you."

I said, "I will just go in and tell my parents that I am here."

He continued to talk and when I finally said good night he pulled me gently toward him. I tried to pull from his embrace but his arms were like steel. I was afraid that he would try to kiss me. However, he didn't try. With his lips close to mine he said,

"There is something I want to tell you. It has been on my mind for a long time. I would much prefer to say nothing but tomorrow may be too late."

"What about tomorrow?" I exclaimed.

He picked up my thought. "I might be sent away from here. Perhaps tomorrow, perhaps the day after. Nobody knows and therefore I have to tell you how much I love you. Life does not have much value these days, and mine has none at all, but having you makes me want to live. But answer me. Do you love me too?"

I couldn't speak. I liked Abek very much. I respected his intelligence and judgment. He was the best friend I had ever had and now I knew that friend was gone. I searched for an answer, for an impetuous, happy, bubbling answer, but there was none.

Then his voice came again as from another world. "You can make me the happiest man in the world." Pointing to the yellow star and the word JEW over his heart, he continued, "In spite of this, love is all that matters. My parents wrote me today that they approve wholeheartedly."

"What?" I said. "You wrote to your parents?"

"I had to," he said, "before I asked you. Please don't misunderstand me," he continued, "I don't want to marry you now. That would be stupid and selfish. All I want is your promise to marry me after the war. It will give me all the courage I need to get through."

60

"Your question is quite unexpected," I said in a hoarse voice, "and you are asking much too much of me. You know I like you but I don't know if that is love. I can't tell you yes because I would be lying and besides, I feel since you asked your parents I am entitled to do the same." My only wish was to escape. "I must go now," I said, "and think about it." There was a lump in my throat.

"I'll see you tomorrow," he said.

I turned toward our house in bewilderment. Instinctively I felt that I could never love Abek. He did not possess the strength that I had known in my father and brother and that I expected in the man I would love. Had he held me in his arms and told me that he would take care of me and shield me, had he not asked me to kiss him but kissed me masterfully and assuredly, I might have given him the answer he wanted. His weakness shattered my illusions.

I went to bed early and pretended to sleep but I kept thinking about the proposal. No, no, it wasn't at all the way I imagined it would happen. There were no gay garden parties and music and dancing in the starlight. What Abek offered me was probably deeper and truer than anything else I could expect, but it wasn't what I was looking for. I hadn't asked for it. He wants to marry me, I said over and over to myself. He said I could make him happy. Then I understood the cause of my sadness. I didn't want to make anybody happy. I wanted someone to make me happy. I knew that there was laughter and I wanted someone who could laugh with me. I remembered the poem that Abek had quoted and I knew that the man at my side could not be Abek. I sat up in bed and called Papa and Mama and I told them about Abek.

"What did you answer?" Papa asked me.

"Nothing yet, Papa. I am supposed to give him my answer tomorrow and I am quite sure it will be 'No.' "

And then I grew angry. I felt that Abek didn't have the right to ask me what he did, he didn't have the right to disturb my peace and that of my family. I dismissed the argument that tomorrow it might be too late, that he might be

61

sent away. I was aware only of my feeling, not of his, and I felt quite sorry for myself.

I must have made a dramatic picture, sitting cross-legged in an outgrown nightgown in the mildewed basement of our home. There were Papa and Mama, too old for their years, looking at their child to whom love had just been offered, and one floor above us was the room where twenty-five years before Papa had offered Mama his love. Papa probably understood Abek best. He had been about to go to the front in the First World War when he had told Mama of his love. He didn't want to marry then for fear that he might leave her a widow. But he too had wanted her word and something to come back to. Looking at Mama now, was he thinking of that winter night when he asked her and she, full of happiness, accepted? And was Mama thinking of that day too, remembering the happiness she had felt, and how the war hadn't really mattered because she had known that she would be his wife?

Finally, I fell asleep. When I awoke at dawn, Mama and Papa were talking in whispers. Mama seemed to be taking Abek's side but Papa was more critical and again and again the words *war* and *abnormal* entered the conversation. Then Papa said, "I am afraid she loves him." Mama answered, "No, she doesn't. If she did, she would be happy."

That afternoon Abek came. He looked pale and tired. I was very self-conscious and could not look into his eyes. Fortunately, Ilse appeared a few minutes later to tell us how the Germans had come for the piano. Much as I sympathized with her, for once I was glad not to have to carry the burden of conversation. After an awkward hour in which Abek and I both felt dejected and ill at ease, Ilse sensed that something was amiss and said that she had to go home. I arose to go with her. To my dismay, Abek insisted on accompanying us.

We walked with Ilse less than halfway when I decided to return home. There was no use, I had to face him. As soon as Ilse was out of earshot, Abek's voice grew soft.

"I am sorry," he said, and I winced—I had known he would

apologize. "I should not have said it yesterday"—his voice betrayed anxiety. "Have you got an answer?"

I could not bring myself to say "No." I hated the idea of losing him completely. If only we could simply be friends . . .

"One does not change one's feelings overnight," I heard myself saying. "I would like to continue seeing you but I think it would be better if you didn't mention love until after the war."

He was biting his lip and there was suffering in his eyes as he nodded silently. I knew that I would not be carefree with him again.

It was getting dark as we approached our house. At our fence I looked wistfully toward my beloved garden, now covered by snow. The trees seemed grotesque, silhouetted against the darkening sky. Only the pines looked merry, spreading their branches like wings toward the heavens.

"How beautiful," I breathed, enchanted with the picture.

"How beautiful," Abek repeated. I was in his arms. I struggled to free myself. His lips brushed my cheek.

"Leave me alone!" I cried out.

Instantly his arms released me. "I am sorry," he muttered and without another word he left.

That was more effective than anything else he could have done. I was sorry to see him go, afraid I might never see him again. By that one abrupt gesture he gained more of me than by all his devotion. He appeared mysterious, desirable.

As I reached the house, he returned. "I forgot to give you something." His voice was steady and quiet. He pulled a small package out of his breast pocket.

"What is it?" I asked in surprise.

"A book I found that I thought you would like."

"Thank you," I said a bit too eagerly. "Good night." I held out my hand to him. He gripped it.

"Good night," he said. "I am sorry about before. I will try not to do it again."

When I stood alone again, I wished he had not come back. I wished he were not sorry. Why hadn't he taken me in his arms and kissed me, not caring about my protests?

I stooped and scooped up a handful of the fresh snow and wiped my face with it. It was refreshing and felt good. Inside, I opened the gift. It was a thin volume of Chinese love poems. As I read the beautiful words I thought again of Abek —with annoyance.

Chapter 9

SEVERAL WEEKS WENT BY AND THE YEAR 1941 WAS DRAWING TO a close. I still saw Abek almost daily, although for a while our meetings consisted chiefly of awkward silences. Then, gradually, I was able to laugh and joke with him once again, even though always aware that he wanted to marry me, that hé interpreted each pleasant word or gesture as a sign that I might be changing my attitude.

In December I got a letter from a former classmate of mine, Erika. Erika, her parents, and little brother had fled Bielitz shortly before the Germans came and were living in a small town in the *Gouvernement* near the former Polish-Russian border. Erika and I looked very much alike and were often mistaken for one another. We had never been close friends, but now, in these tragic, lonely times, as I wrote to even casual acquaintances, I began to realize how much Erika and I had in common. Thinking back to our school days and how she used to rise to answer the teacher's questions, I again saw her straight back, clad in the regulation navy serge, the short bob of her black hair, the dimples in her somewhat pale face. I knew her as Erika who flung her books over her shoulder; Erika who preferred milk hot rather than cold; Erika who had a daring wish to wear a red dress to school just once instead of that navy blue. That was all I knew of Erika. Yet she had thoughts so like mine, which were never spoken. Only now, when several hundred miles were between us, did she sit down in an alien room at a strange table to write these thoughts that I understood.

Her letter was different from so many others. There was no longing for the school years in it, or for friends we both had lost. "I am in love. We want to get married. Henek is everything I ever dreamed of and more, much more. My parents oppose, can you understand why? My own parents who always claim to love me and to want my happiness only. *His* parents understand how we feel. One never knows how many months or weeks we can have together. Why make it hard for us? I wish we could run away, but how? Where to? One needs identifications. But I am sure that in the end my parents will give their consent and I will be the happiest girl in the world."

I brooded over that letter, examining it in the light of my feelings toward Abek. Erika was in love, I decided. I was not.

I waited to hear more from Erika, hoping that her parents would understand her, and then I realized with shock that I, a mere seventeen, would have a married woman as a friend.

Abek seemed to depend more and more on me. I fully realized this shortly before Christmas when he told me that there was a good chance he might go home for the holidays. The guards took a week or so off and since most of them lived in Sosnowitz—Abek's home town and that of most of the boys in camp—they might take the boys home. He was quite excited when he told me about the possibility.

"Oh, I am sure you will go," I answered in my lighthearted manner.

The following day he came later than usual, explaining that he had had to pack for the trip. I told him how glad I was for him and asked when he had learned he would be going.

"You told me yesterday," he said in a matter-of-fact tone.

"What do you mean?" I demanded, bewildered.

"I believe in your intuition," was his simple reply.

He presented me with another book before he left. I found his picture between the pages and an underlined sentence which read, "What the heart and even mind won't do, time will settle if given a chance." I tried to interpret the statement in various ways but it boiled down to the same thing. I showed it to Papa. "Well," he said with a smile, "I am glad that at least you are giving yourself time."

Abek was to stay away for a week, but on the fourth evening after he had left there was a knock on our door and there he stood. Still standing in the doorway he whispered, "I could not stand it any longer. I had to come back."

None of us offered a warm welcome.

"What about your parents?" Mama asked pointedly—we all knew only too well that each furlough might be the last that he would spend with his family.

"Your parents surely minded," Papa said, looking sternly at Abek.

"No, not at all. They understand. They too love you, Gerda."

I looked away, but in a flash I saw Papa's glance meeting Mama's bewildered look. Blood shot into my cheeks—Abek had never spoken of his feelings in front of my parents.

There was a meaningful silence which Mama interrupted with, "I'd better start supper."

I stood at the window, trembling.

Abek took off his coat, then came toward me. "You did come to a decision?"

I did not answer.

"You love me, don't you? When I was away, you knew you did."

I still did not answer.

"That's why I came back." There was pain in his voice. The anticipation was gone.

"Abek, why must you do this?" Why must you do this to me?

After Abek left, I felt uneasiness in the silence. I knew Papa was angry. Years before, when I had been naughty during the day, I had waited for the after-supper hour, when Papa would discuss my offense. Punishment was never severe. To know that Papa was displeased was often enough. This evening, after dinner, Mama resumed her knitting. Papa filled his pipe and tried again and again to light it. The tobacco was poor and would not light. Papa emptied the bowl painstakingly and started to refill it, packing it not quite so firmly. Mama looked up from her knitting; questioningly she looked at Papa. He did not speak, not yet. The pipe was filled now. Papa tore a piece of paper into a long shred, held it over the chimney of the kerosene lamp. The paper caught fire. The tobacco crackled. It caught. I waited. But Papa knows, I was saying to myself, Papa knows everything about Abek. Why is he angry with me now?

Slowly the smoke puffed.

"I don't like it," Papa said.

That set me off. "I don't like it either," I broke out. "What should I do, Papa? What shall I do?"

"He is a nice boy." It was like a justification from Papa.

Then I started to cry. Papa pulled me over toward him, his hand stroking my hair, his frayed sleeve brushing over my eyes.

"Papa, what did I do wrong? I want to see Abek, I told him that, but I don't want to be bound, tied. Papa, am I wrong? Tell me, Papa."

I don't think Papa ever thought me wrong. After a while he said, "That still does not make it right for the boy."

Christmas passed and 1942 began, terrifyingly cold, with lots of snow. I couldn't recall so severe a winter. Early in the new year my mother's uncle died. Papa went to the funeral. Mama stayed with the widow while a grave was hastily dug, a few quiet prayers said, a handful of earth thrown on a crude casket.

I was home alone, waiting for Papa and Mama, when a letter came. There was no return address on it. The handwriting looked like Erika's. I was afraid to open it. Somehow I felt that this letter did not contain the happy news of her marriage. When I finally tore the envelope open, my fears were confirmed. In it were a few tattered pages from a child's notebook, some of the letters big, as if written by a six-year-old, others tiny. Although there were no marks of tears, the letter seemed to vibrate with pain. Here is what I read.

It is dark outside. It is night. A deadly silence hangs over the house where two days ago there was so much life, so much dear life. I am sitting on the floor to catch the little light that is falling from the tavern across the street to a patch on the floor. It is a dull patch of bluish light and in it lies my paper. "They" are sitting in the tavern—"they" the murderers. I am in the dark, alone in the dark, just as my heart and my soul will forever remain in the dark and the light of those criminals, the light of their crime illuminates the paper to let me write about their deeds.

Do you know what happened? No, you don't know. Yesterday, yes, it was yesterday, early in the morning we heard a lot of noise— screams and crying and begging for mercy. They were the cries of Jewish people in the streets. Quickly my father and I ran down the back stairs to hide in the basement, while Mother went to get the baby out of his crib. He was sleepily rubbing his eyes. He was so small, he did not know that you had to be watchful even in your sleep, that night and day you must be on guard, quickly go and hide. Maybe he was dreaming of toys he never had. Maybe my mother did not wake him fast enough. I imagine how he stood, rubbing his baby eyes, when the murderers entered in their gray uniforms and took them both, my mother and the baby. He was not dressed because his little suit is still lying there on the chair. The pants of his pajamas are still lying there. He must have kicked them off and gone half naked. From the cellar we heard screams.

Why does the world go on when things like this happen? We heard distant screams for hours and hours. Only when night fell was it quiet. We hoped and we prayed that Mama and the child had found refuge somewhere.

After it had been dark for hours we crawled out of the cellar. The house was empty. Empty was our flat, empty the flats of all our friends and that of the boy I loved. Where are they? We went to the street. We went to all the homes. We met a few ghostlike people who were swaying as if coming from another world. In one house we found an old man dressed in his garment of white in which to stand before God on the Day of Judgment. He was saying the prayer for the dead. We begged him to tell us what happened. He looked at us wild-eyed, pointed with his finger to heaven, and continued to pray. Like a sacred figure about to enter heaven he stood there alone, around him a world of sin and unspeakable crime. Finally, we met a young man who told us the tragic tale. Old people, young people, and children all had been taken to the market place. There they had undressed and lain naked on the stones, face down, and the murderers on horses and brandishing guns trampled on that screaming human pavement. Many were killed by the horseshoes, the whips left bloody traces. After the initial thirst of the sadists was satisfied, those who remained alive had to march naked outside the town. They had to dig their own grave and stand on the rim until a hail of bullets killed them. Strangers embraced as they went to sleep forever.

We went there. What were laws now, forbidding Jews to leave

the city limits? But nobody caught us or cared. The moon was shining. We saw a great square grave, half-open yet, a mountain of naked bodies in it. Many we recognized. We found my mother. She was all bloody. We did not find my little brother. I found Henek, the one I loved more than life, who was to be my husband. I kissed his dead face. Not one tear did I shed in that grave. Only my heart died. Do you know what? If they would come tomorrow and kill my father I would not care. I would not cry. I would be glad for him. I wish they would kill me. From now on I will walk wherever it is not permitted. I want them to catch me. I want them to kill me because I don't care. There is only one thing that could stir within me. I want a gun. I want a knife. I want to kill, just kill. I have no feeling. It won't be a crime. Maybe it won't even give me satisfaction, but I want to kill.

What are we waiting for? My father's hair is snowy white. He hasn't spoken, or eaten, or slept, or cried. He is watching me while I write this. He is like an animal. I don't think he knows me. My little brother's clothes are there. I can't touch them. There is a brooch on my dress, a little heart that Henek gave me. There are no hearts. All hearts are dead. How does one bury a heart? I am writing something to you. It's good to tell it, but who are you? Are you alive? Didn't they murder you yet? Too bad if you too have died—then you would not get this letter from a girl named Erika who has a dead heart.

I never heard from Erika again.

Chapter 10

Two TENSE WEEKS FOLLOWED WITHOUT NEWS FROM ARTHUR. Troubled with the most horrible images of what might have happened to him, I had a hard battle with myself not to tell my parents about Erika's letter.

Abek came one afternoon when I was alone, and I could stand it no longer. I told him everything: about my wakefulness at night, my nightmares when I slept, my frantic worry about Arthur. Then I read Erika's letter to him. For the first time in years I felt unburdened by talking without reservation. He understood. He offered no empty words of comfort but held me in his arms while I talked. When I finished and rested my head on his shoulder, he stroked my hair with loving caresses, he kissed my feverish forehead, my tear-streaked cheeks. I was comforted and at peace. I never liked him better, or felt closer to him.

"Everything will be all right," he whispered.

Not looking up, not thinking I said, "I know it will be, Arthur." I felt him grow rigid. I looked up. His face was stony. "Abek," I said, but could not finish. Of course he resented my indifference to him.

The next morning Arthur's long-awaited letter arrived. It contained no real news, except a change of address. I thought his hand was not as regular as ever. I seemed to detect a certain strain. Was it only my imagination? Surely, Papa and Mama noticed it too. If they did, they said nothing.

I admired my brother's courage and strength, his ability to conceal everything that was painful. I imagined him sitting in some unknown dark room, late at night, writing home those banal words while listening for dreaded footsteps, fearing tomorrow.

And so the winter passed, with Arthur's frequent letters providing the only relief. Each day brought new announcements of deeper German penetrations into Russia. Far into the night our knitting needles would click in a desperate race against the ever-worsening food and fuel shortages, but nothing depressed us as much as the chilling thought that no army seemed capable of stemming the German advance. Somehow winter seemed to be our enemy. Fervently we hoped for an early spring. Spring would mean that we would no longer need to worry how to heat our cellar. There would be more vegetables, more food, the days would be longer, the fearful nights shorter. But had I known what else the spring of 1942 would mean, I would have prayed that winter should last forever.

On the morning of the nineteenth of April all Jews were ordered to prepare to move to the shabby, remote quarter of town near the railroad terminal. Here, where cattle and produce were unloaded, there were a few unoccupied, decrepit houses. In two short days they would become our ghetto.

Nobody said much. We all had expected it, but for Mama it was the hardest blow. She did not mind the cellar for it was ours in the house of her childhood—in the house where she had been born, and her mother and grandmother before her, where she had married, where her parents had died and her children were born. Now we had to leave it. Was it so hard to leave because we sensed that we would never return?

Very early on the morning we were to leave, long before the hour when we were allowed to go out, I ran down the street to say good-by to Niania. I crept up the creaking stairs and without knocking gently pushed the door. I knew it would be open. Niania was sitting at the window. Her long gray hair lay about her shoulders, the big shawl on which I had fallen asleep so many times was wrapped around her. She held her prayer book in one hand, her crucifix in the other. Without looking up, she continued to pray. I saw her in that early dawn like a figure in a beautiful, long-forgotten dream. At her feet was the little wooden stool on which I used to sit in childhood when she would tell me stories while she sewed dresses for my dolls. Her window box was then full of flowers. She used to say, "Those flowers are for you when you grow up." But Niania said nothing to me now. While she said her paternoster I looked about the room I had known so well. There was the green pillow cover I had crocheted when I was ten. In her cupboard were the gleaming cups I had sipped from so often. I knew them all—the one with the purple flowers, the fat one with the picture of Emperor Franz Josef, the one with the tiny crack that Niania would not pour anything hot into. . . .

In her wooden wardrobe dresses were hanging neatly. The brown one with tiny glass buttons. The black one, a bit shiny and frayed, that she still wore to church. There was the fine black silk dress covered with a sheet. Niania often said she would wear this one only three times. She had it made to wear at her granddaughter's wedding, she would wear it when I got married, and then forever in her coffin. On her night-table there was a large Madonna in blue and gold with a flaming heart. She had brought it from a pilgrimage to Czestochowa.

Niania's room was as orderly as ever; nothing had changed in it since I could remember. I couldn't help but compare her comfortable room to our cellar home. I could picture our few pitiful bundles standing on the floor, several old blackened pots and pans, some mended clothes, a basket with a few dried peas, a loaf of bread, a little salt, a small jar of homemade jam, a little cocoa from before the war, the pot of chives under which the remains of our jewelry had been buried. Now Papa and Mama were tying the bundles in a sheet. That was all that remained from a beautiful home.

I despised Niania at that moment for her security. She could stay, but we had to go.

With a harsh voice I finally said, "I came to say good-by, Niania. We have to go, you know. I hope I will see you soon again."

I wanted to get out fast. Niania's deep voice went through me.

"Gertele, come back."

She called me by my childhood nickname. At the sound of that long-forgotten name I felt a tightening in my throat. When I turned around, her work-worn hands stretched toward me. I ran into her embrace. She sat me on the little stool at her feet, her hard, calloused hands stroking my hair.

"My poor child," she said.

I put my head in her lap, I felt her warm tears on my hair, I felt my own tears start.

Then the picture of our cellar room came back to me.

"I have to go now, Niania," I said finally.

She pushed me back into the chair, begging, "Stay, please, stay a little longer."

"No, Niania, I have to go to Mama and Papa. They send you all their love. You know they cannot come. It is too dangerous."

I embraced her once more and ran out.

At home we sat silently. This was the last morning in our home. I could not stand it in the cellar. I went into the yard and then I jumped over the fence into the garden, the garden which I had so loved. I did not care if anybody caught me, I had to see my beloved garden again. It had rained during the night and the young fresh grass was wet. I looked at the rich moist soil under my feet. Everywhere memories surrounded me. On an old tall branch was a piece of rotted string. I knew it: a few years before, Arthur had flown a kite, it stuck in the tree, and we had never got it down. Wind, snow, and rain had blown the paper away but the little bit of string was still there.

On the old pear tree there was a mark made by a Scout knife driven into it years ago by Arthur. There had been a note under it that day reading, "I am a prisoner of the Cow-Cow tribe." We had played Indians and Arthur had been taken prisoner; that heroic sword and note were supposed to save him. The note was gone a long, long time and Arthur was far, far away. . . .

There were the narrow, now overgrown paths where I rode my tricycle and wheeled my dolls. There was the little garden house, now badly in need of paint; we had used

74

to paint it every spring. From one corner of its ceiling hung some faded yellowish paper. It had been a Japanese lantern in the shape of a full moon, for my fifteenth birthday party. We had left it there because it looked so funny.

Was it really only three years since Mama and Papa, young and gay, had stood arm in arm with Papa watching us eat ice cream and cake? How happy I had been that day!

I ran down to the edge of the brook where I knew I could find violets, and there they were, in their velvety brilliance, fresh, untouched, and fragrant. I picked a bunch and held them tight and then sat down on the moist ground and started to cry, thinking of the velvet lawn, of the yellow dandelions that soon would be blooming in abundance, thinking of the birds that sang in the trees at night, thinking of the blooming cherry trees, the red fruit hanging from the branches, of the rich autumn that would paint the leaves in bright hues, of the gleaming fruit, of the sunshine and rain that would come to my garden in all seasons. And all this we were not to see any more.

There by the brook, thinking and crying softly, I bade farewell to my childhood. Then I walked toward the house, not the front entrance, but the side where the bedrooms faced. I did not care whether I was caught or not, I had to see my beloved home once more!

A shade went up in my parents' room and I saw the familiar cream-colored wallpaper. Soon Mama's head would appear and she would say to Papa, "You had better take your umbrella, Julius. In April one never knows." Then she would come into my room, gently kiss my forehead; I would stretch, turn around, and sigh. "Take your raincoat to school today," she would say.

I started to walk back now, not along the path but over the young grass. Here was the plum tree with the funny twisted branch on which we used to swing; it felt wet, cool, and familiar. I sat on it, closed my eyes. For a moment, for one moment only, I will pretend that nothing has happened. I leaned back, swinging on the old branch. I will go into the house now, I thought. They will be at the breakfast table, Mama pouring the hot coffee, Papa buttering his bun. Arthur will gather his books together and hurry to a lecture. The white cups will gleam on the table, crumbs will be scattered on the checkered cloth. "Look at the lovely violets; oh, they are perfect!" Mama will exclaim. "Go put them in the dining room." "Which vase, Mama?" "Put them in the shallow silver bowl. Short-stemmed flowers look their best like that." Yes, Mama is right, it's hard to tell if the bowl does more for the flowers or the other way around. I better hurry. I will be late for school. . . .

Late? Yes, late. Slowly I creep back to reality. I will be late because we are going away from here. Why is it all so hard? The war will end soon, we will all be back home. Somehow the thought brought no comfort. I felt way down in my heart that I would never be back again.

A bird fluttered in the branches above me. Somewhere a dog barked. I embraced the twisted branch and kissed its rough wet bark. "Good-by, good-by," I murmured.

"Where were you?" Mama asked when I went downstairs again.

"Out in the garden," I answered.

Then I saw Niania sitting on an old kitchen chair. She had braved danger to come to us. Papa was urging her to go. She refused.

A wagon drawn by an old sleepy horse pulled up in front of the house and a peasant with his son started to load our meager belongings. Then Niania embraced Mama and they both cried. She grabbed Papa's hand and before he could protest she kissed it.

"You brought up my grandchild, you gave me a home for thirteen years, I loved you like my own son."

Papa embraced her and kissed her cheek. She wept on his shoulder and looking at me, she said, "It was a morning like this when she was born. You carried her in your arms toward the window. You said she was your princess, our little sunshine princess. Where are you taking her now?" Her voice was terrible. "Where?" she repeated. Then Niania started to pray. Papa and Mama lowered their heads.

The wardrobe and Mama's and Papa's beds were on the wagon. The furniture was mildewed from the dampness in the cellar. It looked strange and unfamiliar on the wagon. We took a last look into every corner of the cellar. How gladly would we have stayed here, how desirable the cellar looked! The peasant snapped the reins. "*Hetta wio. Hetta wio.*" The old horse began to walk . . . slowly the cart started to move. Papa and Mama and I followed the wagon with bowed heads, as though walking behind a hearse. Here and there neighbors looked from behind curtains, waved mute farewells, wiping tears into handkerchiefs. Papa and Mama didn't see them. Papa carried the pot of chives, Mama her black shopping bag with our bread, our salt, the dried peas, the precious cocoa and jam. I still clutched the violets I had picked.

When we reached the bend of the street where Arthur had slowed down, instinctively Papa and Mama slowed down too. They wanted to look back, I knew, but at the crucial moment Papa took Mama's hand and they went on. I looked back though—the only one who did so. No one was in sight. The tree branches swung in the mild breeze. The windows of our home gleamed in the sunlight.

Chapter II

Before I opened my eyes I felt the peculiar strangeness of waking in an unfamiliar room. Most peculiar was the brightness—I was used to the darkness of our cellar. When I opened my eyes, there in the sunlight was our old furniture, shabbier than I had imagined, but at the same time clean and bright. Both Papa and Mama, with whom I shared our one room, were in much better spirits than I remembered in a long time. The thing that we had feared most was done. The act of moving was over.

We had never lived anywhere else before. There had always been our home: the garden, the attic, the shacks in the yard, the garden house. Somewhere in the back of my mind I had always felt that the walls of our home would protect us. Now I fully understood why we had dreaded the move to the ghetto.

The ghetto consisted of a number of buildings of which only three faced the street. Ours was one of them. Another one next door was occupied by the Kultusgemeinde. The one adjacent to it housed several families. The other houses, behind these, were grouped around a cobbled courtyard. Wooden porches ran clear around the courtyard, connecting all the houses on both floors. To me those porches were somehow symbolic of the way our lives were linked and I felt safer in the knowledge that we were not alone.

All the Jews now remaining in Bielitz lived in those few houses and in a huge armory-like building with primitive plumbing, ten minutes' walk from the Kultusgemeinde.

There were about 250 Jewish people left in Bielitz, most of them old and sick. None of our once numerous kin were in this group, and there were few of our old friends. Just a handful of trusting, lonely people who either could not or would not leave Bielitz.

As the days went by and we settled into monotonous routine, we relied more and more on the news and rumors we heard at the Kultusgemeinde. More and more frequently the dreaded word *Aussiedlung* (deportation) crept into conversations. Young people, we heard, were sent to labor camps. The old ones were sent to Auschwitz. Even then we knew what kind of a camp it was. Somehow we never believed that what happened to Jews in other towns would ever happen to us. Each time, however, that I returned from the Kultusgemeinde I would swiftly run up the steps to the apartment that we shared with the Kolländers to be reassured that Papa and Mama were still there.

The Kolländers were very religious. The pious old mother alternately cried or prayed. There were also two unmarried daughters in their late twenties and a son about forty-five years old. He had been paralyzed in both legs early in the war when a tunnel under his home had been blown up. His wife and only daughter were somewhere in the part of Poland still occupied by Russia.

In the adjoining apartment lived a couple by the name of Freudenreich. Mrs. Freudenreich was a frail, sweet, gentle person. Her eyes were always red. The first day I saw her and said good morning she asked me to come in. I was struck by a large number of photographs and paintings in her room, all of a girl of about nine or ten. Her room was like a shrine for her young daughter, who had died in an accident in Vienna a few years before. Mrs. Freudenreich talked in a monotone about her daughter and her tragic death. I said nothing. When I got up she kissed me. "It's been so long since I kissed a child," she said. "You must come often." And I did.

Downstairs lived a young woman with charming twin girls. They were four years old, golden blond and blue-eyed. I loved to play with them while their mother told me about her husband, who had gone with the same transport as Arthur. She showed me some of his letters. They were full of love and

79

anxiety to see his children. Those dreams were never to come true.

In another room near ours a middle-aged woman lived with her old mother. The mother was dying of cancer and the daughter seemed to be losing her sanity. Her biggest concern was her inability to obtain olive oil for her complexion.

When I thought of our neighbors, I sometimes had a feeling that we were the only normal family there.

We got used to living in the ghetto. Ilse, Rita, and Ruth lived close by and I saw them often. Abek came as frequently as before.

We had been in the ghetto for about two weeks when one day, while only Papa and I were home, there was a knock at the door strong enough to break it. We knew it could only be the Gestapo. Papa hid in the wardrobe while I opened the door and faced a husky, red-faced, uniformed man with pistol in hand.

"Where is your father?" he shouted at me.

"I don't know," I whispered.

"Don't you have one?"

I shook my head.

"What are you? A bastard?" he yelled. "All Jews are bastards."

"Where is your father?" he yelled again.

"I don't know." I could hardly move my lips.

"You will tell me right now or I will shoot you like a dog." He pointed his pistol at my heart. I felt its cold muzzle pressing my breast. When I heard Papa move in the wardrobe, I was paralyzed with horror, realizing that he might show himself in order to save me. At this moment there was a tooting of horns and shouting outside.

The intruder lowered his gun and hurried away. We learned later that the Gestapo had combed the ghetto in search of someone and that the sound of the horn was a signal that the victim had been found.

White as paper, Papa staggered out of the wardrobe. He had heard the threats but had not known that the pistol was already touching my breast. Papa's eyes were glassy. He lay

80

exhausted on his bed and I brought him water. When he winced in pain and sweat broke out on his brow, I gave him one of the pills Dr. Reach had left for emergencies.

"Don't tell Mama," he whispered. I shook my head.

"There is one wish," Papa continued, "one wish only—you and Arthur." He fell into a gentle sleep. I wiped the sweat from his forehead. Slowly a little color came back into his face.

Then fear gripped me that my beloved Papa might die. I shut my eyes tight to avoid seeing his gray hair, his lined face, his frayed sleeves—to feel for a moment close to the happy, vital Papa of my childhood.

When Papa woke, after an hour's rest, he seemed a shade paler, a shade grayer and older.

Chapter 12

A FEW DAYS LATER, ON MAY 8, I WOKE UP WITH PAPA AND Mama kissing me and saying "Happy birthday." Mama pressed something into my hand. An orange! I hadn't seen one in almost three years.

"Where did you get it, Mama?" But Mama would not tell. She smiled with the old merry twinkle in her sad eyes. Mama had always loved surprises.

Papa and Mama wanted me to eat all of the orange, but finally they each accepted a section. Later I learned from the Kolländers that Mama had given a valuable ring to obtain the one orange. It was the last birthday gift I was ever to get from my parents.

Abek came and brought me a portrait of Arthur that he had painted from a photo. I was touched by the thought, and the likeness was excellent. I placed it on the table and for a while it gave the illusion that Arthur was with us. Abek also brought roses for my birthday. Roses in the ghetto. How unreal they looked! Somehow they were not mine, but I was tremendously pleased. Ilse, Rita, and Ruth came too. Ilse brought me a pin, a little white dog pin. Ruth and Rita brought note paper. Mama had made oatmeal cookies that tasted just like nut macaroons. "The rations, Mama?" I asked, but she just smiled in her old carefree way. I remember it as a very happy day and I shall never forget it.

My guests departed. I stood alone on the wooden balcony in the dusk. All of a sudden I had an intense longing for my garden. I closed my eyes and almost felt its aroma—the cool white lilacs kissed by a May rain. . . . I wanted to run, run home. If I ran fast I could be there in half an hour. But my garden was as remote as paradise. "I am eighteen years old," I confided to the old wooden post, "eighteen today."

Shortly after my birthday a notice was posted that all able-bodied persons were to register for work, inasmuch as there was a critical shortage of labor. A notice followed proclaiming that those who failed to register would be sent to Auschwitz, described in the notice as a newly created concentration camp about twenty miles away.

Papa, Mama, and I registered. Papa was told that he would work in Sucha, where the Germans were fortifying the river. It was a two-hour train ride. Mama and I were to work in Wadowitz in a shop that sewed military garments, which was about the same distance away but in a different direction. There was a general feeling of newly found security. The wages of course would be ridiculously small, barely enough to cover the train fare. But we would be safe now, and might be able to stay in the Bielitz ghetto.

Papa got up at four every morning. He had to be at work before seven. I trembled when I thought that he would have to push a wheelbarrow and work up to his knees in water. I ran home to our room every evening after work, grateful that he would be there for the all-too-short night. When Mama and I came home from work a little after eight, Papa was usually going to bed.

After a week or so Mama was not needed at the shop; for a while they had enough help. It was good that Mama did not have to go; she could have supper ready for us and keep our room in order. I enjoyed going to the shop, even though we had to assemble and march out of the ghetto under guard, and be counted like cattle at departure and arrival. The train ride was a pleasant break in the monotony. I loved seeing the forests we passed, the mountains in the distance, the meadows strewn with flowers. But best of all I liked to open the train window and shout at the top of my voice. The clatter of the wheels would drown my voice. To shout or sing was a luxury I hadn't enjoyed in a long, long time. There always were people close by, old people, sick people. On the train I could sing off key to my heart's content. I missed Abek, because I didn't see him all week, but he came as often as he could and left letters for me with Mama.

Surprisingly, Papa looked better. The sun gave him a little color. I only noticed that he rubbed his arm more frequently. It bothered him, but he never complained.

One gloriously beautiful Sunday, early in June, Abek came and suggested that we go for a walk. It was a wonderful and daring idea. By crossing the railroad tracks behind the ghetto it was possible to get through the meadow into the forest.

Abek was in an unusual mood. I had never seen him quite so lighthearted. As we crossed into the forest he tried to kiss me several times. I laughingly avoided him. This time he was not too angry with me. He took my hand and we ran down the green slope over daisies and buttercups.

I could touch the grass and the flowers instead of admiring them from a distance. Running down the hill I noticed something quite peculiar: running alongside of me, Abek was laughing too but with the gaiety of a grandfather playing hide-and-seek with a grandchild.

A couple of hours must have passed. It seemed a shame that this beautiful day had to end. Again we raced, this time up the hill. I got to the top first, sat down, and urged Abek to hurry. He came up breathlessly, flung himself down at my side, and started kissing me. I was calmly observing a curiously shaped cloud in the sky. When I pointed it out, Abek exclaimed, "Haven't you any feelings?" I was surprised, not quite knowing what he was talking about. He kissed me and asked me over and over again, "You will marry me, won't you?" but I continued to gather flowers without answering. Finally, we went home.

The following Friday we had to work longer than usual at the shop. It was quite dark as the train puffed through the sleepy landscape. We were not to work Saturday and Sunday and the two free days stretched ahead enticingly. I was in a gay mood, and gave the other girls imitations of people in the shop. I was quite good at it and the girls roared with laughter. The train stopped at a deserted little station. As Ilse and I stood at the open window we heard footsteps on the short platform. Then we heard voices and we saw two young men pass by. One of them said, "Today it's Andrichau, on Monday Bielitz." Ilse and I looked at each other. Was it? I felt a little nudging pain under my heart. We did not speak for the rest of the trip.

At home Papa was still up despite the lateness of the hour. He and Mama were both waiting for me. When I finished eating my supper, Papa motioned me to sit on his bed.

"What is it, Papa?" I asked, unable to bear the silence any longer. He stroked my hair but did not answer. Fear gripped me! Had they heard something too? When Papa said nothing I kissed him good night. He held me longer, much longer than usual. So did Mama.

I lay still in my bed, but sleep would not come. I was terribly afraid. And when finally I fell asleep I had horrible dreams. Toward morning I woke and saw Mama and Papa packing an old knapsack. I sat up in bed, demanding an explanation. For a moment there was silence; then Papa sat down on my bed and told me that in the morning—Saturday —he had to go to Sucha, where he worked. A camp was being formed there. On Monday Mama and I were to be moved to Wadowitz. Bielitz, our home town, would then be *Judenrein* —clear of Jews. Now I remembered what I had overheard at the little station. I wanted to shout, to cry out, to fight, but Papa's and Mama's strength kept me silent. How composed they were, packing and talking so casually!

We got word that Papa and the other men were to leave on Sunday, a day later than scheduled. A strange silence fell over the ghetto. I went downstairs to play with the little twins. I could not stand seeing Papa and Mama, yet I ran back every few minutes to be with them. Abek came. He and Papa embraced.

After supper, pretending to sleep, I listened to Papa and Mama talking. They talked both of the good life they had together and of what was to come—how the war would end soon, how Arthur would come back, and how he would have matured: "It is good for a man to have been away for a while," Papa commented. Presently, they discussed me: how much of life I had missed because of the war. "We will make it up to her," Mama said. "She shall have the prettiest dresses, dancing, and everything a young girl should have."

They talked about their parents, about the first years of their marriage, about waiting through the First World War . . . their reunion . . . when Arthur was born. Listening, I wanted to cry out—to reassure, to be reassured—but I bit my pillow in pain and kept silent.

And so they talked on through the night, animated and happy. They faced what the morning would bring with the only weapon they had—their love for each other. Love is great, love is the foundation of nobility, it conquers obstacles and is a deep well of truth and strength. After hearing my parents talk that night I began to understand the greatness of their love. Their courage ignited within me a spark that continued to glow through the years of misery and defeat. The memory of their love—my only legacy—sustained me in happy and unhappy times in Poland, Germany, Czechoslovakia, France, Switzerland, England. It is still part of me, here in America.

In the morning we did not talk about the train that was to leave a few hours hence. Silently we sat at the table. Then Papa picked up his Bible and started to read. Mama and I just sat looking at him. Then all of a sudden Papa looked up and asked Mama where my skiing shoes were.

"Why?" I asked, baffled.

"I want you to wear them tomorrow when you go to Wadowitz."

"But Papa, skiing shoes in June?"

He said steadily: "I want you to wear them tomorrow."

"Yes, Papa, I will," I said in a small voice.

I wonder why Papa insisted; how could he possibly have known? Those shoes played a vital part in saving my life. They were sturdy and strong, and when three years later they were taken off my frozen feet they were good still. . . .

When it came time to leave, Papa and Mama embraced. Then Papa put his hands on my head in benediction, as he had done for Arthur. His hands trembled. He held me a while, then lifted my chin up and looked into my eyes. We were both weeping.

"My child," he managed. It was a question and a promise. I understood. I threw myself wildly into his embrace, clinging to him in desperation for the last time. I gave him my most sacred vow: "Yes, Papa." We had always understood each other, but never better than in that last hour.

And so we went to the station, across the meadow, taking the longer way, trying to be together as long as possible. A crowd was already assembled. Papa was asked for his identification. We went out onto the platform with him. The train would leave in a few minutes. People were saying their heartbreaking good-bys.

Papa entered the last car and went to the open platform at the rear to see us as long as possible. There he stood in his good gray suit, his only one, his shoulders sloping, his hair steel gray in the sun, on his breast the yellow star and black word.

There he stood, already beyond my reach, my father, the center of my life, just labeled JEW.

A shrill whistle blew through the peaceful afternoon. Like a puppet a conductor lifted a little red flag. Chug-chug-chug —puffs of smoke rose. The train began to creep away. Papa's eyes were fixed upon us. He did not move. He did not wave. He did not call farewell. Unseen hands were moving him farther and farther away from us.

We watched until the train was out of sight. I never saw my father again.

Only after several moments did I become conscious of the fact that Mama was with me. She took my hand like that of a baby and we started to walk toward the ghetto. I didn't once look at her. Only after a while did I realize that she too was weeping.

That night she fixed me something to eat and I ate to please her. She asked me to sleep with her in Papa's bed. I did so reluctantly. I was half asleep when I felt her arms around me, clinging to me in desperation. All my life I shall be sorry that I did not feel more tender that night. When Mama needed me most I wanted to be alone. I pulled away like a wounded animal that wants to lick its wounds in peace. Finally I fell asleep—on a pillow soaked with my mother's tears.

We rose early. While I put on my skiing boots Mama made me a cup of cocoa—the precious cocoa which she had saved for almost three years for a special occasion.

"Aren't you eating, Mama?" I asked.

"It's Monday," she answered. Mama had fasted every Monday for half a day since Arthur had left.

"But today," I said, "you should eat something."

"Today especially not," she answered from the window, holding the ivory-bound prayer book she had carried as a bride. She prayed and watched me—and I watched her. The chives were uprooted on the window sill. Yesterday we had taken out the few remaining jewels, sewed some into Papa's jacket, Mama's corset, my coat.

A shrill whistle blew through the ghetto. It was time to leave.

When we had made our way downstairs we saw the woman with the lovely complexion, Miss Pilzer, screaming and begging to be allowed to go with her mother. The dying old woman was thrown on a truck meant for the aged and ill. Here the SS man kicked her and she screamed. He kicked her again.

On the same truck were Mr. Kolländer, the man with paralyzed legs, and the mother with her little girls. The twins were smiling; unaware of what was happening, they were busy catching the raindrops. An epileptic woman was put on the truck; her dog jumped after her. The SS man kicked him away, but the dog kept on trying to get in the truck. To our horror, the SS man pulled his gun and shot the dog. I looked toward Mama. I wanted to run to her. I wanted to be held by her—to be comforted. Now it was too late.

Leaving the invalids behind, we assembled in a field in a suburb of Bielitz called Lärchenfeld. Here we were left in the rain to wait. After about four hours the SS men finally came

88

in a shiny black car, their high boots polished to perfection. A table was set up and covered with a cloth—a tablecloth in the rain!—and at that table they checked the lists of the people present.

We had all assembled.

Why? Why did we walk like meek sheep to the slaughterhouse? Why did we not fight back? What had we to lose? Nothing but our lives. Why did we not run away and hide? We might have had a chance to survive. Why did we walk deliberately and obediently into their clutches?

I know why. Because we had faith in humanity. Because we did not really think that human beings were capable of committing such crimes.

It cleared up and then it rained again. I was tired and hungry, hot and cold, and still we stood at attention, losing track of time.

Finally, certain trucks were loaded and driven off amid crying and screaming. Mama kept looking into my eyes. Her courage gave me strength. Those of us who remained were lined up in rows of four and ordered to march to the station. Instead of marching us across the meadow directly to the station, we were marched all around town. Oh God, I asked, I prayed, oh God, are they going to do to us what they did to Erika's mother? Will we dig our own grave? Oh God, no, no, NO! Don't let it happen—don't! I am afraid. I don't want to die. Don't hurt Mama. Don't—

I saw Bielitz, my dear childhood town. Here and there from behind a curtain a familiar face looked out. We kept on marching. People went marketing. Guards beat stragglers with rubber truncheons. Oh God, I prayed, don't let it happen!

Someone pushed a baby carriage. Workmen were repairing a street. On the butcher shop they were painting a new sign. We were marching. A dry goods store was decorating its show window. We had bought the flowered fabric for my dress there, but it was not colorfast. Oh God, don't let it happen, don't, I prayed, don't! At the movie theater they were putting up a sign announcing a new feature—and we were marching.

I noticed Mama grow pale. She was gripping her suitcase tightly. I jerked it out of her hand.

"You hurt my hand," she said in a whisper.

Finally we approached the railroad station on the opposite side of town. Beyond the station were open meadows where the annual circus set up its tents. There we waited again.

From mouth to mouth the news traveled: "Merin!" Merin was here. The king of the Jews, as he was called, had arrived. His headquarters had been at Sosnowitz where there were the biggest Jewish congregation, the largest factories and shops in which Jews worked.

Customarily the Nazis established someone such as Merin as head of Jewish communities and gave him the job of liquidating them. It was said that Merin lived in luxury, that he had visited Goebbels, that he was the only Jew to own a car, that he was indescribably wealthy. I imagine these things were true. Certainly he was master of life and death.

I looked at him now. He was short, perhaps a bit over five feet, pale and thin; he had watery eyes, dull brown hair, and he was clad in a brown raincoat. He talked in a hoarse whisper. He pulled a bottle of schnapps from his pocket, drank first and then handed it to the SS men about him. They drank after him. I saw it all and marveled. Yes, he was all right for them, he was their kind.

"I am glad you took the suitcase," Mama said very quietly. We were no longer standing at attention. "I would have fainted," she continued.

"Why didn't you throw it away?"

Her voice was without tone as she answered, "Arthur's picture is in it."

Merin was walking in our direction. Mama prompted me, "Go ask him if we are going to Wadowitz."

I asked him in Polish—it was known that his German was very poor.

He looked at me, his eyes without expression.

"Are you crazy?" was his hoarse reply.

Mama asked me what he had said, but I had no time to answer, for "All march down this way" came the command.

In our clenched fists we held our working cards from the shop, those sacred cards that we thought meant security. As we marched along in pairs we heard cries and screams ahead of us. Mama and I held hands tightly. A cane hit our hands. They unclasped. The cane pointed at me, a voice shouted, "How old?" My answer came, "Eighteen." The cane shoved me aside. Like a puppet I went. I knew Mama was marching on—in the opposite direction. I did not turn around. I could not. I knew she was looking at me as Papa had looked at us from the platform of the train. I knew that if I turned around we would have to run to each other—and that they would beat us or shoot us. We had to go on alone.

I was herded toward a group where my friends Ilse, Rita, and Ruth stood. Our parents were led to the other side of the meadow where a barbed wire enclosure had been set up. I did not see Mama, but we saw how earrings were torn out of ears, rings from fingers, and all thrown into a pail. I pictured Mama's wide wedding band with Papa's inscription in it among them, and I pictured the SS men digging greedily into the gold. Digging into people's love and pledges. . . .

I saw a couple we knew. With their baby in their arms they walked up to the SS man, the judge of life and death. He told them to give the baby to those marching to the right, and motioned them to the group to the left. I saw the couple look at each other. Then I turned away, feeling the wide field revolving around me. When I looked again, sick and limp, I saw the couple embracing their baby—and walking slowly toward the right. . . .

We had assumed all along that we were going on a train, but now a truck came for us. I was the last one to enter it. Then I screamed, "I want to go to my mother!" and jumped down. Just then Merin passed. He looked at me, and with strength unsuspected in that little man, he picked me up and threw me back on the truck.

"You are too young to die," he said tonelessly.

I glared at him. "I hate you," I screamed. "I hate you!"

His eyes were without expression; there was a faint smile on his pale thin lips. It would have been easy for him to order me down and send me with my mother. Why did he not? Strange that the man who sent my mother to death had pushed me into the arms of life!

Someone fastened the canvas across the back of the truck and Merin walked away. Then above all the screams coming from behind the barbed wire I heard my mother. "Where to?" she called. I spread my arms and leaned out of the truck. I did not know the answer.

"Mama! Mama!" I called, as if the word could convey all I felt. Above all the confused, painful cries I heard Mama's voice again.

"Be strong!" And I heard it again like an echo: "Be strong." Those were my mother's last words to me.

As the trucks pulled away, the late afternoon sun came through the gray clouds for a moment. Its rays touched the roof of the church, glistening wet. The church bells were ringing. And then the sun disappeared.

Once more Bielitz was gray and dark, and as the truck rolled on, the city disappeared before my misty eyes.

Part Two

Chapter 1

THE TRUCK ROLLED ON FOR PERHAPS AN HOUR OR TWO; I HARDLY bothered to wonder where they were taking us. My thoughts were with Papa. I feared what might happen to him when he heard about Mama. His heart would not stand the shock. Our truck, and the others, stopped at a little station and we were put on a passenger train. For hours the train stood on a siding. I looked out of the window, pressing my forehead against the cool glass, and wondered where Mama might be. I prayed, lost in thought, clinging to the faint hope that she had been taken to Wadowitz to work in the shop, after all.

As the evening shadows crept over the little station I felt the jolt that precedes the starting of a train, and then we rolled toward our unknown destination. A vivid picture formed in my brain. . . . Mama sitting on a crowded floor in the corner of a dirty freight car, also in motion. I could see her hands pressed together, her face white, her beautiful eyes filled with tears. I knew she would be praying with all her might; praying for Papa and her children, praying for our strength because she herself was no longer afraid. I felt the serenity that had come over her, the strength that had emanated from her during our last hour together. And then a picture, cruel and unthinkable, started to revolve in my mind: about the tortures she might have to endure, about the heat that might burn her to ashes, which would then be scattered to the winds. My beloved mother . . . I felt both the heat and the cold of the horror. Finally, I could suffer no longer. My eyes remained dry. I felt my features turn stony.

"Now I have to live," I said to myself, "because I am alone and nothing can hurt me any more." And the picture of

95

Papa's and Mama's mute farewells—those two faces suffering without uttering a cry—was imprinted in my heart forever.

Ilse sat next to me at the window, her lips repeating "Mama, Mama, Kitty, Kitty," tears running down her face. None of the girls spoke. Each was alone with her tragedy, suffering in her own way, as the train sped on through the evening.

I felt remote and alone. A piece of broken bottle was lying under a seat. I picked it up and played with it. Then I drove its sharp edge into my palm. The blood trickled onto my cuff, but the wound did not hurt. There was no pain.

It does not matter, I am going to live. Mama and Papa are going to live. I am going to live to be with them. And if . . . if it happens to them—I am going to live for revenge. I am going to live! The wheels of the train, beating in rhythm, were saying over and over, "I am going to live, I am going to live."

We passed through Kattowitz and I knew that we had traveled fifty-six kilometers to the north of Bielitz. We were not going to Auschwitz. . . . But where then? After another twenty kilometers the train slowed to a stop and we read a faintly illuminated station sign: Sosnowitz. Our guards ordered us off the train and marched us through dark, empty streets. It occurred to me that Abek's family lived in Sosnowitz. Abek? I had not thought of him at all: he now seemed as far away as someone I had known a long time ago. I wondered fleetingly if I would be able to see his family.

Finally, exhausted, we halted in front of a tall building that turned out to be the headquarters of the Militz. The Militz, an auxiliary police, was a Jewish force established by the Germans, headed by a notorious SS commander and a subordinate Jewish commander. Young Jews were conscripted to fill its ranks. We were marched inside, led through dim passages, and finally into a large hall upstairs. Everywhere Militz men were milling about and an excited exchange of questions followed. They were curious to know where we came from and we in turn asked anxiously where we were going. A shrug of the shoulders and "Probably to camp"—this was our small satisfaction.

"Come lie down," Ilse whispered. She had spread her coat on the floor near a window. I lay down but sleep would not come. After a while I got up and started to walk about again. On a shelf I spotted a stack of paper. I took a sheet. Under the faint light of the single bulb, hardly conscious that I had taken a pencil from my pocket, I wrote these words, "My beloved brother." Then slowly it trickled into my mind that I had to write him and tell him . . . and the wish that was dearest to my heart and which I could not consciously express wrote itself down in the letter. I told Arthur that Papa was in Sucha and Mama in Wadowitz, that I was on my way to a camp, and that he had no cause to worry. I reminded him that our parents were young, that they would be able to stand the hardships, and that we would soon be together again at home. "Young? Yes, young," I answered myself. Mama was barely forty-five and Papa fifty-five. They were young people, much too young to die, but too old to bear more suffering. They had already suffered too much. "But they are young," I answered myself in defiance. "They must live"—and I continued my letter to Arthur.

When I had finished it I put it in my bosom and felt comforted. There now was a link with Arthur, a link with Papa, Mama, and home. I lay down next to Ilse and instantly fell asleep.

There were gray shadows in the room when I opened my eyes, and on the opposite walls the naked bulb gleamed dimly. I heard whispers around me, some stifled crying. The picture of yesterday's events came into my mind. I was in Sosnowitz. And Mama?

I looked out of the window into the misty street below. In the bleak light of dawn shadowy figures were going somewhere. Then I distinguished their yellow stars of David. I marveled at how many Jews I saw. There had been so very few in Bielitz. Sosnowitz, I had been told, had the largest Jewish community in all of Germany. There had been a large Jewish population before the war, but now all the shops and factories in which Jews worked were located here. Sosnowitz was just inside the border of the *Gouvernement* and many Jews had fled here, in the hope of finding work and safety.

I decided to try and see Abek's parents and I asked one of the Militz men how to get permission to leave the building.

"You have to go to the Commander," he said.

"Where is he?"

"Here in the building."

"When can I see him?"

"Listen," the Militz man said, obviously tired of my questions and lack of comprehension, "you have to register ahead for an appointment. Do you think you can just walk in and see him?"

"I am going to see him this morning," I said quietly, more to myself. The guard shrugged his shoulders and smiled.

I walked out into the corridor. We were not restricted within the building but I noted through a glass panel that the outside door was guarded by Militz men and one SS man. Walking along the corridor, I suddenly felt a new freedom born from the realization that no matter what action I might take, only I would have to bear the consequences. Nothing that I might do now could harm Papa and Mama. I felt elated.

A long line of fearful people with a hunted look on their faces stood in front of a door that was blocked by a guard, begging, offering money to get an appointment with the Commander. I stood there, hardly believing what I saw. Still, I was sure that I was going to see the Commander. I noticed a second door marked PRIVATE and decided that it was the one to try. I went back to our room and told Ilse my plan.

"Please don't do it," she begged.

"But Ilse, I am not afraid," I told her. "I will be all right." I went out into the corridor again. The air of excitement indicated that the Commander had arrived. The guard was frantically driving people away from the door. Thinking fleetingly that Papa and Mama would scarcely recognize their shy little girl of yesterday, I went quietly to the door marked PRIVATE, turned the knob, and entered.

There, at a littered desk, sat a fat, bald man, his forehead shining, his eyes small and piercing. His fleshy lips curled in a vulgar, greedy manner toward the glass of tea he was lifting. He turned to me, startled, amused, a bit angry. "Yes?"

What a picture I must have made in my heavy ski boots and schoolgirlish tweed suit and with long black braids falling over my shoulders.

"Are you the Commander?" I asked pleasantly in German.

"I certainly am," he answered in Polish, then checked himself and repeated it in German, which I noted at once was faulty. The few words he had spoken betrayed the fact that he spoke neither language correctly. I felt that this man hated his ignorance, and that my mastery of both Polish and German somewhat compensated for the power of his position. I chose my words with care and spoke slowly in German.

"I would like a permit to visit my relatives who are living here in town. Their name is Feigenblatt. Could you please give me one?"

I said it without begging in my voice. He leaned back in his chair and scrutinized me, his fleshy lips twisting into a smile. I went on.

"And I might as well tell you that I have neither money nor jewels to pay for it." What was dictating my words? I felt like an actress on a stage.

His smile vanished. He was sitting upright now. I sensed that nobody had spoken to him like that in a long time. Apparently I had caught him off guard. He opened his mouth and closed it again.

"Can I see your *Ausweis?*"

"I have no identification," I answered. "Why do you have people crying outside your door? Do you like it? You can't like it." He stared at me. I wondered if I had gone too far. Staring right back at him, I lowered my glance to the star of David on his chest.

"Could I have the permit, please?" I repeated, my voice soft and steady now.

He was still looking at me when his fingers pressed a bell.

A young Militz man came in. The Commander wrote something on a piece of paper.

"Your name?" he asked, his voice gruff; then, after a moment, he added, "Please."

Silently he handed me the permit. "Thank you." My voice held although my knees felt weak and I was shaking. The Commander told the guard to accompany me. Then he did me an honor that he probably accorded no one else but the SS: he got up and stood while I left the room.

I was thoroughly shaken. I hardly knew myself. I had never spoken like that. I had never felt like that. I was different in a thousand ways from yesterday. But the knowledge that such strength was within me gave me the courage to go on.

Chapter 2

IT WAS A BRIGHT, WARM, SUNNY DAY AND I WALKED ALONG THE streets of Sosnowitz, the Militz man at my side. Almost everyone I saw wore the yellow star, and this gave me a feeling of comfort.

After perhaps half an hour's walk we came to a large apartment house on which I saw an enameled sign which read BESKIDENSTRASSE. Under it was a small number 6. I rubbed my eyes. This looked quite different from what I had imagined while writing to Abek at this address. To me, home meant a house like ours, with a garden and flowers. I couldn't associate a large apartment building on an unshaded street with "home."

As we walked up the stairs I rehearsed what I was going to say—how I would explain who I was—but before I could knock, the door was thrown open and Abek's dark-haired, pretty sisters, Paula and Lola, rushed out to embrace me. They seemed to be expecting me.

A tall, gaunt, erect woman in black came forward. Her resemblance to Abek was striking, though her features were softer. Her face was pale, her eyes red as though she had been crying. She embraced me without a word and slowly stroked my hair.

"My poor child," she said finally, "we are not going to let you go anywhere. You are going to stay here with us."

The guard broke in immediately, pointing out that my permit expired within two hours. Abek's mother did not answer him. She just went on stroking my hair.

"Come, child," she said after a while, "you must eat something and get some rest."

101

"I am responsible for her and must be with her all the time," the Militz man insisted.

"Let her wash," Paula said firmly. Her voice had a melodious quality. "I will stay with you as hostage, if necessary."

Abek's mother led me into a bedroom and hovered over me while I took off my jacket and proceeded to wash and brush my hair. When Lola came into the bedroom carrying warm food, I suddenly realized that I had not eaten since the morning before, when Mama had fixed me the precious cocoa that she had saved since before the war.

Yesterday . . . Was it only yesterday that I was with Mama? It seemed so far away. Everything that had happened since yesterday was like a monstrous dream.

While I ate, Abek's mother asked about him. She had not seen him for many months and was of course anxious to hear and know all about him. Although I had seen him only two days before, there seemed to be little that I could remember to tell her. She seemed to sense it, for she soon excused herself and left me alone. I felt very tired now. All I wanted was to sleep for a long, long time.

I rested my head on my arms on the table and closed my eyes. After a bit I heard soft steps approaching. I opened my eyes and saw Abek's picture before me. It was a warm gesture to make me feel welcome and at home. I looked at him. He seemed strange and aloof and again I had the sensation that he was someone I had known a long time ago and half forgotten. Abek's mother was watching me. Ashamed, I lowered my eyes.

Abek, it turned out, had telephoned to the Kultusgemeinde in Sosnowitz and sent a message about me to his parents. I had no doubt that to make the call he must have bribed a guard, for Jews were not allowed to use telephones. An uneasy feeling came over me that Abek had not merely asked, but ordered his family to help me. It was this thought that kept crossing my mind while Abek's mother talked of her plan to get me out of the transport. The important thing, she said, would be to secure a working card for me. That meant that I would need a certificate of employment. Paula

102

and Lola had come up with an idea, however. They were sewing underwear for a German shop at home. A quota had to be met, of course, and twice a week they delivered the required number of garments to the factory. They hoped that in exchange for one of their machines they would be able to obtain a working card for me. They would then take turns on the remaining machine and fill their quota by working day and night.

I was taken aback by their generosity and stammered a protest at their proposed sacrifice. "Abek's happiness is at stake," his mother said simply, tears streaming down her cheeks. I took her hand and kissed it. She leaned over, embraced me, and touched my forehead with gentle lips.

There was a knock at the door and the guard entered. My time was up. Despite the sisters' pleading he remained adamant; I would have to leave before Abek's father returned from work.

"Until tonight then," Abek's mother said as the guard hurried me down the stairs. "We may have good news for you by then."

When we got close to the Militz headquarters I saw that all the girls from Bielitz were assembled outside. In the last row I spied Ilse, frightened and on the verge of tears. When I had made my way to her she whispered, "I thought that you wouldn't come back any more." I noted that she was the only one who stood alone. We clasped hands silently.

We were marched through the streets of Sosnowitz, the sun beating down unmercifully and the asphalt feeling soft underfoot. After an hour we came to a large, unfinished red brick building, obviously meant to be a school. Work apparently had been stopped when the Germans had invaded Poland. We were led to the rear of the building, to a large yard that had been fenced in by barbed wire. Signs of construction were still in evidence: mounds of sand, gravel, and cement were scattered about the yard as they had been left by the construction workers. Two SS men guarded the entrance and counted us as we entered. Once inside we stood at attention. My temples throbbed after the hard march.

We were in a so-called Dulag, an abbreviation for *Durchgangslager*, or transit camp, which in this case served as a labor pool. We were to be chosen for work in the German war industry and would be trained by the people who had requisitioned us from the SS. We learned later that industrialists paid the SS three and a half Reichsmark (approximately $1.00) for each worker, plus a small fraction of what constituted normal going wages, according to the services performed by their slaves.

Finally we were herded into the building and assigned to a large room upstairs. In neat rows throughout the room were crude four-tier bunks, some of which were already occupied. Ilse and I managed to find two vacant neighboring bunks on the fourth tier, just under the ceiling. The heat was most oppressive, despite the fact that we were near a barred window. There was a bit of straw scattered over the bunks and we soon discovered that vermin nested in it. It was unbearably hot just under the ceiling—even the wood felt hot to our touch. Still, I wore the woolen suit and ski boots that Papa had insisted on. Because I felt nauseated by the vermin and the heat we climbed down from our bunks.

As I started to tell Ilse about my visit to Abek's family, we were ordered to assemble downstairs in the yard again, together with a group of girls from Cieszyn, Czechoslovakia. When we got downstairs we found that more groups like ours were lined up, altogether perhaps a hundred girls. After what seemed like half an hour's *Appell*, or roll call, a sleek limousine drove through the gate. Two giant SS men and one elegantly clad civilian got out. *"Achtung!"* thundered one SS man, and we snapped to rigid attention.

The three men stood near us, talking. I could hear fragments of their conversation. One SS man said "Bielitz," and pointed to our group; then I heard the word *Weberei* (weaving mill). After a while the civilian was handed a cane. Walking up and down the rows, he pointed to the girls who were to step out of line and walk over to the other side of the yard. He pointed to me. After I crossed the yard, I looked back with longing to Ilse. To my great relief she soon joined me, and so did all the other girls from Bielitz. Altogether fifty of us were picked for the same camp: the girls from Bielitz, the ones from Cieszyn and vicinity, and a few others whom we saw for the first time in the yard. We were told to go back to the room.

As we passed through the downstairs hall we heard feeble voices calling from behind a closed door. A few of us tried the door and went in. What we saw was sickening. Several living skeletons, clad in rags that crawled with vermin, stretched out begging hands. Some had only one leg, or were maimed in other ways. Their faces were drawn, their eyepits burned feverishly. They told us that they had come from camps where they had become ill or had been injured in accidents. Most of those who had lost limbs had been working in a quarry. They knew they were now going to Auschwitz to be gassed and cremated. They were useful no longer to the glorious Third Reich. They had given their strength, their youth, their health, and now they had to give their lives. They were hungry, they said. On impulse we ran upstairs to our bunks and gave them all the bread we had.

Late that afternoon we were again called to stand *Appell*. We formed in separate groups just as we had been picked. Some of the sick crouched near the fence.

A steaming kettle of food was brought and one by one we marched by. Each of us was handed a rusty, battered bowl filled with ill-smelling potato scraps and an unwashed greenish vegetable. Ilse, who was ahead of me, stopped to talk to someone from Bielitz. I took my food to the end of the line near the fence, where one of the sick girls sat on the ground, scraping her empty bowl with a dirty aluminum spoon.

"Do you want mine?" I asked, offering her the bowl.

She looked at me stupefied, her eyes burning. Slowly she set her bowl on the ground, rose, and with both her hands gripped my empty hand and was about to lift it to her lips. Then she stopped, seeing my bewilderment. Her head was closely cropped. High on her cheeks were two red spots. Her body was pitifully emaciated, her neck overly long. We looked at each other. For a fleeting moment I thought, She must be my age. I did not know her name or where she came from. I only knew that she was going to meet her death. She stood there against the wire fence with the light of the setting sun on her face. She looked at me, perhaps wondering about the past, and I looked at her wondering about the future, the bowl of unsavory food between us. I closed my eyes.

"God bless you, may you never know what hunger is," she said to me. When I opened my eyes she handed me her empty bowl. I looked at her, not understanding.

"Turn it in," she said. "If they find me with two bowls I might be beaten because they will think I stole it."

I still think of her, that nameless one, standing against the barbed wire fence, of her blessing and her wish.

Evening came, followed by a restless night. Ilse and I could not sleep. We talked and talked. We had heard rumors about the camp we were going to. It was said to be a textile mill, a good place to work, and we would be the first Jewish girls there. We were wakened early and stood *Appell* in the yard. We had no idea when we would leave and I had no way of knowing what Abek's family had accomplished in the meantime.

Around noon most of the ill were put on a truck and driven off, some crying, others in pitiful resignation. I ran up to my bunk and wished desperately that I could cry.

In the afternoon I was called before the supervisor of the Dulag, a Jew, in charge under the supervision of the SS. A Militz man in his office handed me a suitcase, telling me that Abek's family had sent it. I hurried to Ilse to open it with her. We found clothes from Lola and Paula and at the bottom, bread. The sight of the bread made me realize how hungry I was, for I had not eaten since I had been in Abek's apartment more than twenty-four hours before. I broke off two pieces of bread and handed one to Ilse. She started to devour her piece and then stopped abruptly. Taking the bread out of her mouth, she swiftly unrolled a piece of thin cardboard. Written on it was a message that I should be set free soon. My heart skipped a beat. Ilse embraced me.

"I am so happy for you," she said, and I knew that she

meant it. She possessed the rare quality of never being envious. Late in the afternoon I was summoned to the supervisor's office again. He beckoned me toward his desk. His hands were well groomed and his dark hair was very neat. He must have been about Papa's age, but looked much, much younger.

"You are lucky," he said. "You are free to leave. A working card has been secured for you."

"But I was picked for camp," I said, nothing else coming to my mind.

"You were chosen in number only. The rosters are not yet made up. We can easily substitute someone else. This is a new camp, you know. The new ones are usually better and some other girl will be glad to go in your place. In about an hour a guard is going to town and you can leave with him."

"I don't know, I just don't know," I was saying, half to myself.

"What do you mean, you don't know?" the supervisor asked in disbelief. "You mean you don't want to get out?" He looked at me penetratingly . . . "Well, you have the hour to think it over."

I don't know why I hesitated. Perhaps it was intuition. All of a sudden I didn't want any special privileges. I wanted to be with the others. But I knew, too, that there was another reason. Slowly I climbed the stairs, returned to my bunk, and sat down next to Ilse. She had already bundled up the clothes I had received from Abek's family and was ready to say good-by.

"Ilse," I said, "I don't think I am going."

She looked at me in bewilderment.

"Are you out of your mind? You have to go! You owe it to Abek!"

In all my confused thoughts, the word "owe" hammered on in my brain.

"Go, go, before it's too late," Ilse urged me.

"Leave me alone!" I barked at her. "I have an hour to think it over. Just leave me alone."

The bunks between ours and the window were empty. Ilse moved up to the window and I saw her sitting there, her forehead pressed against the bars, her arms folded, and above her the square window, the broiling hot gray-blue sky.

I sat alone, hugging my bundle. In my mind, Ilse's words kept spinning over and over. "Owe," I felt, was the one that held me back. I knew as I never had before that I did not love Abek. I could love his family, but what place would I have in their household? His mother had already called me her child, and she was making a tremendous sacrifice, spending possibly all their money for me. The whole family had taken it for granted that I loved Abek and that our happiness together was worth their sacrifice.

A frightening thought crossed my mind. If I accepted their offer, it was clear that I must marry Abek. I visualized how it all would happen. I would be in Sosnowitz with Abek's family for a while, working in a shop, while Abek would paint day and night to secure a furlough. Then he would come home and get permission for me to go to Bielitz and work there in the camp kitchen. It might take weeks or months, but in the end Abek would get that permission. I imagined a hurried wedding in Sosnowitz before a rabbi, quickly before the Gestapo might knock, and everyone crying because my parents were not there. I imagined girls envying me for going to Bielitz, the camp where there would be no hard work and no hunger. I imagined the trip back with Abek. A guard would accompany us on our wedding journey. Perhaps he would be kind. Perhaps he would look away so we could exchange a kiss. At Bielitz we would get off at the station, across from the place where Mama was taken away from me. . . .

I had visions of standing in the hot camp kitchen, preparing meals, looking through the windows over blooming meadows toward the home of my childhood. I saw myself standing over steaming tubs, washing clothes drenched with sweat and sometimes blood.

So vivid were these pictures that I felt nauseated. I thought of Papa in Sucha, the miracle of Mama being in Wadowitz, and my chance of being with them. I remembered the girl to whom I had given the food yesterday—who might no longer

108

be alive. I remembered those breathing skeletons who had been shipped to Auschwitz to meet their death.

It occurred to me that if I refused to marry Abek, he would never demand it against my wishes. But I couldn't accept his family's sacrifice and reject him. The certainty remained that if I accepted freedom now I would have to marry Abek.

I was young, a child in emotions and dreams. If I should live, I wanted perfection in marriage. I wanted the kind of love that I could imagine, accompanied by flowers and laughter. With the vivid picture in mind of what the beginning of my married life with Abek would be, I ran to the office of the supervisor and told him that I would stay with my group. I watched him substitute another name on the shop permit.

"I want to ask you a favor," I said, barely above a whisper. He looked at me. "Please don't let the family know that it was my decision."

"I won't," he replied, still looking at me and blotting the fresh ink.

Dazed, I went back to my bunk. Ilse was still at the window.

"Ilse," I said, putting my hand on her shoulder, "I am staying with you." I heard my voice telling Ilse of my decision, but when I heard myself saying, "I am going to camp," the words became reality and I was panic-stricken. In a frenzy I rushed back to the supervisor and begged him to allow me to leave, dreams and reasons forgotten. I had only one wish now—to get out from behind that barbed wire. But I was too late: the girl who had been given my permit had already left.

When night fell I felt strong pains tearing my abdomen. I had always suffered during menstruation. How I wished for a little hot water. I looked at Ilse. She was sleeping soundly, the first sleep she had had in several days. The night was hot and sticky. The straw in my bunk made it worse. The bristles stuck to my flesh and the vermin gave me no rest. I tossed uneasily and in pain and desperation I called, "Papa! Mama!" But there was no comfort—only pain and loneliness.

Then suddenly, there was a slight breeze. It quickly grew

stronger and a few heavy raindrops fell to the baked earth. The rain came faster and faster. The stifling room became cooler. I felt myself slowly relax and breathe more easily. The pain ceased and the flow began, releasing with it some of my tension. Calmer now, I cried to the accompaniment of the falling rain.

Chapter 3

ON JULY 2, 1942, WE WERE ROUSED FROM OUR SLEEP AND marched to the station to board the train that was to take us to camp. The streets were wet from the night's rain, the first rays of sunlight were breaking through, and the day gave promise of being a warm and brilliant one. Our marching feet echoed on the cobbled pavement as our column of fifty girls neared the station.

While we waited under the canopied enclosure I managed to send a note to Abek's family, telling them that I was sorry their plan had not worked and that I would be forever grateful to them for their efforts. I wrote on the only piece of paper I possessed, a crumpled sheet in my pocket, and I asked one of the Militz men who accompanied us to mail it for me.

I did not write to Abek. The gesture his family had made for me called for a different letter than I felt I could write. Although I was closer to Abek in this hour than ever before I did everything to separate myself from him.

We were about to board the train when I saw the Militz guard who had taken me to Abek's apartment hastily entering the station platform. He came directly to me.

"The Commander is interested in your staying in Sosnowitz. He did not realize that you would be sent out of the Dulag so soon," he said a bit breathlessly. "Here is a message from him." He slipped a closed envelope into my hand. The girls in front of me were boarding the train. I was caught up in the shuffle and mounted the steps, Ilse close behind me. As we both stood at an open window the Militz man called up to me from the platform, "The Commander is a very influential man, you know."

With an impulsive gesture I tore the Commander's un-opened envelope into shreds and let them drop out the

111

window. I enjoyed seeing the baffled expression on the Militz man's face. I smiled in triumph. It was wonderful to feel so important.

As the train started up, Ilse and I sat next to each other, glad to leave Sosnowitz, even though we were uncertain about our future.

The day must have quickly grown warm, for people we saw from the train moved slowly and with effort along the roads. Cattle were lying lazily in their pastures. We did not feel the heat because our window was open, letting the wind blow in.

I almost enjoyed the journey. The two old SS men who accompanied us looked into our compartment every so often, but as the hours passed they no longer bothered to come, perhaps because they had fallen asleep in another compartment. Our group occupied a whole car. When we stopped at stations, our doors were locked. People stared at us curiously through the windows.

Ilse kept complaining of a headache. I noticed a tall, lovely girl in the corner of our compartment looking through all her pockets. She finally found what she was searching for and offered Ilse an aspirin tablet. After thanking her, Ilse introduced herself and then told her my name.

"I am Suse Kunz," the girl replied with an accent that to me seemed Viennese.

When I asked her about it, she told us that she had been born and raised in Vienna, but that the last few years she had lived in Czechoslovakia with her grandmother. She had a wonderful matter-of-fact cheerfulness about her.

"I am not worried a bit," she said. "Everything will be all right—much better than living in a ghetto, for sure. We are young and strong, and we can take a lot. What have we got to lose, except our lives?"

Suse was young and looked very strong. She had a healthy, tanned complexion, flaming chestnut hair, and sparkling eyes. As I looked at her shyly, I wished she would become my friend.

Ilse fell asleep, lulled by the motion of the train. Suse moved up to the window and leaned her elbows on the ledge beside me.

112

"You know, I feel pretty good, in spite of everything," she confided.

I knew exactly what she meant. The thing we feared most was done. We each had only ourself to worry about. There would not be any more decisions to make.

We spoke easily and understood each other. She asked about my parents, and then she told me that she and her father had been separated in Cieszyn. Her mother had died when she was born. She was an only child.

The train puffed on. It became cooler as we approached the mountains. We talked away like old friends.

"Won't it be fun when we make the journey back?" Suse said dreamily. "We will be free. Can you imagine how wonderful that will be?"

"Yes!" I was eager to agree.

"It may be longer than we imagine," Suse said, her gaiety vanishing.

"No, no. It won't be!" I spoke quickly.

"Let's bet on it," she challenged. "It will be longer than a year."

"Shorter than six months." I was confident. "Let's bet a quart of strawberries and whipped cream, payable after the war."

"I hope you win!" Suse shouted over the clatter of the wheels.

Somewhere in the mountains of Silesia we made a bet of strawberries and cream and solemnly shook hands. I lost that bet, but I never paid it, for gay, laughing Suse died on the very morning of liberation day. . . .

My new friend and I remained at the window, thinking of liberation. Away from the Dulag, I could believe that my parents were well, and that it would be only a matter of time before we were reunited. I wished the journey might never end. There was safety in motion.

We seemed to be traveling in a southwesterly direction through eastern Germany. Late in the afternoon, after having covered perhaps two hundred kilometers, the train stopped at a tiny, spotless station. The sign read "Bolkenhain."

113

The two SS guards got off and lined us up on the platform. A woman of about forty briskly walked up to the SS men and in a barking voice identified herself as the *Lagerführerin,* or camp supervisor. Her first command to us, *"Achtung!"* thundered through the station. We snapped to attention and looked into the face of the woman who would be in charge of us. She appeared grim and forbidding, with the face and jaws of a bulldog. Her brown hair was tightly curled and she was dressed in mourning.

Looking at her uncommunicative face, I could feel fear creeping into me. Her harsh appearance turned out to conceal a kind heart, but we did not learn this until much later.

We were counted and marched out of the station and through the little town. It was hilly and reminded me of Bielitz. So this was the homeland of Nazism. People looked at us as though they had not expected us to be human. Children were called into houses. One young blond woman stood at an open window watering flowers in the window box as we passed. She interrupted her task and looked at us wide-eyed. The thought came to me that she had probably never seen a Jew in her life. Brought up under the Nazis, she expected us to be monsters. What a shock it must have been to find us looking very much like herself, some of us quite pretty.

One woman stood in front of her home, broom in hand, and glared at us with cold hatred. Perhaps, I thought, she had lost a son in the war. Their propaganda told them the Jews were responsible for the war—so she hated us. I saw an old man on a porch, smoking a long-stemmed pipe. We passed close by. There seemed to be pity in his eyes, and I noticed a slow, almost imperceptible shaking of his head.

As we approached the factory, we turned off the road where it widened, and marched into a paved yard before the long, modern, well-kept buildings. I read the firm's name in large gold letters over the entrance: "Kramsta-Methner-Frahne," and under it, *Weberei*—weaving mill. After we lined up, one of the SS men disappeared into the factory. He soon reappeared, bringing with him the man who had picked us in the Dulag in Sosnowitz. I heard the *Lagerführerin* address him as "Herr Direktor."

The director handed the *Lagerführerin* a roster and told her to read off our names. We were to reassemble in alphabetical order, he said. When he handed her the list he called her Frau Kügler. Frau Kügler read off our names. We were all present. Then the director signed a sheet of paper handed him by one of the SS men. The merchandise was delivered. The SS men clicked their heels, lifted right arms. "Heil Hitler," they boomed. "Heil Hitler" echoed the director and Frau Kügler. Without wasting a moment, Frau Kügler marched us alongside the factory. At the end of the long building we came to a stop. A high gate with barbed wire strung along the top stood open and we marched through into another courtyard which ran along the end of the factory. I was one of the last in the column and behind me the gate of our prison clanged shut. Frau Kügler locked and bolted it.

Locked up . . . I felt deprived and helpless.

Beyond our high wire fence stretched beautiful gardens, reaching far into the pine-wooded hills. There, against the slopes, stood the stately white villa of the director.

Presently, the director appeared in our enclosure. I watched him as he stood near me, a tall, handsome man in his early forties, with sleek dark hair and a small, carefully clipped mustache. He smiled a bit ironically as he let his eyes wander about our group.

"Let us pick the personnel," he said to Frau Kügler. They conferred a while, scanning the roster for suggestions that must have been made in the Dulag.

"Malvine Berger," Frau Kügler barked, and a tall redhaired woman, much older than the rest of us, stepped forward. "*Judenälteste!*" We knew that there always was a senior Jewess in charge of a group like ours, and that she would be directly responsible to the *Lagerführerin*. The cook was chosen, a slender woman of about thirty with light blond hair drawn back into a bun. Two girls for kitchen help were next, both wearing glasses, then the *Sanitäterin*, or nurse. There were two girls among us who had been nurses. Both

115

were told to step forward but only one was chosen. Although I did not catch her last name, I made out that her first was Litzi. I liked her; she had jet-black hair, smiling eyes, and dimples. Her appointment made me glad: apparently they cared about our health.

The director announced that we would be taught to weave. If we behaved and worked hard, all would be well; if not, we would be sent back to the Dulag.

"And I can get enough replacements from the Dulag," he observed with a smile on his lips. "You are to obey your *Lagerführerin* and your *Judenälteste!*"

With that he turned and summoned Mrs. Berger. He spoke to her for a moment and I saw Mrs. Berger nod assent. Then she stepped in front of us and said, "Girls, I hope you know what our position is here. How we feel is beside the point; we have to please the people here. Whoever breaks the rules will be punished by me personally, in addition to all other punishment, since one can do harm to all of us by her behavior. I will be stern." Her speech was clipped, her German excellent. She made it clear where we stood. She dared to say, "How we feel is beside the point." At that remark I saw how the director knit his brow. Thus, she made our captors understand that we were no fools. Nor was there any humble begging in her manner. Whatever else she might be like, I could tell that she possessed intelligence, integrity, and courage, and I liked her very much. In the months to come, when in the course of our trials I got to know her better, I was often annoyed by her pettiness and her desire to shine, yet the qualities I had first recognized in her never fell short of my estimate. She had daring and she often baffled people so that they could not refuse her requests. I am convinced that in part, at least, we have to thank Mrs. Berger for a relatively easy time at Kramsta. Bolkenhain soon gained a reputation as one of the best labor camps for women in Germany.

After Mrs. Berger had addressed us we were led to our quarters in a building joined to the factory by means of the fenced courtyard. I entered the low building with a prayer in my heart. I had expected another Dulag but was pleasantly surprised to find that everything was fresh and clean. We were obviously the first occupants. Our room was large, perhaps forty by fifty feet. Near the entrance stood several long tables flanked by benches. The remainder of the room was mainly taken up by rows of three-tiered bunks, with clean gray blankets and a straw-filled pillow on each, as well as a coarse towel. The far right end of the room was divided into two parts. One of these was the kitchen, the other a washroom with a row of faucets over a long trough, three toilets, and three showers. Near the entrance to the kitchen was a separate small room for Frau Kügler. At the far left end of the main room was a tiny cubicle which was to be known as Mrs. Berger's room, and next to it was another larger room where Litzi was to sleep with three bunks reserved for the ill.

We called our quarters the *Lager,* or camp, and I promptly named our bunks the "Catacombs." Somehow the name stuck. Ilse and I had adjoining bunks two up from the floor. Beneath us were two girls from Bielitz and I noted with pleasure that Suse Kunz was assigned the bunk above me.

We were given warm soup in new bowls and hunks of well-baked bread. If only we could be certain that our parents were in a camp like ours . . .

After supper we were allowed to wash. The water was cold. We learned that it was heated only once a week. After that we were free to go to sleep, for which we all were grateful. However, few of us slept. After the lights were turned out I heard girls toss and turn and here and there weep quietly. The night was starry and beautiful. From my bunk I could see the hills through a window. Slowly the full moon rose. I spoke dreamily to her. I asked her if she saw Papa and Mama. It seemed as if she said yes. In the years to come the moon became my loyal friend, my only friend that was free. Each month I counted the days until she returned, and often when she hid behind clouds I thought that she was avoiding the horror on earth.

That first night in Bolkenhain I whispered to her, "Say good night to my loved ones," and went to sleep under her watchful gaze.

117

Chapter 4

A SHRILL WHISTLE SOUNDED AT 5:30 A.M. I SAT UPRIGHT IN MY bunk, rubbed my eyes, and had to think where I was.

We went to wash. When I returned to my bunk I saw Mrs. Berger slap a girl. I turned away; suddenly I hated her. There is nothing I despise more than physical violence. Later Mrs. Berger told me that she had to do it, to establish her authority. The girl had not gotten up when called, therefore she had to be punished immediately. I disagreed, but I must admit that in the next three years, she rarely used violence. That first morning she won respect, or rather fear, from us, but a great deal of hatred as well.

We were marched past the kitchen and handed a slice of bread with beet marmalade and a cup of "coffee," a bitter brew made of wheat. After breakfast Frau Kügler handed each of us three yellow stars, each with the inscription JEW. One was to be fastened on the breast, one on the back, and one on top of a kerchief tied around the head, so that one could tell who we were from any angle.

Shortly before seven we marched to the factory with Frau Kügler, entering a hall containing about twenty-five looms. We lined up along a wall and waited. After a few minutes, Meister Zimmer, a man in a clean blue working uniform, entered. As he stood in the center of the room, his hands on a loom, he seemed grotesque; he reminded me of the big posters plastered on walls at every street corner: "The Men Who Turn the Wheels for Victory," "The Pillars of the Reich."

His voice was harsh, precise, and well trained. He told us that we were here to work for Germany and the glorious Nazi party. If we did our share, we would be able to stay for the

118

rest of our lives, and be well treated. If we failed, or did anything that would not conform to German ideology, we would be looked upon as traitors.

"And what is done with traitors, you know!" he thundered. "Those who cannot work for our victory are not needlessly fed. Those we exterminate."

Our parents—useless, not worth three and a half Reichsmark any more. . . . Anger shot through me. I clenched my fists.

He kept on talking, repeating that we could stay for life. He was so positive, so reassuring, that I felt myself falling under the spell of his words. Not only would he teach us to weave, but he felt he should teach us decency and how to be a part of the program for the glory of the Führer and the Fatherland.

Decency was a word by which my parents lived: used by this man, it became ugly. I tried to concentrate on what he was saying. He talks about staying here forever, I thought. He is at least thirty years older than I; he will die long before I do.

With pleasure I imagined how he would look dead, worms eating his ears. What strange, confused ideas crossed my mind! I must have smiled because Ilse poked my side.

"Are you crazy?" she whispered. "You smiled! Luckily he did not see you!"

Those first days in Bolkenhain were difficult. We worked in the factory classroom from 7 A.M. to 6 P.M. The heat bothered us, our ankles were swollen from standing, our eyes strained from watching the thousands of threads. I was afraid that if something went wrong with my loom I should be blamed.

Meister Zimmer watched us constantly, popping up in unexpected places. But though he was fairer than I at first thought he would be, I always hated him with all my heart.

Sunday came, the first at Bolkenhain. On Sundays we got meat stew and we were permitted to write one one-page letter.

I wrote to Papa at Sucha, in care of the head of the Jewish Community. I described our camp in glowing colors. I expressed my opinion that Mama might be with him or in a camp similar to mine. Somehow I believed it. I asked him to write to Abek and tell him where I was and I told him how wonderful Abek's parents had been to me. I begged him to write to me right away, to tell me how he was, and to take good care of himself. And I think I closed the letter on a cheerful note.

Ilse and I washed our clothes, fastened the stars back on them, and cleaned around our bunks. Those were tasks I did not like and Ilse urged me to leave them to her. "Go talk to the girls," she would say, "then tell me about them. You can't clean properly, anyway."

I loved to talk to the girls, to hear their stories, and gladly I let Ilse spoil me.

After a week's training in the classroom we began work on the factory's regular looms. We were especially tense and frightened when Meister Zimmer told us that each mistake would or could be counted as an act of sabotage. He had been an excellent teacher, I had to admit, but I was sure that he had been chosen for his position as foreman not only for his practical knowledge of weaving, but also because of the fanatical way in which he loved to spread the Nazi doctrine.

We worked hard. At first each of us tended one loom, then we were assigned two, then three looms, and finally, we watched four. Experts who had spent their lives weaving never handled more than three looms. It was grueling work, necessitating constant running, and it caused severe eyestrain; the noise of the looms deafened us for hours after we stopped working. The material we worked with was bad. Sometimes we wove paper. It would tear and break constantly; in the heat it became dry and brittle, in damp weather it became moist and fell to pieces.

How I worked those first weeks I will never know. My fingers worked without conscious direction. I worked mechanically and watched the movement of the clock's hands. I waited for the evening, for the mail call.

In time most of the girls heard from relatives in cities which had not yet met the fate of Bielitz. Ilse corresponded with an aunt who remained in Bielitz. Having been married to a

Christian, the aunt had been allowed to stay. I waited anxiously every night when Mrs. Berger came in with the mail, but I waited in vain.

Our second Sunday came and this time I wrote to Abek. I thanked him and his parents for all they had done for me. I asked him about Papa and Mama, and begged him to write to Arthur. It took three or four days for our mail to leave Bolkenhain, for Frau Kügler censored it all.

The following week, I waited for mail from Papa, but night after night nothing came.

Then Saturday came.

"Oh God," I prayed, as Mrs. Berger came out of her room with a pile of mail.

Mrs. Berger started distributing the letters. When I heard her call "Gerda," I jumped up, but it was for another Gerda: Gerda Feldmann.

The pile of letters grew smaller and smaller. Mrs. Berger looked at her last letter. Quite a few pairs of eyes watched her anxiously. I felt a burning and twitching inside. Then her eyes wandered over the girls. She halted when she saw me, and said the unbelievable, "Gerda Weissmann!"

I grabbed the letter from her hand. My moist eyes spotted Papa's name. I ran to the fence outdoors, I wanted to read it alone. As I started to tear it open, I suddenly realized that the beloved name on the envelope was written in my handwriting. Over it, in black ink, was: "Return to sender, moved without forwarding address."

I wanted to scream, but no sound came. I wanted to cry, but no tears came. I clutched the barbed wire and shook feverishly. I wanted to run out—to run and look for my father.

Ilse joined me. She did not ask any questions, but looked instead at the unopened envelope in my hand. She wanted to talk to me, but I would not listen, and I couldn't speak. Finally she went to Mrs. Berger and told her about the returned letter.

Mrs. Berger summoned me to her room. I stood there and she questioned me, but I could not answer her. Finally, she told me to sit down on her bed. As I did so, she slapped me.

121

Instinctively my hand went up to my cheek. I shook my head.

"I am sorry," she said, "I wanted to jolt you out of it."

I started to leave, but Mrs. Berger took me by the shoulder and turned me around. With her cold eyes she looked into mine, and she held me.

"Talk, Gerda," she said. "Speak to me."

I shook my head.

She released the pressure and pushed me toward a chair. She showed me a picture of a man and a boy.

"This is my husband and my son," she said. "I don't know where they are, either of them. We are all in the same boat. Have you any pictures?"

I went to get a couple of snapshots which I had in my coat pocket.

"Show me your father," she said.

I had a picture of Papa taken a few years before, when he had gone to Turkey for my uncle's wedding. The picture was taken during a boat ride on the Bosporus. It was Papa at his best: young, handsome, and energetic. Not my poor sick Papa. Full of pride, I held his picture out to Mrs. Berger, while in my other hand I held the letter he had not received.

She looked at the picture a while and then she put it back into my hand.

"Look at the picture, Gerda," she commanded, "for your father is dead."

I looked at the picture, I looked at her.

"He is dead," she repeated. "You will never see him again, nor your mother."

"Dead" imprinted itself in my brain. My lips formed to say the word, but no sound came.

"Cry, Gerda," Mrs. Berger persisted. "Cry for your dead father."

Then something within me snapped, something wild and horrible. I made a terrible sound, the sound a dying animal might make, the sound Papa made the day Arthur left. It shook me out of my muteness. Without a tear, I cried for my father. My sobbing tore my insides, it pulled at my heart, but my eyes remained dry.

122

When I calmed down, Mrs. Berger sent me to my bunk. Ilse was most understanding—she said nothing. Finally the lights were put out. Some of the girls whispered a bit. Then silence fell, and in this silence I started to think of home again. Not of the ghetto nor the cellar, but our home as it had been before the war. I thought of Papa, Mama, and Arthur, and all the happy times we had had together.

These happy thoughts were comforting. Memory upon memory, things long forgotten, came back to life. And from that night on, whenever I thought of my parents I thought of them in the happy times before the war, their faces perfect, not distorted by sorrow and hurt—too perfect, perhaps, for ordinary life, too perfect for an adult eye and mind, but so right for me.

Slowly I fell into an exhausted sleep on that horrible day. My parents were so alive in my mind that I could see them coming into my room and bending over my bed to kiss me good night. I smiled, stretched my arms out to them. My lips formed the first word that I had ever spoken: "Papa."

Chapter 5

IT WAS IN AUGUST THAT I FIRST WROTE TO ABEK, BEGGING HIM to tell me if he had heard from Papa.

Shortly thereafter I received mail from Abek and from then on his letters came almost daily. Abek had heard from Papa right after our separation. He told me that he had tried and failed to get Papa into the camp where he was interned in Bielitz. Papa had written me a letter and left it with Abek. I asked Abek to forward the letter to me, yet I waited for it in vain. In his next letter he told me how distressed his parents were about their failure to keep me in Sosnowitz, but he made no mention of Papa's letter. When he finally sent it, I knew why he had not wanted me to read it. The nervous scribbling only faintly reminded me of Papa's firm, energetic hand. Papa asked me why I had left Mama? That question, written in his shaking hand, burned within me for years, for Papa never learned the answer to it.

Abek's letters were mostly romantic and far removed from everyday life. Sometimes there would be only a couple of lines such as: "It is 528 hours since I last saw you. How am I to stand it much longer?" I remember the day when he wrote that he had been one of a group to go the Bielitz ghetto, to clean out several rooms. He came across a few family photographs in a drawer in our former apartment and he said that he would send them to me in his next letter.

It was a hot, hot day late in summer, and I had a splitting headache. The looms were behaving badly, the brittle yarn kept breaking, and I wasn't able to maintain the required rate of production. The harder I tried the more I fell behind. My feet and ankles were swollen. I felt utterly discouraged.

Then the worst possible thing happened. I heard a noise and crash, and the shuttle leaped up from the cloth web like a silver fish. As it dropped it tore thousands of warp threads. I stood speechless, unable to imagine how it had happened. I examined the shuttle and saw that the lid was off the bobbin holder. Either it had broken off or perhaps in my haste when refilling it I had not closed it securely.

Desperately with shaking fingers, I tried to repair the damage before I was discovered. But I knew that it would take hours. When the whistle blew at quitting time my loom was still not in order.

That night I didn't feel like eating and went to my bunk to lie down. Mrs. Berger came by and handed me two letters from Abek. As I opened the first, a few pictures fell out—the ones that Abek had found. One was of Papa's father taken when he was a very old man. He had a high forehead and a long white beard. I had never known Grandpa Weissmann, because he had died when I was less than a year old. Papa had told us many stories about his father but the one which I remembered filled me with new miraculous faith. He and my grandmother had ten children, five of whom died at an early age. My father was the oldest of the remaining children. During the First World War, my grandparents lived on the Austro-Russian frontier. Anna, their only daughter, lived with them and their four sons were in the Austrian army. The border area changed hands frequently and in 1915 became Russian again. One day Grandfather, who was then in his seventies, went for a walk in the woods. He met a group of drunken Russian soldiers who accused him of laying telephone wires through the woods. I am sure Grandfather had never seen or heard a telephone in his life. Nevertheless, without a trial, he was convicted and sentenced to life imprisonment in Siberia.

I recall my grandmother telling of the day when she and my Aunt Anna said their last good-by to the kindly old man with his long white beard.

Years passed, the war ended, my father's three brothers returned home. Papa had married meanwhile and moved to

125

Bielitz. Then one windy, cold evening, my grandmother, who was living with her younger sons and daughter, heard a knock on their front door. They opened the door and an old man staggered in. He first went to his precious Bibles and kissed them, then he embraced his wife and children. My grandfather had come back! After the Revolution the Bolsheviks had granted amnesty to Czarist prisoners and Grandfather, after many months' journey, had returned home. He had hardly dared to hope that all his sons would survive the war. They all had.

Always with a quiver in his voice, Papa would tell how he, Mama, and Arthur (one year old at the time) had traveled four days by train across the war-ravaged countryside to see Grandfather. The old man had greeted Papa with the words Jacob had spoken when Joseph had brought his children for benediction. "I had not thought to see thy face again and lo, God hath shewed me also thy seed."

As I looked at the picture in the dim light of my bunk, my kindly old Grandfather seemed to be saying: "Have faith, my child, have faith in God."

Meister Zimmer appeared at my looms the next morning. Before he spoke he looked first at me and then at the damage. He must have realized how hard I had worked to repair the broken threads, for he only said in his most abrupt manner: "See that this never happens again."

Early in September I got my first letter from Arthur. "At last," I whispered to myself, tearing it open. Yet, this letter that I had looked forward to so long left me troubled. Arthur wrote that he was working and was well and that his only worry was for my welfare. However, there was something about the letter that was not Arthur; strength, hope, and vitality seemed to have been drained from him; even the writing of the message seemed to have been a tremendous chore. When I answered him the following Sunday, I tried to be cheerful in order to break down the barrier that had risen between us. I asked whether he was ill, whether there was something he

126

was keeping from me. His next letter was the same, almost word for word, as the first. I was distressed.

Ilse's warm friendship and the long talks I had with her and Suse helped a great deal to overcome my worry about Arthur. Talking with the other girls and hearing their problems helped, too.

There was one Bielitz girl, Greta, whom I liked in particular. She was always cheerful. "You know," she said to me one day, "I actually was never happier than now." I gasped in sheer disbelief, and then she told me her story. She had been born out of wedlock. Her mother had always worked and Greta had never had a home. She had drifted from family to family. Some children were not allowed to play with her. "I looked at all those kids," she said, "and you were probably among them—with your frilly dresses, your patent leather shoes, your fretting nannies and doting parents. I always was on the outside. Now finally we are equals. Yes, it's true, I have never been happier than I am now."

We had been in camp for three months when Yom Kippur, the Day of Atonement, came. We all said that we would fast. Meister Zimmer somehow heard about it. He warned that severe punishment would be meted out to anyone who feigned illness or did not produce the prescribed amount of material.

Nevertheless, we all fasted. We worked harder than ever but no one touched food until there were three stars in the evening sky. There was a proud serenity about every one of us, a sense of accomplishment.

That night the heat was unbearable. I could not sleep, and after tossing in my bunk for a long while, I went out into the courtyard. The air was heavy. In the distance, the hills were dark against the rising full moon. The stillness was frightening. The world seemed to be awaiting Judgment Day.

I pressed my head against the wire fence and prayed. Then I noticed two girls clinging to the fence near me. One of them was named Tusia. She was tall, thin, and ugly. I am sure that I never quite understood her but when she spoke I could not help but listen. She reminded me of a giraffe: her small head

127

was set on a long neck, her round eyes were far apart, her mouth was full and wide. She walked toward me and looked down in her peculiar way. "I was very much like you," she said. "I hope you will never be disillusioned. To you life still means beauty, and that is how it should be. Continue to go through mud without dirtying your feet." She spoke without explanation or introduction and without finishing, and then she stalked away toward our quarters.

I heard stifled crying and turned back to the fence. The second girl was still there. She was Lotte, one of the girls who worked in the kitchen. I walked over to her and waited without saying a word. Her sobs stopped and she wiped away the tears from behind her thick glasses. "It would have been so different, so different," she whispered. Then she told me her story.

"My mother left my father when I was a few weeks old. We went to live with my grandmother. Mother was wealthy, but my father gambled. The night I was born, father lost our house playing cards. Shortly after that Mother left him. She never spoke of him until one day when I was seven, she called me into her room and asked if I wanted to meet my father. I had often thought about him, but never dared to ask mother if what the servants had whispered was true. My heart beat wildly—I had never dared to hope that I would meet him. I had heard that he traveled a lot, but that he never came to our town. 'He is not here,' Mother said. 'You will go to another town to see him.'

"I couldn't sleep that night. Would I really see my daddy? What was it like to meet one's real father? How would he look? What would he say? What would he buy me?

"I made the journey with my nurse. We came to his hotel and when she knocked at father's door I held onto her firmly. Suddenly the door burst open and before I could utter a word, a tall man lifted me high, and kissed me over and over again. I felt a peculiar tickling on my face. It was Daddy's beard. I had never felt the face of a man before. It was the most wonderful day of my life. I got more dolls and toys that day than ever before in my entire life. He bought me sweets and

128

let me eat all I wanted, something Mother never permitted. It was like a birthday and a circus rolled into one. I had found my daddy.

"When we left and I cried, he said to me lovingly, 'I shall see you soon again, my darling.'

"Mother was anxious to hear all the details of my visit. Soon letters, cards, and presents started to pour in. From faraway places Daddy sent everything that a little girl could dream of. He was an engineer. He built bridges and traveled from England to many countries in Europe. Then, more than a year later, he wrote that he was coming back home, and would Mama and I meet him? Mother was very excited. She bought a new green hat and looked very pretty. We met Daddy and had dinner together. How happy I was!" Lotte stopped talking. Her hand clutched the fence as she gazed into the starry night as if to recapture that dinner when she was eight years old, and for the first time sat at the same table with both her parents.

"How happy I was," she repeated, tears glistening in her eyes behind her thick glasses.

"Before Daddy left, he saw Mother alone. Then he called me and said, 'I am going back to England to wait for a letter from your mother. When it comes, we shall always be together.'

"In the next few days Mother wrote the letter. A few days later an enthusiastic telegram came. Daddy just had a few business details to take care of, and then he would come to get us. We started packing feverishly. We were to make our home in England with Daddy. Then a few days later a second telegram came. Mama tore it open quickly. She went pale. Daddy had been killed in a train wreck on his journey to us. On his body they had found Mother's letter with an address."

That was the story of Lotte's childhood. The rest of her life story I can tell in its entirety. We went from camp to camp. In February, 1945, on the infamous death march to Czechoslovakia, I saw Lotte's corpse thrown into a hastily dug mass grave: her glasses gone, her eyes half-open, a sad smile on her lips. I saw the frozen earth thrown onto her. That was Lotte. I cannot help but want to tell her story, for I might be the only one left in the world who knows it.

The days grew colder. Fall came. In November Abek sent me a big parcel containing warm clothes, a coat, a sweater, a scarf. He thought of everything. I still had my skiing shoes Papa had insisted I wear and so I was prepared for cold weather. One evening as we marched from the factory to our quarters it was snowing. Later that night, when the lights were put out, I got up from my bunk and walked noiselessly to the window. I watched the first snow fall softly to the ground.

Pictures from the past came to me: a crackling fire, Papa smoking his pipe, Mama embroidering in exciting, bright hues, silk wound around her white, swiftly moving fingers, Arthur reading, I playing with my cats—Schmutzi, my favorite, purring gently. Wonderful days and evenings. I marveled that we had taken life so for granted. . . .

Christmas approached—we could feel the hustle and bustle in the factory. Goebbels was feeding his people with reports of new victories to make Christmas more pleasant.

The day before Christmas we were assigned to clean the looms thoroughly. It was bitter cold and the vast halls were not heated. My fingers froze to the iron bars suspended between the looms. My throat filled with the year's accumulation of lint and dust that we brushed away. I was cold through and through and I looked eagerly forward to a shower and something hot to drink.

When we got back to our quarters late Christmas Eve, the hot water had been turned off. We learned that we had to get up early and finish the cleaning on Christmas morning, and that after that we would get two days off. Frozen and shivering, we went back to work in the early hours of the morning, and were done by noon. Then we were allowed to take hot showers. How delicious the water felt on my body! It warmed me and made my pale skin glow; it washed away the dirt and fatigue. Ahead stretched two full free days! As I

130

combed my hair by the window, I saw bright sunshine on the snow. Quickly I put on my coat to go out to the courtyard. On my way I met Mrs. Berger.

"Oh, Gerda," she called, walking back toward her room, "there is mail for you from yesterday."

It was a letter from Arthur. I passed several girls throwing snowballs, and walked over to the fence before I opened the envelope. It contained a frayed, dirty piece of paper, covered with a few uneven lines. Arthur was in a camp, I should not worry, he would try to write again.

A strange sensation came over me. That piece of paper seemed alive. Like Erika's letter of long ago, it throbbed with suffering. I knew that Arthur was not in a camp like Bolkenhain.

"Arthur," I whispered, "why were you not spared?"

And there in Bolkenhain on Christmas Day, 1942, when the sun stood high at noon, the snow brilliant at my feet, I heard people outside the gates laughing as they came from church, children jingling gay sleigh bells. And there in the glaring sunlight I suddenly knew that I would never see Arthur again.

Every jingle, every laugh, brought back a picture of my brother to me. Arthur painting, with a green stain on his thumb; Arthur skiing over the brilliant snow, his navy-blue sweater showing his powerful muscles; Arthur the center of a group, laughing, frowning, forehead wrinkled, then a flashing smile; Arthur swimming, his hair wet, sunshine flecking his merry eyes; Arthur kissing Mama's hand when he left us; Arthur leaving home that morning without looking back. Arthur, my rock of strength! I fumbled for the little sack that I wore around my neck under my blouse. I opened it and looked at the piece of broken glass that we had gathered from the ruins of the temple. Arthur, Arthur. . . .

Upset and bitter, I wrote to Abek, and poured out my grief to him.

After New Year's, I got his answer. He could not understand why I carried on so. I knew that he loved me and would willingly have endured hardships for me, yet because he and his immediate family were still safe, he could not comprehend.

He told me that he had been home over Christmas and he described how happy his family had been to be together. He was not callous, he merely shared his experiences with me. But I was jealous of his being home. I was bitter that I could not see Arthur, for I felt that only he could fully understand me. I was hurt by Abek's letter, sorry that I had not stayed in Sosnowitz, sorry for myself.

A week or two later, I began to feel ill. I went to see Litzi, the nurse. She told me that my temperature was high, but that nothing else seemed wrong. So it went for a week or more, until the nails of my hands and feet became infected and full of pus. My temperature rose again and Litzi said that I had better not go to the factory, but stay in the *Krankenrevier*. I felt no pain, only terrible fatigue. Yet I could not sleep. I wanted to cry, but no tears came.

I had been in Litzi's room two days, when in the morning after the girls had marched off to the factory, Frau Kügler hurried in, flushed and excited. There were two other ill girls in the room with me.

"Get dressed," she said. "Quick, quick!"

"Gerda can't," Litzi told her. "Her fever is very high."

Frau Kügler ignored Litzi and pulled me from my bunk.

"Hurry, hurry!" she urged, and they all helped me dress. Frau Kügler tied my shoes.

My knees trembled. The few feet to the door seemed to be an enormous distance. Cold sweat ran down my forehead as I walked. I felt cold all over.

Frau Kügler led the three of us to the factory. We kept close to the wall as we went. She followed me to my looms and set them in motion.

"Keep going, Gerda," she muttered under her breath as she turned to go.

I felt as if I had just gotten off a merry-go-round. I could not see the looms. The light fell queerly in ugly yellow stripes. The machines seemed to stand at an angle. At times the looms seemed far away, as if I were looking at them through the wrong end of binoculars. The next instant the threads rushed

132

toward me as if to entangle me. I started forward and then I swayed.

Someone caught me in strong arms, and shouted into my ear, "Pull yourself together, Gerda, it is a matter of life or death!"

As the words reached me I shuddered, almost beyond caring. Then I gripped the beating loom and looked into Frau Kügler's eyes.

"Pull yourself together," she repeated, and then vanished. After a few minutes I saw the factory director walking nearby with a tall, stern-looking SS *Obersturmführer*. I knew he must be Lindner. I had heard in the Dulag that he was the most notorious sadist of them all. Those who were ill he sent directly to Auschwitz. Then I knew why Frau Kügler had hastily led us to the factory. My hands felt steady; when Lindner passed me I stood erect, my looms all in motion. Somehow I lived through that day.

The last thing I remember was the coolness of a sheet against my burning body. When I woke up there was a great stillness that I had not experienced in many months. I sensed that it was late and that I was again in Litzi's room. Frau Kügler came in. I looked at her, remembering.

"Thank you," I whispered.

"It's all right." She touched my hand. "Who knows—?" She broke off there, and as she went out of the door I looked after her in wonder. The German woman who worked for the SS had saved my life.

I got well fast, resumed the old routine. In a way I began to like my work. I found a new security in it, for the intricate process of weaving gave me a sense of satisfaction and accomplishment.

Late in January I got another message from Arthur. I was shocked, so sure had I been that the letter I read on Christmas Day was his farewell to me. I hardly recognized his handwriting. The words looked as though his hands were stiff or frozen, or as if he had written in darkness. He just said that I should not worry and that I should be strong. He did not say what he was doing or where he was. Somehow that jumbled little

133

note reassured me; it had some quality of the Arthur I knew and I was calmer after I got it. It proved to be the last message I ever got from my brother. Perhaps he knew or sensed it would be, perhaps he paid for writing it with life itself. His quiet words gave me the strength and trust to go on and face what was to come.

Chapter 6

SEVERAL DAYS LATER ABEK WROTE. THE THING HE HAD HOPED would not happen—had happened. His parents and sisters were gone. The Jews of Sosnowitz had met the same fate as those in Bielitz and elsewhere. He had managed to get to Sosnowitz but by the time he arrived no one was left. Even the young people had been sent to Auschwitz and not to work camps. Abek described what he thought had happened, down to the last cruel, unthinkable detail. He told me that he had seen the large field where his family and thousands of others had stood before their last journey. He imagined how the place must have echoed with cries only the day before. He described the bodies still lying in the field, dead from cold, starvation, or suicide. There were many bodies of children, whose parents had given them poison or sleeping pills, so that they could be spared Auschwitz. I lived it all through Abek's eyes until I felt that I could take no more. I forced myself to read all his letter.

"My life is a desert now," he wrote. "I go on living only because I have you. Only you can make a future possible for me. When I hold you in my arms again, we will both cry our bitterness away. You will wipe away my tears and make me happy. You will teach me to smile again. Through you I might yet know some happiness. . . ."

When I put down the letter, I felt anew all the pain I had suffered at separation from Papa and Mama. I was afraid of the future. Abek's parents were gone too, and I felt closer to them than to Abek. They were no more. I could hardly grasp it. With horror I remembered how I had battled with myself in the Dulag. Had I stayed in Sosnowitz and not been able to get back to Bielitz, I would have been sent to Auschwitz too.

135

I sat down at once and wrote to Abek. I wrote what he would want to hear: that I would be with him, that I would never leave him, that I would make him happy. I wrote slowly and deliberately, not in my usual swift, careless way. I was halfway finished when the lights in our quarters were turned off for the night. In the washroom, in the dim blue light there, I wrote the rest. I wrote without looking back, without correcting. I had to finish it without stopping.

Timidly I knocked on Frau Kügler's door and asked her if my one weekly letter might be mailed ahead of time. To my surprise, she was not angry; she promised to send it off in the morning.

I returned to my bunk, undressed slowly, and neatly folded my things away, something that I had never done before. When I got into the bunk, I felt Ilse's hand reaching for mine. The gesture annoyed me. I turned away and gazed into darkness. Only then did I start thinking of what I had written to Abek and realize that it was false. In that hour when I should have felt closest to Abek I felt remote. When my feelings should have been strongest for him, there were none. He looked to me for strength and I had no strength to give. I wished I could tell Ilse how I felt, but Ilse would not understand. I was sure that she would think me cold and unfeeling.

As I stretched under the blanket, my body felt young and slim. I felt strangely accomplished, even beautiful. I was glad to be eighteen, glad to be alive, glad for my youth, and thankful that I had not stayed in Sosnowitz. I realized for the first time that I could live deeply and I was ashamed of my feeling of contentedness. I thought of Abek again, and I knew that I could not love him as he wanted me to. But I will have to marry him, I thought. What will happen to him if I don't? And then suddenly, sweetly, I imagined unknown, gentle eyes looking at me. A happy, full, generous mouth that had never known bitterness or pain smiled at me. I smiled back. How easy it was! I felt my blood racing. I embraced my hard straw-filled pillow. With a happy smile, I closed my eyes and whispered, "Whoever you are, wherever you are, I love you!"

On February 8, his birthday, Abek wrote me a letter and

enclosed a picture of himself. On the back of it he had written this dedication: "On my twenty-fifth birthday, my life, which is so lonely, is yours. You shall form it for me." I did not like it. I was more disillusioned than ever. Why, oh why, did he love me so much?

Winter passed and spring came again. Spring which always brought hope for the end of the war. The days stretched longer, I felt more restless. I particularly hated Sundays, when through the gates we could see the townspeople walking, their children laughing and playing.

If only I could be free! I felt myself clutching the bars of the fence. To be free, free—oh, God, how wonderful it would be!

Actually, we were well off. The work, once we got used to it, was not as difficult as it had seemed in the beginning. Frau Kügler was good to us, and never resorted to physical violence. We had food; there were no black market dealings in the kitchen as we heard there were in other camps. We could, of course, have eaten much more, but we were not really hungry and we were not cold.

Early one afternoon, a foreman came and told me to shut off my looms and go to the director's office. My heart skipped a beat. "Why?" I asked. The foreman shrugged his shoulders. What could it be? I wondered, appalled. I had delivered my quota of goods. Besides, Meister Zimmer handled cases of individual quota failure.

I walked through the labyrinthian corridors. Arrows pointed the way to the office. I trembled as I approached, tugged at my blouse, adjusted the kerchief on my head, made sure that my stars were in place.

In the outer office four stenographers were sitting at their desks. They stopped typing and looked at me in amazement. "What do you want?" one asked.

"I'm called to see the Herr Direktor."

They looked unbelievingly at me. One of them giggled. I felt their curiosity.

One of the girls rose, opened a door and called, "Hilde!"

The director's secretary appeared, nodded at me, and indicated the pale green door. I trembled, knocked, and went in.

It was a spacious room. The light fell, not from a skylight, as in the rest of the factory, but through large, open windows that looked out on rows of tulips and toward the street on a side of the factory that we never saw.

In the center of a thick carpet was a single black desk, very much like Papa's. I walked up to the edge of the carpet, hesitated, and stopped.

Director Keller was looking through some papers, and did not immediately lift his head. I saw a miniature loom on his desk and a square frame in which he kept a picture of his family. Samples of material were displayed in glass cases hung along the walls. But what struck me most was that in this big, luxurious room he was alone. We fifty girls had to share space no larger than his office.

The director lifted his head. "Oh, it's you," he said. "What's your name?"

I told him.

"Hmmm." With a curious smile he eyed me from my heavy ski boots to my kerchief. "Come closer."

I stepped onto the thick carpet, my heart beating wildly. Two steps from the desk I halted.

"Aha!" he said again. "So that's you."

I felt blood shooting into my cheeks. What does he want? I thought in panic.

He held up a letter. The postmark looked familiar; on the letterhead were three lions holding a crown. I almost shrieked with joy and relief. I knew it was a letter from my uncle in Turkey!

"I want to ask you some questions." The director's voice was not as stern as when he lectured us.

"Yes." I waited, checking my excitement.

"I have a letter here from someone who says that he is your uncle. Do you have an uncle in Turkey?"

"Yes, I do."

"What is his name?"

I told him.

"Do you know his address?"

"Posta Kutusu 530, Istanbul."

"So you wrote to him," he said sternly. "You smuggled a letter out of camp!"

"No, I did not," I answered quietly.

"How else would he know where you are?"

"Perhaps my brother, who is in the *Gouvernement,* or friends in Bielitz, wrote to him."

My explanation must have satisfied him.

"You may write to him," he said then, "but give Frau Kügler the letter."

"Thank you," I answered, realizing what a big thing it was, for we were not allowed to write to foreign countries.

He put the letter in a drawer—I was not to have it. Thinking that I was dismissed, I turned to go.

"Wait a minute," he called.

I turned and faced him again.

He hesitated. "No, never mind. Go now."

How I wished I knew what was in the letter! I wondered if by chance my uncle knew the director. It was possible: my uncle, who had a textile factory, came to the textile conventions in Europe every year.

"Oh God, I am so lucky!" I exulted.

I wrote a letter to my uncle. Shortly after, surely before it reached him, I was called to Frau Kügler. She had a package for me from Turkey. It was more than three-quarters empty.

"It was open when it arrived," Frau Kügler told me. "It was probably not properly packed because things are missing."

I could not help but notice that the neat wooden box would surely have taken effort to open. The few things that were left in it were wonderful—burnt almonds, sugar-coated nut clusters, and halvah. I called Ilse, Suse, and some other girls and we shared those delights. They were quickly eaten, but I was so happy with the idea of getting the package that I would not have cared even if I had not tasted anything at all.

Frau Kügler eagerly urged me to acknowledge the package. Her eagerness confirmed my suspicions that she and the director were guilty of opening it. As the result of my letters, more parcels came from Turkey, but each one that reached me was opened and more than half empty.

Then May came, the month I particularly loved.

When I woke on the morning of my nineteenth birthday Ilse embraced me, saying, "Happy birthday!" She led me to our table where, on a doily made of the paper in which the white yarn for the looms was wrapped, was a white china cup. Ilse had borrowed it from one of the girls. And my slice of bread was spread with margarine! That was indeed a treat, for only on Sundays did we get margarine. Ilse had scraped it from her bread and saved it for me.

I got other wonderful gifts that day, more precious and harder to obtain than any I will ever get: shoelaces made from factory yarn; three bobby pins made from the wire on which spools were suspended over the loom; a pair of stockings not too badly darned; a new kerchief (or rather a triangle cut from a square—the girl who gave it to me wore the more bleached and worn half); and a few green leaves with one posy, plucked from the director's garden through the barbed wire of the fence. I felt a lump in my throat—the girls had been wonderful to me!

That afternoon two parcels came from Abek, one with clothing and groceries, and the other with books. I was most pleased with the latter. There were dried flowers on the bottom of the box.

I thought and thought of how I could repay the girls in some way, and then I hit upon a plan. When I asked Frau Kügler if I could arrange a play, she liked the idea. She herself was bored, and welcomed a change. So at night, in the washroom, I wrote a skit.

When I announced it to the girls, the whole camp was alive with expectation. Volunteers took parts. One girl had a wonderful voice; she sang classical pieces. Two girls offered to act in a sailor skit. One of them had studied ballet.

My play presented Ilse and me as old grandmothers, knitting and remembering the old times in Bolkenhain, gossiping about what happened to the girls, bringing out each weakness and peculiarity, and predicting, of course, a brilliant future for each.

Frau Kügler enjoyed the play immensely, laughing until she cried. Here and there I inserted a significant word or two in Polish, not meant for her German ears. The girls howled in appreciation.

When our two granddaughters (one was Suse) appeared, and we tried to tell them a bit about our lives, they winked at each other knowingly.

"Come, let us talk about our boy friends," they whispered, taking advantage of our deafness, "for the old ones like to exaggerate a bit."

Ilse and I strained to catch their remarks, and we smiled at each other with understanding. When our granddaughters left the stage we smiled indulgently after them. The play was over. There was a moment of complete stillness and then came a hurricane of applause.

We knew we were understood. After the merrymaking and fun, that note of hope was the right one to strike. The hope for a normal life, for children and grandchildren who could live in a world where our experiences would seem too fantastic to be believable—that was our dearest wish.

I was urged to arrange more performances for Sundays. I spent many a night writing in the washroom. I loved every bit of it. I loved the applause in my ears. I loved the single light burning on our improvised stage when the rest of the room was in darkness. I loved that light falling upon me and illuminating my figure. I loved to hear my voice in the hushed silence. But best of all I loved those upturned faces between the bunks, the smiles and sudden laughter, the knowledge that it was in my power to bring them an hour of fun, to help them forget.

When I look back now over the years, thinking of their happy faces, I remember too how pitifully few lived to know the joy of freedom. When I remember the forests of Czechoslovakia, where most of them lie in unmarked graves, I thank God that I was able to make them forget. Even now, when I meet the few girls who survived and they remind me of those performances, I feel humble and grateful. I know that that was the greatest thing I have done in my life.

Toward the beginning of June workmen started to erect a barracks at the far end of our courtyard and Frau Kügler told us that fifty more girls were scheduled to arrive. We lived in feverish anticipation during those next few days. Would there be someone we knew among them? Finally, the day came. After work we all rushed to meet the new girls. They were mostly from the vicinity of Sosnowitz. We were eager to hear what was happening in the outside world and they were of course anxious to find out what sort of camp Bolkenhain was. They told us that more and more people were being sent to Auschwitz, that the political situation was not good for the Germans, that the English were bombing cities in Germany in ever-increasing force. We listened hopefully to this last, praying that it might be true.

The new girls were trained by Meister Zimmer just as we had been, and after a week they joined us in the plant.

Toward the end of June, suddenly and without warning, our mail was no longer handed to us and we were not allowed to write. We were soon to discover a probable reason: on the Eastern Front, all was not well. We now had to stop our looms, often in the middle of a bolt of material, for lack of yarn. The machines stood idle for days. Finally we were told to remove the unfinished bolts and clean the looms. There was not enough raw material, not enough work. They said we had not produced enough and our punishment was not to have our mail. Incoming mail did not get to Frau Kügler; it was being burned outside the front offices of the factory. We were given odd jobs to do, such as cleaning windows and oiling machinery. Meister Zimmer ran about like a wild tiger, slapping whomever he could reach. He had never done that before.

Toward the end of July, for no reason that we could fathom, we were suddenly given mail again. I had a letter from Abek. Apparently he had written often, although he had not received any mail from me.

Abek's next letter came a week or so later. He was leaving Bielitz and was going to another camp. He wanted me to know, in case he couldn't write any more, that he would love me always and that if he should die, my name would be his last word. How odd, depressing, and pessimistic his letter sounded! I felt terrible. His letters now meant more to me than I ever admitted to myself, and when they stopped coming, I took out the old ones and read them over and over. I omitted the ones in which he sounded weak and discouraged.

The best of his old letters seemed precious and wonderful now. I missed him, and thought about him all the time. I saw Abek as he was, unaffected by my moods, writing to me for months, not even certain if I received his mail, sending packages that meant depriving himself. How many nights did he have to paint to be able to buy the goods he sent me? I surely must love him for all that, I said to myself, over and over again.

Then, in the last hot days of August, 1943, we saw uniformed men walking through the factory. The director was excited. We were called into the courtyard, divided into three units, and told that we were leaving Bolkenhain.

Chapter 7

How differently I had pictured my departure, with the high gates thrust wide open to freedom, and how gladly I would have stayed in Bolkenhain until the war's end.

When we assembled in the courtyard, we found Frau Kügler and the director engaged in discussion and we heard the words "Landeshut" and "Märzdorf." These names came as a great relief, for we knew that in these towns were subsidiaries of Kramsta-Methner-Frahne, the firm we worked for. During our months at Bolkenhain many bolts of material had arrived in crates, their markings indicating that they had been sent from these towns. Now they sounded like old familiar places that we had known all our lives. "Thank God," we whispered one to another, "we are not going back to a Dulag. They will let us work—that means we will live."

Ilse and I clasped hands tightly and together we were assigned to the group destined for Märzdorf. Suse and Lotte were to go to Landeshut, along with Mrs. Berger and Litzi. We had no idea whether Frau Kügler was going with any of the groups.

There were a few minutes when we all embraced, then one by one we mounted our different trucks. There was silence while the gate opened, then the engines started with a roar. With the inevitable grinding of gears and a jolt we were on our way. I looked back at the fence that I had clutched so many times in desperate prayer. It did not look so confining now. Our truck swung out into the main street of the little town that we had seen only once, the evening when we first arrived, more than a year before.

It was late afternoon. We had been riding for a couple of

144

hours and we were on a dark forest road. Low-hanging fragrant pine branches brushed our faces. It grew quite dark.

Ilse took my hand and whispered, "Gerda, I am afraid." I did not answer, though I knew what she meant. There was something frightening about the stillness of the forest. Where were the Allied planes that were supposed to be destroying Germany? Where were our liberators? The fields we had passed earlier in the day had looked rich, the cattle contented. Orchard trees were heavy with fruit. The villages seemed calm. Germany suffering and hungry?—it was only we who suffered.

The truck's headlights threw a low beam on the road ahead. "Gerda," Ilse whispered again.

"I am afraid too," I whispered back, not knowing how to comfort her. She started to cry, pressing her hands to her eyes.

It must have been about ten that night when we reached Märzdorf and could see the tall factory chimneys rising toward the sky. There were about thirty of us and I sensed that all of us were apprehensive about what was ahead.

The truck drove into the factory courtyard, enclosed by three six-story buildings. On the fourth side was a high fence topped by barbed wire and a gate guarded by an SS man. We were met by the new *Lagerführerin*, a girl of perhaps eighteen or nineteen, tall, blond, and vulgar-looking. Whip in hand, she was in the midst of a tirade directed at the *Judenälteste*, a sloppy, cow-eyed woman. My heart sank. This was not Frau Kügler, not Mrs. Berger, who was never afraid to stand up for her girls. This was different, so different. We were counted with the whip by the *Lagerführerin* and I noticed that she wore a ring on every one of her short, red fingers. How repulsive she was!

Roll call over, we were herded up to the sixth floor of one of the buildings. In passing, I noticed that the other floors of the factory were equipped with unfamiliar machinery. Some seemed to have looms but it was different, very different from Bolkenhain, much older and in disrepair. On the top floor a heavy iron door was opened and we looked into a large, nearly dark room filled with rows upon rows of three-tiered bunks. From some of the bunks girls' heads popped up. "Where

145

from?" they asked us, and immediately the whole room buzzed with life and the usual asking about news of relatives and friends.

"Quiet!" the *Lagerführerin* yelled hoarsely, and her whip smashed against the bunks, hitting girls all around her. It was quiet now. Again Ilse and I were lucky enough to be assigned adjoining bunks near a window. We were told to go to sleep, but sleep would not come. I rolled over on my stomach and looked out of the window, into the factory courtyard. It looked much smaller from so high up. The thought of the heavy iron door being bolted from the outside was heavy upon me. There was no escape from here!

As I dozed off, I heard Ilse calling me. I was too tired to answer but could not fall asleep again. I looked out the window. A rocket, shot into the sky, illuminating the strange countryside. I looked at Ilse, but she was sleeping.

Maybe it's the English, I thought with hope. Maybe they will drop a bomb. What if they did? We would be trapped here on the sixth floor! The flare vanished like a dream.

In the morning we were awakened by a shrill "Auf! Auf!" and a whip cracking against bunks. This was a woman guard, simply called Frau Aufsicht (Mrs. Overseer) because she supervised us on the way to and from work. Formerly, we learned, she had been a prison warden. She was small and thin, always dressed in gray; her face, her eyes, her hair, everything was gray. She seemed to have no mouth and never once did I see her smile. She was a creature born to hate and to be hated. She used her whip and profanity as if they were the only language we could understand.

Märzdorf was badly organized. There were about a hundred girls, including our group, but few worked at regular jobs, as we had in Bolkenhain. Each morning, after we were handed a chunk of bread and a bitter ersatz coffee, Frau Aufsicht marched us down to the courtyard where we stood roll call. Then several supervisors would appear to pick a number of girls for whatever work there was to be done. It was like a slave market.

From time to time, the young blond *Lagerführerin*, with

her bejeweled fingers, would commandeer three or four girls to pull a child's wagon in which she sat. As she rode around the courtyard, rickshaw-fashion, she would crack the whip over their backs.

The first day I was picked for a bricklaying detail along with four more girls. We were marched out of the courtyard and behind the factory where some construction was going on. A high pile of bricks was on the ground. We were told to form a line and throw the bricks from hand to hand until they reached a man who apparently was an experienced bricklayer. At first I thought I would never be able to do it. The bricks came too fast, their weight exhausted my arms, tore at my hands, and threatened to crush my fingers. Soon my shoulders began to ache and once when I missed a brick, it landed on my foot. I felt tears of pain welling up in my eyes and I wondered how I would last through the day.

Before long, however, I caught on to the rhythm of the work and then it became easier.

When we marched to quarters that night, I felt deathly tired from the fresh air, the unaccustomed work, and the excitement of the previous two days. All I wanted was to sleep.

The brick work was comparatively easy. The flax detail was what everyone dreaded and it was only a few days later that I learned why.

We had been at Märzdorf a week when I was chosen to work inside the factory, to clean and oil delicate parts of machinery which was being dismantled. I was glad for the change, for it permitted me to sit down. Besides, it was raining.

I was busy cleaning little screws when I sensed that someone was watching me. I started to feel more uncomfortable when I saw the blue cloth of a supervisor's coveralls. Then I heard a voice above me.

"Well done," he said, as he examined some screws.

I looked up, for surely it was rare that one should be praised. Then he asked me a tricky question.

"Are you hungry?"

I could not very well say yes and so accuse the Germans of

147

mistreating me. Yet I did not want to say no, because it was true that I was hungry. I just said, "I eat in camp."

"Come, come. Surely you don't get enough to eat there," he said in a fatherly tone.

Feverishly I continued the cleaning, my thoughts running wild. Perhaps he was not a Nazi; perhaps he was one of the partisans from the underground. My cheeks flushed, my lips quivered, as my hands continued to polish mechanically.

"You can't get enough to eat," he insisted.

I wished that he would go, but he stood there stolidly.

"Perhaps bread and butter," he suggested. "Apples, sausage, warm soup."

He mouthed those words so easily that I realized the disgusting truth. He was no partisan, for if he truly wanted to help me, he would not tease me.

He continued, his voice unctuous and dirty: "And for all that, I don't want much from you—"

"What do you want?" I demanded.

His voice changed abruptly. "Don't pretend to be stupid, or one might think you are a lady."

I was on the verge of crying, but I looked at him with all the hatred I could muster, and continued cleaning. There was so much I wanted to say, but I knew that my life was in his hands. I was afraid even of silence. I rubbed the machine furiously. Out of the corner of my eye, I saw him standing there watching me, as a cat watches a mouse.

He started to walk away, hesitated, and came back.

"You will be sorry!" he said before he left.

He could have taken me by force, he could have made up a story for the *Lagerführerin* and I would have been sent to Auschwitz, but evidently he decided to break my resistance. From that day on, Märzdorf became hell.

Next morning I was picked for the flax detail. We were marched to the freight depot just outside the factory. Freight car after freight car arrived, loaded high with bundles of flax. A huge crane lifted the bundles one by one from the cars, and dropped them at ten- or fifteen-second intervals. A human line quickly passed the bundles until they reached the barn.

There they were stacked until they mounted three or four stories high.

The crane operator would throw the bundles systematically, accurately, with brutal precision. He did not care how we sweated under the dropping weight. The operator was completely indifferent to the frail girls who kept up the inhuman pace, with arms that were bloody, swollen, and infected, whipped by the prickly fibers. The dust flew thick, irritating eyes and wounds, and making it difficult to swallow or breathe. We had the sensation of the ground moving under our feet.

This was the loathsome flax detail. Slowly, the freight cars emptied. The piles in the barns grew high.

We had company on my first day. Four women were brought from a nearby prison to work for half a day, severe punishment for them. I wondered if they had been convicted for murder. It would not have surprised me, the way they swore! They said that they would have preferred to be locked in solitary confinement. I understood their choice.

The day dragged on but it finally came to an end, and we marched to camp. Sweat mingled with blood and the fine dust from the flax covered our bodies. Our eyes were red, our throats tight.

I did not even have the desire for washing and food, all I wanted was sleep. But that day was not over yet. Just as we got to our bunks, Frau Aufsicht came by and yelled at certain ones of us. "Get up, you dirty lazy swine, up to work!"

To work? But it was night! Yes, to work. A few were chosen, and I was among them. The supervisor kept his word.

We were marched back to the freight yards, to unload coal. I stood on the freight car, the black mass of coal under my feet, my blistered fingers grasping a shovel. I shoveled the coal onto a high pile on one side of the platform. There, tired hands shoveled it into round baskets; others carried the heavy baskets on their backs to storage.

There was a little break. Slowly my eardrums cleared. My hands and clothes were black. My throat felt dry. When I tried to clear it, the spit came black.

I looked at the railway signals flashing stop and go, red

149

and green. The tracks were silvery gray in the moonlight. They held me fascinated. Bending over my shovel, I looked down, fully aware that I could not stand this life for long. The days at flax, the nights unloading coal. I knew now what the supervisor meant when he said, "You will be sorry."

I could wait until a train approached, then jump. How fast it would be over, I thought. A few seconds, then quietness forever. No more roll call, no more the horrible *Lagerführerin*, no more smirking supervisor trying to buy me with soup and a piece of bread, no more flax, no more coal. Just one fast, stabbing pain and then . . . stillness. . . .

As I gazed down at the tracks, I felt a strange sensation on my neck. Suddenly I realized why it was so familiar. I remembered my thoughts about death when I stood in my parents' bedroom shortly after Arthur had left, and how Papa had turned me, grasping my neck to make me look into his eyes, forcing me to promise that I would never give up. Strange that my neck should trouble me now, at the precise moment when death seemed the only solution!

Beyond us the main station became alive with lights and whistles. Slowly a train puffed by. From behind curtained car windows came muffled cries of suffering. We deduced that this was a hospital train filled with German wounded. Watching it, I was not even glad with the knowledge that Germans suffered too. I was only sorry for the promise that I had given my father.

By the time dawn came the freight cars were empty of coal, and we marched back to quarters. We weren't even allowed to wash, and it seemed only seconds until we were awakened again. Again I was chosen for the flax detail.

The same never-ending day continued and melted into the night and coal. Flax dust, coal dust, blood, sweat, all mixed together into a crust that covered my body. We were only a handful of girls who were chosen for both the flax and coal details, but I was always among them.

Ilse was jittery. She kept most of her meager rations for me. "You need all the food you can get," she insisted.

Then Sunday came. We didn't work. To be away from the

hateful flax was a most wonderful feeling. Locked up on the sixth floor we sat on Ilse's bunk and looked toward the distant hills.

Ilse asked gently, "How are you going to stand it?"

I knew that she wanted me to reassure her, but all I could say was, "I don't know."

That night coal trains came again, and again I was chosen. During the night it grew cooler. Other freight trains passed, from them we heard faint cries and pleas for water; in those trains were Jews making their last journey to Auschwitz. Those trains rolled by swiftly. Like snakes, they rolled into the night, taillights blinking sadly, and with them disappeared lives, thousands.

Another four days and nights and I felt myself weakening. My mind grew dull. There was no longer any satisfaction in showing the supervisor my pride. The tracks became more inviting each night, the promise given to Papa less meaningful. I wasn't myself any more, and that Thursday night I told Ilse that I couldn't take it any longer.

She squeezed my hand and didn't say anything. The next day, Friday morning, when I was again chosen for the flax detail, I felt Ilse's hand in mine. She had either been selected too, or had traded places with someone.

That day the flax train did not arrive on time, so we were led to a swamp where we had to open bundles of flax and spread it in the water. My back felt broken, for we had to crouch in order to perform our work. Mosquitoes feasted on us.

All at once Frau Aufsicht appeared, wanting to know whose number had been thirty-two in Bolkenhain. Thirty-two had been Ilse's number. For a second I saw her hand start to go up, then I saw her motioning to me to lift my arm.

"That's her number!" she said, pointing at me.

I knew what she was trying to do, but my mind still was not entirely clear. I only heard Frau Aufsicht yell at me, "You idiot, don't you know your own number?"

I was led away by the guard before I could say anything to Ilse.

We arrived at the factory courtyard where, to my immense relief, I saw Keller, the director from Bolkenhain. As much as I had always hated him, I was glad to see him now.

A few girls, all of whom had formerly worked at Bolkenhain, were standing near him. As I was led toward them, I saw Ilse coming. Her eyes were enormous with fear. Her clothing was wet and dirty. She was shaking. Frau Aufsicht hissed at her, asking what she was doing, but she ran up to the director—shy, timid Ilse—threw herself at his feet, and started to beg. He seemed amused. Frau Aufsicht raised her whip, but let it fall at a sign from the director.

"What do you want?" he finally demanded.

Wringing her hands, Ilse pointed in my direction and stammered, "My sister, my sister!"

The director turned to me. "You worked on four looms in Bolkenhain, your name should be on the list." Frau Aufsicht started to check the roster but the director said impatiently, "Both of them can go." He frowned at us. "Go wash, you look like pigs."

We clasped hands and with new-found energy we raced up to the sixth floor, cleaned up as fast as we could, and gathered up our bundles.

A truck entered the yard. Ilse and I and ten other girls, all formerly from Bolkenhain, stood in readiness. We were going to Landeshut. . . . In a matter of minutes we were settled on the truck. Why, oh why, did it take so long to get started? After an eternity the heavy gates opened and the truck roared out. I hardly realized that it was beginning to rain, I was so lost in my desire to get away as far as possible from Märzdorf.

As we climbed higher and higher along the mountainous road I made out that we were traveling southwest. For several hours, while it grew colder and colder, Ilse and I held hands without speaking. I still had not thanked her for what she had done—for the risk she had taken. I had no words.

It was evening when the truck pulled up at a building that looked like a large stable. A familiar voice sounded through the rain and darkness.

"Get inside. Quickly! Quickly!"

152

We mounted the stairs, illuminated by a single, faint bulb, and at the top found Frau Kügler barking, "Get in, get in!" Behind her were Mrs. Berger and Litzi. Beyond them I spotted Suse. In the kitchen, Lotte, beaming, was putting steaming bowls of something that looked and smelled delicious on the well-scrubbed table. I felt a lump in my throat. We hugged and kissed each other again and again. This was home! The stable, converted into a camp with the familiar three-tiered bunks, seemed so dear and safe. There were the girls from Bolkenhain but also some others, new girls. Suse took Ilse and me aside and led us to two empty bunks in the lowest tier. "They are right next to where I sleep," she said. Her smile illuminated her face and I could see how happy she was. There was much milling about. We all talked simultaneously. Finally, the lights went out. I took Ilse's hand.

Märzdorf was behind us, but I could still remember those silvery tracks beckoning in the moonlight.

I must have murmured aloud, "I'm glad I didn't jump."

"What did you say?" Ilse asked, half asleep.

"I said I am glad," I answered, and holding hands we went to sleep.

Chapter 8

THE WEAVING MILL IN LANDESHUT WAS A BRANCH OF THE ONE in Bolkenhain. Director Keller came on periodic inspections; thus we learned that he was in charge of all mills owned by Kramsta-Methner-Frahne.

Although everything in Landeshut was much more strenuous than in Bolkenhain it was heaven compared with Märzdorf. We worked the night shift only, from 6:00 P.M. to 7:00 A.M., with an hour at midnight when we returned to our quarters for a bowl of soup. The Germans worked the day shift. We were weaving white silk for parachutes and time and again were warned against possible mistakes which would be considered sabotage. Handling four looms was very hard since the thousands upon thousands of fine silk threads shone like liquid silver and reflected millionfold the lights overhead. It was most difficult to notice when a thread broke and got entangled in the fabric. During those ten months on the night shift in Landeshut my eyes suffered seriously and always burned and itched unmercifully.

The man in charge of the plant, who was addressed as Herr *Betriebsführer,* or plant supervisor, was not older than twenty-five. He walked with a limp, was short, stocky, and blond, and had one blue and one brown eye. Before the war he must have been a minor bookkeeper in the firm. Now, because of the manpower shortage or perhaps because he was a good Nazi, he had reached a position for which he obviously was ill suited but which he relished. He spoke to us as if we were all mentally deficient, punctuating every sentence with, "And if you don't do it, you know I have a big stick." I would have been amused had I not been sobered by the thought that our lives were in the hands of this moron. On the other hand, we

154

now knew beyond doubt that we were valuable. The factory owners did not want to send us back to the Dulag; we were trained weavers and skilled labor was scarce.

Bolkenhain, we heard, had become an aircraft factory. Many unfinished bolts of fabric were turned over to us for completion in Landeshut. We sensed that the war was growing worse for the Germans when our rations were cut. We were convinced that it was when we noticed the factory was heated less and less. But we had learned one lesson well: we realized that our lot could be far worse. We would have been willing to stay in Landeshut until the end of the war.

As at Märzdorf, there was no mail privilege. For weeks now we had not heard from friends and relatives. We did know, however, that each Polish town in turn had met the fate of Bielitz, and that the only Jews who remained were in camps.

We had no contact with the outside world, yet, strangely, I did not miss the mail. There was relief in not having to wait for good news that would never come. I thought of Papa, Mama, and Arthur and spun dreams of our reunion at home. At night, alone with my looms, I dreamed of the future. As each night passed, my dream became more vivid, more real. In a way, I looked forward to going to the factory in order to dream through my waking hours, to think of the people whom I would see when I would return home. I designed new dresses, planned trips to faraway places. During those long fall nights a new thought came more and more insistently into focus—the thought of a baby, warm, new, clean as freedom itself. How wonderful it would be to have my own baby!

We had heard that in some camps girls had been forcibly sterilized. That thought filled me with unspeakable horror. Many girls in our camp no longer had their monthly periods because of their poor nutrition. Few of them seemed concerned. It was always a problem to contrive sanitary supplies, to collect sufficient paper and sometimes bits of wood shavings to be wrapped in paper. Of course, no sanitary supplies were obtainable officially.

I spoke to other girls about my fears but they shrugged it off. Survival had become their most important thought, shutting out all else. Yet the thought of sterility did worry me. More forcefully as the long nights passed, the idea returned that someday I must have a baby of my own. I felt that I would endure anything willingly so long as that hope was not extinguished.

Saturday was a hard day for us for we worked as usual through Friday night, then went back to camp for three hours' rest and were back in the factory at 11:00 A.M. to work another twelve hours. But Saturday midnight we felt rich, realizing that we did not have to go to the factory again until Monday at 6:00 P.M.

Sunday was our day of leisure. We usually sat around and talked, slept, or invented games to play. A favorite game was called "Adventure." Each girl said where she would like to travel and why. The walls of the camp seemed to slide away as each of us wandered over the wide world. The war seemed far away and a life of adventure unfolded. One Sunday in late fall we played a variation of the game. The question was posed: "If you could choose, what qualities would you have in a husband?" Ilse nudged me constantly as some of the answers were given, and Suse could hardly suppress her laughter. Some wanted wealth, and swore if given a chance they would never so much as lift a finger again; the word *work* would be stricken from their vocabulary. To many, the most important attributes were good looks, combined with gaiety and the ability to dance. One voice, unforgettable, boomed, "Give me a grocer!"

There was a lot of talk about educated men, for we all craved learning. One girl wanted a husband who was a textile manufacturer and explained, "I could see the looms all the time and would never have to touch them."

Then it was my turn. Eyes centered on me. Before I had time to organize my thoughts, it came out: "Before I marry, I will ask myself if I want that man as a father for my children."

There was a burst of laughter.

"Gerda, you of all people!"

I was angry at the girls, angry at myself. I felt that I was

156

misunderstood. The discussion became gayer and gayer; they did not let me explain. I walked away, furious. I thought I had expressed my feelings well but the girls had not understood my dreams about a baby. I was the butt of much good-natured joking for a long time after that.

November came. As we left the factory one morning we watched a column of men march by, on their backs and chests the Jewish star. We saw the SS guards shouting commands, swinging their whips. We were speechless—there was a men's camp nearby! The men marched across the meadow that adjoined our camp. When almost out of our sight, they halted and began to build something. There was excitement in our camp, a kindling of hope that fathers, husbands, and brothers might be in the group.

Frau Kügler soon found that there was a dentist among the prisoners and summoned him to repair her teeth. When he came with his equipment, we learned from him that the men were housed about an hour's march from us in what had formerly been a tavern on a hill called Zum Burgberg. It was shortly to be known as one of the most horrible men's camps in Germany.

The dentist, Dr. Goldstein, was a dark-haired man of about thirty-five, with a dimple in his chin. He still had the air of a jolly person, yet when he spoke of the Burgberg, horror came into his eyes.

A few girls learned by means of the messages that Dr. Goldstein smuggled out that their loved ones were close by. I saw girls breathlessly wait for his visits and I saw them at the windows, anxiously watch the passing column of prisoners, throw their precious bits of bread to the men when the guards were not looking. Some girls waited in the yard next to the outhouse, where they knew the column must pass. Sometimes a boy would step out of line for a second and risk being whipped to touch a girl's hand, or to get a piece of bread.

From the time the men came there was no peace. The girls could see the column dwindle daily. When a loved one failed to pass by for two or three days running the girls knew what had happened. I often awoke to their sobbing or to a cry of

157

despair so piercing that I could sleep no longer. Dr. Goldstein kept us informed of the incredible excesses the SS guards indulged in: the slaughter, the wild orgies, the transports to Auschwitz.

One stormy dawn late in November, after we marched back from work, I was about to fall asleep when I felt somebody touching my shoulder. It was Mrs. Berger. "Come to the kitchen," she whispered. I followed her. She took a folded piece of paper from her pocket and handed it to me. I recognized Abek's handwriting.

"Where did you get it?" I stammered.

"Abek is here," Mrs. Berger replied.

I shook my head in disbelief. He must have come with the new group that was to replace those sent to Auschwitz. Then the impact of Abek's being so close hit me. Abek was on the Burgberg!

"Read your letter," Mrs. Berger urged. "Then I will tell you something."

It was a strange letter, so inappropriate for that environment: "At last I am breathing the same air as you, seeing the same sky as you. When we are free nothing can keep us apart. When will I see you? How many seconds? Hours? Days? How I prayed for this hour, to be where you are."

I looked up at Mrs. Berger.

"You will see Abek at noon," she told me.

I learned later how it had been arranged that morning. Frau Kügler had gone with Lotte to get a supply of coal, which was kept not far from the construction site where the men were working. Abek had been there and asked Lotte to get a message through to me. Lotte told Frau Kügler. I can well imagine how astounded he must have been when Frau Kügler approached him and said, "Around noon, cut yourself; I will come around and find an excuse to take you to camp to see Gerda." I was deeply touched. I woke up Ilse and told her. Quickly word spread, for Abek was well known. The girls insisted on dressing me up. One friend begged me to wear her white sweater, the most elegant garment in the camp. I waited for noon, looking out toward where the men were working.

158

At times I thought I spotted Abek, but I was not sure. Finally, around noon, Lotte came running from the kitchen, to call me. Then I saw Abek, his face white as snow. He seemed very tall. His head was shaven, he was thinner than ever. He held onto the railing as he slowly walked up the stairs; apparently it took great effort. I stared at him from a distance, watching him enter the kitchen and speak to Mrs. Berger. He had not seen me yet. I stood still, as though frozen, wishing with all my might that I did not have to face him. The last time I had seen him I had been with Papa and Mama.

Mrs. Berger came out of the kitchen, Abek turned around and followed her with his eyes. Then he saw me. He stretched his arms out. I closed my eyes and ran to him. He held me tight.

"My little darling!" he whispered. "At last, at last!"

He buried his face in my hair, whispering over and over again, "At last, at last!" I did not utter a word.

He took my face, as something precious, between his hands, and looked at me as if not believing I was real. I could read love and unbearable sadness in his eyes. Then I realized that I had not said one word, not shown by one gesture that I was glad to see him. I wanted to embrace him but he pushed me away roughly. I thought he misunderstood. I stretched my arms toward him, but he gripped the edge of the table, an odd look in his eyes, his hands and lips trembling.

"Go away," he whispered hoarsely. "Go away!"

I could not understand. I stepped forward. Abek sank on a bench, and cried. I watched him cry. It was heart-rending. I could not speak, nor could I wipe his tears. I wished that I could have cried, but there was no such relief for me.

Mrs. Berger came in with a bowl of food and a cloth for Abek's wounded hand. Only then did I notice the wound that he had inflicted on himself with a shovel. I saw the blood that slowly trickled from it, I saw his tears. That blood and those tears because of me, I thought. Why must there be this bloody war?

"Eat, Abek," I urged him.

He lifted a spoon but put it down.

"I can't," he said, and then I knew how very hungry he must have been.

"Lonek is here at the Burgberg too," he said after a pause, adding, "He came along." Lonek was his nephew.

"Came along?" I echoed. Then I realized what Abek had done.

"Abek!" I gasped. "You did not come *voluntarily?*"

He nodded.

"But why, in God's name?"

"Need you ask?" he said with a catch in his voice.

"We have to go," Frau Kügler called into the kitchen. She had been talking to the guard in her quarters. Either the guard never suspected her motive or perhaps he too was a bit human.

I kissed Abek's cheek.

"Good-by, take care of yourself." With pain in my heart, I watched him go.

The girls waited, excited for me. What could I tell them? I only wanted to be alone. I was not happy that Abek was here, that I could see him, perhaps daily. I wished that he had not come. I felt incapable of such love and sacrifice. I was responsible for his coming, I thought, for his misery and for Lonek's as well!

Oh God, I prayed, watch over him! Let nothing happen to him!

Chapter 9

Bit by bit I pieced together the story of Abek's coming to Landeshut. When the camp in Bielitz had been disbanded, all the men went to Blechhammer since the Dulag in Sosnowitz was no longer in existence. In Blechhammer Abek met a former classmate of his who held the position comparable to Mrs. Berger's in our camp. Through him Abek got into portrait painting again and his lot in Blechhammer became an easy one. One day he overheard two SS men say that Bolkenhain was being dissolved. From that day on he knew no more peace. Aided by his painting and through his friend's influence, he somehow persuaded one of the guards to check the rosters. Thus he learned that I was in Landeshut.

Later, when he heard that a men's camp had been opened in Landeshut, he begged to be sent there in a transport, much against the advice of his friend, who knew of the camp's reputation.

No longer did I look forward to dawn, to going to sleep, grateful that another night of work was over. Now each night seemed never-ending. I waited for Abek every morning and Ilse waited up with me. She insisted on doing everything for Abek that I did. For her he was truly a shining hero, an ideal. Each morning that we saw Abek we threw one of our breakfasts down to him and shared the other. Ilse was usually animated and happy when we had seen him, but I was just glad that another day had passed in which no harm had come to him.

At about four in the afternoon the men would march back to the Burgberg and I usually waited downstairs near the outhouses. Abek would steal away from his group for a moment and run to the fence and I would hand him some bread

161

or a potato. Then he would touch me gently. It was a new pain each day, that little caress through the barbed wire, and I would be glad when his column marched away. Sometimes he would turn and wave, and then he would become lost in the gray, tired column, walking away in the dusk.

Toward the middle of December we saw something new on the factory grounds: dark-haired, dark-eyed foreign men, in bright green uniforms, with funny green felt hats, elegantly slanted to one side. Such smart uniforms! We caught snatches of their conversation. They were Italian prisoners. We knew now that the war had taken a different turn. Apparently the Italians were no longer gallant Axis partners. New hope rose high. Had we known, that winter, that the war would last another year and a half, we would not have been so cheered by the sight of the Duce's subjects in their new role.

The Italians did not last long. We saw them eating out of garbage cans in the factory, shivering in the frost of the mountain winter. Soon their uniforms were soiled, their gay hats crumpled. The sparkle left their eyes. Their numbers decreased rapidly.

I pictured them under the sunny skies of Italy, at grape harvests, singing in gondolas in Venice, walking through the Forum in Rome. How they must have missed their land.

On Christmas Day, as we cleaned the factory, we heard a running to and fro in one of the halls beneath us. We caught sight of a lifeless body in a bright green uniform. Accident? Suicide? Nobody seemed sure. His family would never know that he died without glory on Christmas morning in a place called Landeshut.

Things were getting worse at Burgberg; we could see it in the faces of the men when they marched by. Whenever the dentist came, which was not often these days, he told us of new horrors. In January there was an epidemic of pneumonia. Day after day I waited apprehensively for Abek, grateful when I saw him, fearful and in despair when I missed him. During the long nights at my looms the fear gnawed at me that he might become ill.

A few days after the epidemic started we heard that we

were going to do laundry from the Burgberg camp in our factory laundry. Each Monday morning eight girls were assigned to the laundry; those chosen went without sleep all that day and the following night. I always volunteered for this detail for there was a strong possibility that Abek would be among the men who brought the clothes and he usually was.

I looked forward to those Mondays and dreaded them at the same time. I was somehow ashamed to meet Abek. I was ashamed of my clean clothes, ashamed and pained by the kiss that he planted on my cheek when he could. And always there were the dirty, bloody, vermin-filled bundles of clothes between us. I looked for Abek's clothes, and at the same time I hoped that I would not find them. I sought opportunities to see him and dreaded the moment that I would have to face him. I was sure now that I would marry him, although I did not want to. Yet I was comforted by the knowledge that through that long and frightful winter he never doubted my love for an instant.

Day by day, night by night, the weeks passed. Toward the end of April, 1944, spring showed signs of coming. Then it was upon us. The snow melted, the sky turned blue, grass and flowers seemed to come out overnight. It was as if nature wanted to compensate for that cruel, long winter with one sudden, generous gesture.

I was so glad for that spring, yet with its coming Abek's outlook seemed gloomier rather than better. Whenever I could, I wrote him cheerful notes, but he either began to sense my true feelings about him or like so many others, he was losing the desire to live.

I begged him to pull himself together for my sake—the winter was over, the worst part of the battle over—but a shroud of resignation was closing upon him. His replies were halfhearted.

On May 6, without warning, Frau Kügler told us that we were to be transferred to a large concentration camp. We were to leave Landeshut in two groups, on the eighth and the ninth. The news filled us with horror.

In the first group to leave was Suse. As we embraced, I felt devoid of tears. We had cried too often. Ilse, Lotte, Mrs. Berger, Litzi, and I were to go in the second transport. I desperately wanted to see Abek again and with Frau Kügler's consent, it was arranged that Ilse and I should deliver some laundry to the Burgberg. Acting as our official escort, Frau Kügler planned it so that we would arrive at the camp shortly before the men came back from work.

Thus, on May 8, my twentieth birthday, I saw the dreaded Burgberg for the first time. The place spelled horror to me, from the machine gun over the entrance to the tomblike, windowless walls that housed the men. In the yard we encountered Dr. Goldstein, and I had a few words with him while Frau Kügler talked to the SS guards in charge. I begged him to look after Abek and he promised that he would. I saw Frau Kügler glancing at her watch. Trying to delay our departure, she suggested that she would like to see the whole camp.

"You'd better stay right where you are," she barked at Ilse and me. As she left she winked at us.

Suddenly I knew that I couldn't face him. I feared that he might break down. I didn't want to see him. I drew a piece of paper out of my pocket and while Ilse and the dentist stood guard I huddled against the grim stone wall of the Burgberg and wrote a few last words to Abek, begging him to be strong for my sake. I gave the note to the dentist.

A few minutes later Frau Kügler and the SS men returned. There was a question in her eyes and I realized that she intended to stall some more in order that I might see Abek.

"I would rather go now," I whispered.

She did not seem to understand. She pointed to the ground to indicate that we would stay. I shook my head. She understood.

Descending the hill from the Burgberg we heard the men coming up another road, heard the shouting of the guards, the noise of the whips. Abek was there in that marching column. Was it possible the news had reached him about our departure? How would he take it? For a second I hesitated.

Should I beg Frau Kügler to return for just a moment under some pretext? No, I had already taken the best course.

I had a glimpse of the men marching into the camp.

"Good-by, Abek," I whispered.

At dawn we went one by one through the narrow corridor just off our barracks to be counted and turned over to the SS. Frau Kügler stood in the corridor, under the pretext of searching our meager bundles, but in reality she did not look at any of them. She stood there to speak to each of us. Her face was wet with tears.

"Good-by, Gerda," she murmured under her breath. "Don't forget me."

In the courtyard, as she handed over our papers to the SS, I saw her battling with tears. She stood there grim, her voice barking as it had on the first day when we met her in Bolkenhain twenty-two months before.

She was supposed to withdraw after the SS took over but she went to the station with us. She stood there, a solitary figure, and waved a soundless farewell. I think I have described her with justice. She was a good woman. She made the time that we spent in her charge as bearable as possible. She displayed humanity, she gave us hope that perhaps not all Germans were cruel.

Chapter 10

LANDESHUT DISAPPEARED. THE IMPERSONAL TRAIN CREATED A welcome sense of isolation for me. Sitting in the tiny compartment I belonged to myself, my thoughts had more freedom, my dreams became keener. It was a May morning in all its glory of dewy, fresh grass and budding trees. This was a setting for love, for romance, for a young, gay heart. And—I was twenty years old.

We were traveling in a northerly direction. The rumor was that we were going to Grünberg, about two hundred kilometers from Landeshut. In the early afternoon we reached a large city whose name I no longer remember, where we had to change trains. They herded us onto the station platform. Porters were running to and fro, people streamed past, and the green-gray uniforms of German soldiers were everywhere. Life was going on, a war was being fought, and many people walked about in their busy, free lives. Only we were slaves.

I yearned to mingle with the crowds that had homes and families. Instead, I stood next to Ilse, hugging my bundle of threadbare belongings, waiting to be shipped somewhere, the yellow star ablaze on my breast, back, and head.

People stared at us curiously. A porter approached, carrying luggage and a neatly folded traveling blanket. Following him was a young girl, perhaps my age, slender, tall, in a gray suit and a fresh white blouse. She wore a white beret on her carefully groomed hair. She walked rapidly toward the compartment of her train. I watched her enter it, saw the porter put her luggage into the net over her seat, saw her give him a tip. I heard the porter's muffled, *"Danke, Fräulein!"*

The girl looked out the window as if searching for someone. With fascination I followed her every move. An older man approached. She waved and called, *"Hier bin ich, Papa!"*

I felt a quick, stabbing pain. How many years was it since I had said those magic words, since I heard anyone say "Papa"?

The man entered the compartment. As the girl turned toward him, for a fleeting moment our eyes met. I saw her picture in a thousand fragments, I saw her snowy blouse a hundredfold reflected, I saw her blurred, for now I saw her through tears.

The engine of her train started to puff, the train moved. Daughter and father started toward their destination. I would never know their names, their lives, their lot, but at that moment I would willingly have exchanged my life for hers. How foolish we are!

A few minutes later we boarded our new train. In my imagination I tried to re-create the scene I had just witnessed, I reached into an imaginary purse, looked out the window searchingly, knowing that the beret sat perfectly on my hair, but when I came to the part where I should call, "Here I am, Papa!" the spell was broken. In silence we rolled toward Grünberg.

When I think of Grünberg I grow very sad. It was cruelty set against a backdrop of beauty. The gentle vineyard-covered hills silhouetted against the sapphire sky seemed to mock us.

The vast camp had been built as part of a textile mill not long before the war. The sun shone through the glass roof. The camp was modern, well scrubbed, clean, and filled with suffering.

That day in 1944, when we arrived, there were approximately a thousand girls there. Some were bursting with health and color, others were half-starved and walked about with bent backs, decaying teeth, the pallor of death already on their faces. Those who worked outdoors looked healthy and fresh, the others seemed to be gray, moving parts of the infernal machines. Though clean, the camp was badly run. The staff, appointed by the factory authorities in the days when the plant had first become a camp, consisted of a particularly evil and stupid group of girls who feasted while the rest

167

starved as they wove and spun. The contrast was sharp; there was no in-between.

There was one SS man who guarded the entrance, one *Lagerführerin*, very different from Frau Kügler, and several helpers, vicious and ignorant. The SS guard and the *Lagerführerin* checked and double-checked us in the yard in front of the building in which we were to be housed. Finally, when they had established to their satisfaction that all were present, we were admitted to the building, which consisted of three enormous halls with concrete floors. Two of the halls contained our bunks. The third was the dining hall. It was isolated from the kitchen by a partition with a window through which the food was handed.

Suse came running to embrace Ilse and me. "I have saved you bunks next to mine," she said. "I met a friend here, a girl I used to know back home. You will like her."

We approached the bunks and there stood a beautiful girl. She held out both her hands.

"I am Liesel Stepper," she said in a silvery voice, and as we clasped hands I knew we would be friends. Liesel, who was from Czechoslovakia, told us about herself. She smiled a great deal and when she did her round eyes, brown and soft, always lit up. She reminded me of a fairy-tale princess. When she walked, her movements were so graceful that she hardly seemed to touch the ground.

The conversation inevitably got around to conditions in camp and so we learned about the horrors of Grünberg, and the part of the camp that spelled disaster and death, the *Spinnerei*. Whoever worked there did not last very long.

In the morning we girls from Landeshut assembled in the courtyard. Again we stood *Appell* for a long time, and were snapped to attention when the *Betriebsleiter*, as the director was called here, arrived. The girls had told us about him already. I looked curiously at the man who was so feared. He was tall and slender. His face was large and pale, with a square look and hollow cheeks. His eyes were deep set and water-blue. They seemed to have no lashes at all. He had grotesquely

168

long arms and large hands; on his right hand he wore a large signet ring.

"That must be the ring," I thought—the girls had told us how he would make a fist and beat his victim with the ring until her face or body was covered with blood. It was not long before I had to witness such a scene.

Every two weeks we took showers. On that first morning we waited in line in the long corridor, which was dimly lit, warm and moist. We could hear the hiss of the water and the steam knocking in the pipes overhead. I looked forward to having the warm clean water touching my body. I pressed tightly against the moist wall when I saw the *Betriebsleiter* coming, like a huge, soft-footed cat. The girls who saw him froze into silence, but those with their backs turned continued talking. We could not warn the girls. I saw him stand motionless, like a snake eyeing his prey. Then he leaped forward, digging his fingers into a girl's face. I saw it all, I did not turn away. I was hypnotized, frozen with horror and rage. I felt that I could have killed the man and enjoyed the sight of his blood. Then he walked away swiftly without wiping his hands.

After it was over, it seemed like a nightmare. There was deathly silence. The beaten girl pressed her torn face toward the wall without a sound.

When I got into the shower and felt the warm water on my skin, I started to shiver. My teeth chattered. I leaned against the tiled wall of the cubicle and vomited while the water ran over me. When my stomach was empty, I carefully washed the floor. I prayed that I should never be assaulted, for I knew I would strike back, even though I would have to pay for it with life itself.

But this was still our first morning in Grünberg. We stood in the courtyard, waiting to be picked for our first jobs.

"*Spinnerei!*" the *Betriebsleiter* announced, and I felt a shiver go through my body.

Suse was the first one to go. A few more of the tallest and prettiest girls were chosen next. Then he pointed to me. I detached myself from my group, and walked over to where Suse and the others were standing.

169

A dozen or more girls followed—then Ilse. Our eyes met. The worst had happened, but somehow now I was not afraid. It was always uncertainty that I feared most.

We were marched to the factory. It was a model German factory. In previous years, it was said, they had brought foreign visitors to see it. The architecture, layout, and machinery were beautiful, I had to agree. The office building in front, with its multitude of spotless windows, overlooked vast star-shaped flower beds, and against the factory walls were hundreds of rose bushes. Along the paths were beds of tulips in full bloom.

We were taken to the spinning room. There I saw the girls, living skeletons with yellowish-gray skin drawn tight over prominent cheekbones; there were gaping holes in their mouths where teeth had either been knocked out or rotted out. These girls ran to and from huge spinning machines, repairing broken threads with nimble fingers. Their tired eyes and sallow jaws seemed to belie the swiftly running feet and dexterous fingers.

I was put to tending one of those monstrous machines. I thought I would never learn to operate it, to tie the knots before the machine, which moved rapidly, could smash my fingers. Wherever I looked, the threads tore. I kept running from one break to another until I reached a point of complete exhaustion. Worst of all, my throat felt dry and itchy from the dust and lint in the air. But time went fast. Before I knew it, we were marching back to camp. After another long roll call we fell on our bunks.

The next day the work went more smoothly, and in less than a week I mastered the machine. However, my throat continued to bother me, as did my ankles, which had been swollen for several days. But I preferred the spinning room to staying in camp, where one did not know what might happen from one minute to the next.

About every two months the spinning-room girls were X-rayed. Each time a number were found to have contracted tuberculosis; they were immediately sent to Auschwitz. The

170

spinning room had the greatest turnover of girls, and these bimonthly examinations came to be dreaded by all of us.

May passed, and June came. Thousands of roses burst open in a marvelous range of colors. In the early morning, when we marched to the factory, the dew was still on the fragrant petals. Sometimes the first rays of the sun would make the drops glitter like diamonds. Day after day I had to resist the desire to run out of line and touch those beautiful blossoms.

The day we all feared most came toward the end of July. We were called to have our X-rays taken. We marched through the factory gates and out into the street. I felt a strange animation, felt color shooting to my cheeks. I remembered the girl in Sosnowitz to whom I had given the bowl of food, the first girl whom I had met from a slave camp. I could still see the two red spots glowing on her cheeks and I felt spots burning on mine.

This must be it, I thought. This is the end! I want to live, I want to live!

In the physician's office we were told to strip to the waist. I removed the little sack from my neck, with the piece of broken glass and charred wood that Arthur and I gathered from our Temple the day before he left Bielitz. It might show as a dark spot on my chest. I kept the sack in my hand.

"Arthur," I whispered, "be with me, I am so afraid."

I shivered in the summer heat. Slowly the line crept forward.

"Your name?" a female voice asked.

"Gerda Weissmann." My voice sounded high and unnatural. I heard it trail off in the dark room and there was the sound of the pencil scratching over the paper, checking my name.

As in a dream, I stepped onto a platform. From far away I heard the doctor's voice directing me how to stand. The cold plate touching my bare breast roused a familiar sensation of horror, reminding me of the time when the SS man had pointed his gun at my chest, demanding to know where Papa was. I closed my eyes. I held my lids tightly shut. There was the clicking of a switch, then another.

I waited in another line while my plate was developed.

Why did it take so long? Then I heard the doctor snap. "Clear!"

I saw him pointing at me. "Clear! Clear!" he said, pointing to others.

We returned to camp. Ilse was sitting on the bunk, her face white.

"Ilse!" I called frantically.

She jumped up.

"Are you all right?" she whispered hoarsely.

I nodded. "And you?"

She nodded too.

We embraced. We had a lease on life for another two months!

A week later the tubercular girls departed. There was one among them whom I had gotten to know fairly well. I went to see her before she left. We embraced, there was nothing to say. What does one say to someone who knows that in a few days she won't be alive any more?

It is often said that it is best that we cannot know the future, but this case was an exception. About two years later, when I was working in Munich, I was in the German Museum, looking through some lists of refugees that were published there daily, when I heard a gay voice call to me.

"Isn't that Gerda? It's me, not my ghost," said a rosy girl in a blue sweater.

As she came closer, I remembered our sad farewell in Grünberg before she had left for Auschwitz. As she embraced me, we both started to cry. Then she told me what had happened. When her group reached Auschwitz they were taken to the death house, but traffic was heavy there. Things were so busy, they had to wait for death. As she sat on the ground she idly dug into the soil of which she was soon to become a part. The gesture was her salvation, for she unearthed a handful of gems. To what forgotten soul had they belonged?

The girl was momentarily dazed. Then she ran up to an SS guard—what had she to lose? "Help me," she pleaded, and gave him the bundle. "I want to live."

172

Somehow he got her and two other girls from her group places to work in the kitchen. That parcel of gems saved three lives, even though the guard could have taken the gift and refused to help the girls. When she finished her story, I asked the girl about her lungs.

She smiled. "That is another strange story. I went to a number of doctors, but they found nothing wrong. Perhaps that is another miracle, or perhaps the doctor in Grünberg made a mistake."

Whatever the explanation was, the girl had been given back her life.

As the hot summer wore on, conditions in Grünberg became worse. Working hours grew longer; there was less food; the transports to Auschwitz were more frequent.

For a time I worked on the night shift. Here I became friendly with Liesel Stepper. We talked many hours in the daytime when we should have slept. She told me she was in love with a boy from Vienna, and though she had not heard from him in years, she thought of him constantly. She was relatively free of bitterness. Together we dreamed of the wonderful life we should have when the war would be over.

One day a heavy summer rain fell; thunder and lightning tore the sky. I woke and saw Liesel lying motionless on her bunk, her eyes wide open. I called her.

She turned slowly toward me. "I will put on the red raincoat," she said. "No, the blue one is better for today. I will go out into the garden; the grass will be wet. I will pick up the apples that the storm blew down. It tastes wonderful, that cold wet apple. But I better hurry, I have an appointment later."

"With the dressmaker?" I interrupted, falling in with her mood.

We played the game to perfection.

One morning in September I was returning to camp from the factory, looking forward to some sleep. My head constantly felt heavy and dull, my legs hurt from running all night after the devilish spinning machine.

Suddenly, when our guard had his head turned, a piece of bread was thrown over the fence into the courtyard. The girl ahead of me quickly picked up the bread and as she did, I heard her faint, terror-stricken voice whisper, "Don't give me away!"

The SS man saw the incident. He demanded to know who threw the bread. We knew there would be a penalty—head-shaving, beating, or worse. One by one we were questioned.

"I don't know," was each answer.

Then the husky SS guard with his heavy arm would hit the tired face, again and again. I was frightened. I would rather have gone without food, or worked twenty-four hours straight through, than bear physical punishment.

But my turn came, and I muttered an exhausted, "I don't know."

I felt a heavy blow over my eyes.

"Who?" he demanded.

"I don't know," I repeated.

Another blow fell, deafening my left ear. I swayed and staggered toward the building. When I finally reached my bunk I sat there without undressing. My face was puffed and bruised, my skin and lips were moist with blood. I must have cried without knowing it.

Thirty girls were beaten that morning. I don't know what the blows did to the others, but they shattered the wall of strength that I had built for myself. Neither propaganda talks, designed to break our morale, nor hunger, nor work, no matter how hard, had affected my resistance as had the brutal blows of that guard.

If only they don't touch my flesh, I can survive, I thought.

Survive? All of a sudden it did not seem worth while. All the suffering and agony, for what? How could I be free when they would kill us first? How much longer would it last? It was now September, 1944—five years since the Germans had taken Bielitz—and there was still no end in sight.

How long could we go on? When would it be my turn to

174

go to Auschwitz? How many more X-ray examinations could I pass before I would be doomed?

Ilse, who worked on the day shift, came back at noon. She walked quietly past my bunk, thinking I was asleep. I called her. When she turned around she was smiling. I hid my bruised face under the blanket. She turned away from me so that I could not see what she was doing, and dug into her pocket.

"I brought you a present!" she announced triumphantly.

There, on a fresh leaf, was one red, slightly mashed raspberry!

As I sat up, she stared at my face. The raspberry rolled under the bunk. I crawled under to get it. I ate it slowly, dust and all; its sweet juice mingled with the saltiness on my lips.

A few days later fortune smiled at me. The incredible happened.

Suse Kunz and I were chosen for different work. There was an old German in the spinning room who weighed the finished crates of yarn, recorded the weights in a ledger, and put each crate on a conveyor belt which carried it to storage. One day we noticed that the crates remained piled up at the end of the row of machines; the man who kept the production records had not come. The *Obermeister,* or head foreman, went from machine to machine several times that day. In the afternoon he called Suse and me, and asked whether we could write. We both said we could.

"Now," he said, shaking a bony finger, "that requires thinking; I don't know if you would be able to do it."

I wondered if he wanted to hurt us, or if he really thought that we were some type of animal. He showed us the ledger columns in which each machine was listed by number, with spaces to note the weight of material each machine produced. Then he made us enter a few figures.

"Lightly," he cautioned, "so we can erase it, in case of error. Think," he repeated. "Think!"

With serious faces, we both thought. We almost burst into

175

laughter. We passed the tests well, and were told that one of us would work days, the other nights. The foreman then took us to his office and gave us each a folded piece of paper.

"Give them to the *Lagerführerin*," he said.

Out of sight, we looked at the messages. We had been given hard-labor cards, entitling each of us to an extra bowl of food daily. An extra bowl—we were rich! That meant that Ilse and I would not be hungry any more and it meant the same for Suse and Liesel.

The work was very hard. We had to lift the heavy crates and carefully place them on the running belt; a crooked crate might tangle with the yarn or cause congestion, and this would have meant sabotage. But I liked the work. I was not confined to one machine. Instead, I went all over the vast halls. Other workers envied me, and stared when they saw me walking around with the ledger.

It was interesting to walk through the spinning halls. Huge machines tore the raw materials to shreds. These shreds were beaten into a loose, cotton-like substance that a carding machine then combed into loose strips that could be spun. Each spinning hall had its own carding machine.

During the long hours of the autumn nights, while the machines hummed busily and the sleepwalking skeletons ran after the threads, I walked through the plant, weighing the heavy crates, entering the amounts of yarn that helped Germany's economy—helped Germany fight us.

Deliveries of old clothes arrived daily from Auschwitz to be shredded up and converted into yarn. A number of the girls who ran the shredding machines insisted that they had recognized their parents' clothes. We had heard that in Auschwitz prisoners were told to undress for showers; that they were then handed bread rations and sent into the "showers"—only when the vents opened it was not water but gas.

Once as I passed the shredder I thought I saw Mama's coat. I turned away, praying, then forced myself to look again. It was just a black coat. It could have been anybody's—hundreds of people wore black coats.

176

And as always when in despair, I started to think of my homecoming. I placed and replaced details upon details, playing with the fragments of my dreams. Who would come home first? I always wished that I should come last—walk into the house to find them all there. At times, I thought I would reach home late at night. The house would be dark. I would not wake them. I would go to the garden and wait. I would watch the sun rise. Then I would approach the house. Mama would be wearing her flowered housecoat. No, she wouldn't— we had given it away for a pound of margarine and a loaf of bread. Well, anyway, breakfast would be on the table. Arthur wouldn't be there and Mama would say to me, "Go wake Arthur, you know he never gets down in time."

I would run up the stairs. My brother's hair would be tousled, as it always was in the morning. "Arthur," I would whisper. He would mutter something and turn over and pretend to go back to sleep. Then, realizing I had come back, he would sit up with wide-open eyes, stretching out his arms. It would be as it had always been, from the time when I had brought him my book of fairy tales to read. He had read them to me for years before I learned to read. And we would come downstairs together, holding hands as we had done when we were small, so I should not stumble. We would come down, and Papa and Mama would be holding hands too. We would approach Papa for benediction, as we had done as children. We both would have to bow, for we had gotten so tall. And Papa would kiss the Bible even as his father had before him, when he returned from Siberia. And Papa would speak the words of Jacob: "I had not thought to see your face again, but God . . ."

The night wore on. The horizon became lighter. Another day was coming to Grünberg. The machines seemed to go faster. The shredder rolled louder, tearing to bits the clothes from Auschwitz—and I held in my heart the picture of my homecoming.

Chapter 11

ON THE LAST DAY OF NOVEMBER WE DIDN'T MARCH TO WORK. I was now on the day shift and after the morning roll call, for which we usually assembled shortly before 5:00 A.M., we were kept standing in the cold courtyard for several hours. Finally two open trucks drove through the gates, halted, and thirty or forty young women in smart, trim SS uniforms dismounted and waited in the outer yard.

Then came a staff car. A few high-ranking officers got out and went into the building that housed us. Our names were called in alphabetical groups. Those who were called went in but did not come out again. Panic mounted. We could not imagine what was going on inside and of course we assumed the worst. The morning wore on. Around noon Ilse's name—Kleinzähler—was called. She embraced me, her eyes filled with tears.

"Stop it, Ilse!" I snapped. "Stop it, or I will go crazy. Nothing will happen!"

But I was not at all sure. Inwardly I was afraid, and when Ilse was gone, I nearly gave way. The thought that something was happening to Ilse and not to me at the same time drove me into a frenzy. The hours until I was called in the late afternoon seemed endless.

I was among the last twenty-five girls. We were told to undress completely. I was rebellious and furious, but we all did as we were told. We were then marched into the dining hall. I clenched my fists and stood erect.

The army officers and the SS women were seated at a long table. In the center of the floor was a circle drawn with chalk. I felt as if I were stepping on hot coals as I stepped into the circle. My body burned. I closed my eyes to blot out their staring.

I was given a number—895A—and told to dress and go to my bunk. When I got there I was relieved to see Ilse. No one was yet sure of the meaning of the examination.

The officers departed and the SS women took charge of the camp; they were everywhere and watched us every moment. In time rumors began to circulate: it was said that there were many, many sick and wounded soldiers who needed the amusement that pretty and healthy girls could provide.

"Never," I vowed. "Rather tuberculosis and Auschwitz than that!"

The situation led to my discovering that one of the girls from Sosnowitz had some poison and that she was willing to sell some of it for a price.

I wanted that poison. I had no money, but I still had the diamond and pearl pendant Mama had sewn into the padding of my coat. With Ilse on the lookout for intruders I went to my bunk and carefully removed the pendant from my coat. I kissed it quickly, remembering how well it had looked on Mama's throat. Then I went in search of the girl with the poison. After some haggling, I surrendered the pendant for two tiny, white flat packets. One I gave to Ilse. We folded them in cotton padding and inserted them in our shoe linings. My ski boot felt uncomfortable at first, but after a short time I was hardly aware of the packet.

Two weeks passed and nothing happened. Nobody was called out or sent away and we were not taken to be X-rayed. Nothing much changed except that we were now awakened at 4:00 A.M. instead of 5:00 and made to stand a long *Appell* in the courtyard before going to work. The SS women counted us over and over. Each morning the process became more and more drawn out until they started to wake us half an hour earlier. It was bitterly cold during those morning hours.

One morning in December there was snow on the ground when we awoke. Winter was here again.

A few days later there were several air-raid alarms. They were the first we experienced. The German workers ran for shelter while we stayed in the factory with the current turned off and the machines idle. We tried hard not to look too pleased. Then we were told that we must go to the shelter when the alarm sounded. Apparently nobody wanted to risk his skin watching us.

The sirens began to howl more and more frequently. The Germans threw frightened glances toward the sky and hatefully looked at us. Let them worry now, we gloated. Let them sit on the charred remains of their homes. Let them see their families killed. Then will they shout "Heil Hitler!"?

"It's coming," whispered my heart. "Their downfall is coming!" But I was not naïve. I knew that it would not come without increased suffering on our part.

Christmas passed. There was no Christmas spirit that year. The new year came—the year of 1945.

In January the sirens blew almost daily. Less and less production was entered into the books. At noon one day the electricity went off. The supervisors stood talking excitedly. The SS women took us back to camp. Something drastic had happened. Perhaps the war was over.

That night we were ordered to take all our belongings and go into the dining hall. The door to our sleeping quarters was barricaded. After being given food we huddled together, waiting.

It was snowing heavily. After a time we heard the courtyard gates burst open. Every heart beat faster in expectation. There were shrieks and screams and cries outside. We could hear running feet and shouting from the other side of the barricaded doors. Those of us who sat next to the doors started calling to the newcomers in our sleeping quarters.

They were Jewish girls. They had come from another camp and had been walking for five days. Now we were to join them. They thought we were going to Oranienburg, a concentration camp like Auschwitz, to be gassed. Auschwitz, they said, had been captured by the Russians, who had reconquered Poland and were crossing the German frontier. The English and Americans were invading Germany from the West. Would a miracle happen before we reached the gas chambers?

180

And so the last stretch of the war began. Not in peaceful Bolkenhain, not in the coal cars of Märzdorf, the night shifts of Landeshut. Nor were we to endure it in tuberculosis-ridden Grünberg. I was certain that we would meet freedom somewhere in the open, and that we would meet it soon.

"You are crazy!" Suse said. "We will never see the liberation, for they will see to it. They would leave us here if they did not want us killed."

"We will be free," I insisted. "I know it, I feel it."

Ilse and Liesel sat in silence. Suse's big eyes filled with tears, the first tears that I ever saw her shed.

"How can you believe so strongly?" she murmured. "But then, you always believed. Remember when we met on the train?"

I nodded.

"Well, you lost that bet," she reminded me.

"I know," I said.

"But you still believe?"

"I do!"

"Tell me, Gerda," Suse whispered urgently, "what is it? What makes you so sure?"

"I don't know. It's something I cannot explain, but I know somehow that we will be liberated."

"And I feel," Suse stammered, "I feel that I will not be."

All that last night in Grünberg I coughed. I think I had a temperature. Ilse, Suse, Liesel, and I cuddled together closely.

"Gerda, don't get sick," they begged, as if I could decide.

At dawn we were given three portions of bread, which we carefully placed in our bundles. We saw the kitchen personnel pack big parcels of food in their bundles.

At the last moment before we assembled, the four of us decided to put on most of the clothes we had intended to carry.

The SS women came for us. We lined up. Ilse was on my left, Liesel and Suse were on my right. We stood erect.

"Let us be strong," Liesel whispered.

"Yes," I answered.

"*You* be strong," Ilse whispered back to me. I was now the least fit of the group.

As we squeezed through the door, we gripped hands for a fleeting moment. Then we marched out into the bright snow.

The outer gates were open when we reached the courtyard. Stretching as far as we could see were columns of girls. I was shocked to see so many. We learned later there were about three thousand from other camps; with our contingent from Grünberg we totaled nearly four thousand. We were divided into two transports amidst much whipping and screaming by the SS. Many girls tried to shift from one group to another, in the hope that it might be the better one.

We four were in the column which was doomed; out of two thousand only a hundred and twenty survived. The other column was liberated much sooner. Had I been part of it my fate would have been different. Less suffering, yes, but less happiness, too, I am sure.

Although I had seen misery, I was utterly unprepared for the picture that the girls who had already been marching for a week presented. Covered with gray blankets, they reminded me of drawings of Death when, winged and garbed in loose sheets, he comes to collect the living. Some of them were barefoot, others wore crude wooden clogs. Many of them left a bloody trail in the fresh snow.

Suse looked at me and I looked at my feet—clad in the ski boots that Papa had insisted I wear on that hot summer day. Papa, Papa, how could he possibly have known. The boots were still in good shape, and I had precious things hidden in them: snapshots of Papa, Mama, Arthur, and Abek, wrapped in a piece of cloth, and the packet of poison. In Grünberg they had taken away all pictures, papers, and letters. Germany, we were told, needed all scrap paper she could get. Ilse and I had managed to hide our pictures. Our only worry now was that water might soak through our shoes and ruin them.

"Forward march!" shouted the SS *Wachtmeister* at the head of our column.

"Forward march!" echoed SS men. Carrying rifles, they were stationed along our column at intervals of about thirty feet.

"Forward march!" came the high-pitched voices of the whip-armed SS women.

We took the first step. I thought: I am marching to death or to liberation. It was the morning of January 29, 1945.

We marched all day, with a break at noon. Ilse and I shared one of our portions of bread, guarding the rest carefully.

At the head of the column we saw the commandant of the SS with a Hungarian-Jewish girl who, we were told, was his mistress. She and a few of her close friends knew no want; they had plenty to eat, and slept always in peasant houses, rather than in barns or in open fields as the others did.

"How could they?" I asked myself over and over again.

Toward evening, as it grew colder, we were herded off the road and into a huge barn. We huddled together in the darkness and again Ilse and I shared a portion of our bread. It wasn't enough.

"Ilse, I am terribly hungry," I confessed.

"So am I," Ilse admitted. "I would like something warm to drink. We can't eat any more bread, for who knows when they will give us more?"

"Careful, careful!" somebody called in the darkness. "The Magyars are after our bread!"

Yes, the poor Hungarian girls were hungry. They had been marching a week already.

"My shoes, my shoes!" another voice cried. "They took them from right next to me!"

Many of the Hungarian girls had no shoes. To save their lives they stole shoes off the feet of those who slept. How much I learned that night!

When the doors of the dark barn were thrown open in the morning I could see a flood of wintry sunlight on the glittering snow. Two SS men stood at the entrance and with their rifles prodded us as we emerged four abreast.

A little distance away stood the SS commandant with his girl friend and her court of privileged friends. They were eating bread and drinking something steaming out of a large thermos. How good it must feel, I thought, the warm drink in that cold!

We assembled and were counted and recounted. A girl from Grünberg was missing. A few others were beaten bloody because of it, but either they did not know what had become of her or they would not tell.

We learned the story later. A German from the factory who was in love with the girl had followed our column, and under cover of darkness had snatched her quietly away.

We marched many miles that second day, often plowing through untouched snow. Again we rested at midday.

"I wonder when they will give us something to eat," Ilse said to the three of us as we nibbled our dry, frozen bread.

We did not answer.

Girls who had lagged behind that morning had been beaten by the SS men with the butts of their guns.

After the midday pause, a couple of girls just sat motionless on the snow, refusing to go. We marched on. Behind us there were pistol shots.

"God!" I said, "God!" looking up to the sky. The sky was blue, the snow was clean, the snowy pine trees were beautiful in the sunlight.

Chapter 12

YET ANOTHER DAY WE MARCHED ON IN A WESTWARD DIRECTION. It was the last day that we had bread. We were no longer counted. They could not keep track of how many were shot or died during the night. I was cold and hungry but for the time being I minded the cold more. At night I felt Ilse's hand in mine. I took off my shoes and curled myself over them, for fear that someone might steal them. There was muffled crying all around me. I did not cry, but there, in those barns, I stopped praying. Through all the years I had prayed to God ardently and with hope. Now I prayed no more. I did not consciously know why, for I was closer to my Maker than ever. One short shot away . . . I wanted to be at peace with God, but I could not pray.

But later, much later, I thought about my way of praying. It started in school with a play about ancient Egypt. Each character uttered a prayer: the mighty Pharaoh prayed for a victory, his opponent asked for his own success, a sick man begged for health, the doctor asked for people to be ill, and each prayer, clean and swift, like a white bird, shot upward. In Heaven, it met with the other prayer that had asked for just the contrary. They turned against each other in bloody battle, and usually both fell back lifeless to the earth. A large number of girls had taken part in that play. I thought I had a beautiful role. I was a poor little boy, the son of a fellah. My mother told me to pray, but I didn't know how. I had no wishes, so I just looked at the river that fertilized our field, at the warm sun, at the ripe fruit in our garden, and I said, "Thank you, God, for the warm sun, for the blue Nile, for my father and my mother," and my little-boy prayer, like the others, sailed straight up to the throne of God. Nobody de-

185

fied my prayer, and nobody else thanked the Maker. They were all asking Him for things. He turned His face upon the little barefoot boy. . . .

I was about twelve years old at the time. From then on I had always thanked God for the gifts He bestowed upon me, and they were many. There had always been something to be grateful for, even after 1939, but during that cold march, when we rested in the icy barns, hungry, afraid, I could pray no more.

On the fourth day of our march we heard artillery fire. It was rumored that the Russians were moving forward rapidly. Once I think we were almost overrun by them. We heard two SS men discussing the destruction of the railroad, and thus we learned that we were to have been shipped by rail to the death camp. Now we would have to go all that way on foot.

On the fifth morning a number of SS women were missing. Apparently they had no mind to march on. Perhaps they wanted to return to their homes.

The war was coming to an end, we thought, but so was our strength. We had now gone four days without food. It was over a week since we had left Grünberg. It was an icy day. A sharp wind bit at our faces. We marched longer than usual before the midday break, and when we took it, we were anxious to get moving again.

That afternoon, as we were marching through a thicket, we heard shots. A moment later one of the SS men pointed a gun at me. "Come along!" he shouted.

I stepped out of line. The SS pulled out three more girls. I heard the column marching on. I no longer felt the snow whip my face. I felt no rebellion, no wild pounding of my heart. I just felt at peace. Oddly enough, I thought of a winter's day. at home, and Schmutzi, my cat, bringing her newborn kittens into the kitchen to warm them by the stove. I tried desperately to remember what we had named the kittens, but I couldn't. After a few steps—I had been day-dreaming for only a moment—we came to a clearing. There were two bodies in the snow.

"Take them to the woods," the SS man commanded.

My arms felt unequal to it.

"Take her head," snapped the girl nearest me.

I looked at the dead girl's face. I did not know her. Her eyes were open. I lifted her head. The snow beneath was red. The two of us were too weak to lift her, so we took her by the arms and dragged her into the trees. When we left her, she looked alive. I scooped up snow to wash her blood off my hands. We did not see the other girls.

The SS man stood smoking a cigarette. I thought our turn was next, but he made us hurry to join the column. Ilse looked relieved when I returned. We held hands silently. I was in a state of shock.

We walked for a long, long time that evening, passing through tiny villages. Here and there a light showed. Smoke came from chimneys. We could see women preparing supper. How snug and warm everybody looked!

We entered another town. It was dark now. Nobody was in the streets. The wind was howling as we were led to a low hill where a church stood. The SS women and the favorites were lodged in town. The three SS guards who accompanied us told us to lie on the frozen earth in front of the church. The wind swept the snow over us. After a few minutes we were covered. Ilse and I cuddled close, trying with our bodies to warm each other.

Towering over us, the church stood silent, not even with its bell ringing the hours of our misery. The bells had probably been melted to make bullets.

"I am so cold," Ilse chattered.

We pressed our cold cheeks together. The snow did not even melt on our faces.

I thought of the girl I had dragged into the forest. By now the snow had given her its decent burial.

"Ilse," I said.

She didn't seem to hear me. I remembered a lamp burning softly under the yellow shade in my nursery, Niania reading to me the story of the Little Match Girl. I could hear Niania's warm tones: "And the little match girl smiled, she did not feel the cold any more. . . ."

187

"Ilse!" I shook her.

"Leave me alone!" she protested.

"Ilse!" I shouted. "Wake up. You are not going to sleep!"

She was awake now. I rubbed her face, her stiff hands. I called to Suse and Liesel. They responded. We passed the word around not to sleep. The SS men were stamping and blowing on their hands. Here and there a girl stood up.

"Lie down!" the SS men would shout.

We did everything we could think of to keep each other awake and encouraged. Finally, dawn broke and the wind stopped. In the gray morning light, we could see the miserable faces, the deep, hungry eyes. Those of us who had the strength brushed the drifts from silent mounds: there were a number of Little Match Girls.

"How foolish we are!" Suse exclaimed. "We should have all gone to sleep."

The frost broke. The air felt warmer. We were thirsty and started to eat snow.

Late that afternoon we came to Camp Christianstadt. We waited before its gates a long time. Then we were admitted, put into one huge room, and given something warm to eat. I don't know what it was, but no meal was ever more welcome.

We dried our clothes, and most of us in the warm room began to itch. The lice had already started on us. The taste of food and the warm camp made most of us optimistic again. We did not have to stand roll call. They just left us as we were, gave us something to eat twice a day, and we were happy. We knew the war was almost over.

When we had been in Christianstadt three days we heard that we were to move again. Ilse was beside herself. I had never seen her like that. Before, I had had the power to make her moods change—her belief in me was so strong that it embarrassed me at times—but I failed to help her now.

We marched west again, and that first evening the streets and roads were full of people, all moving in the same direction. They were fleeing before the Russian advance—horses and buggies, children in their parents' arms. We could hear the steady firing of artillery behind us.

I was elated. It is coming! This is the end! The circle is drawing to a close! The Germans are beginning to pay the penalty for their crimes.

The sight of refugees fired my imagination with new hope. That first night after we left Christianstadt we slept in another barn. A few more girls did not rise with us in the morning.

The next day we saw more refugees. From their speech we knew that they were from Silesia.

We began toying with the idea of escape. Several girls had already slipped away under cover of darkness when we marched at night. From various sources we learned that some survived and were taken in by peasants but that others were found and shot.

Our column got smaller and smaller. Probably only half the girls who had left Grünberg remained. We would not be able to stand much more. Hearing a peasant woman speak to another in the dialect of Bielitz inspired me with what I considered a wonderful idea.

That evening I told Ilse my plan. In one or two days we would disappear into the woods and wait there for night. When we were sure that our group had left the region, we would rip the stars from our clothing. Our coats were shabby, but we counted on my ski boots to make an impression. No one in camp had shoes like that—perfect for the season. Now came the hardest, but I felt most effective part of my plan. We would go to the nearest police station. We feared the police as we feared death itself, but I banked on their awareness of our fear. In their arrogance, I thought they would not think Jews capable of overcoming it. We would say that we were evacuees from Silesia—Ilse and I both spoke that type of German—that we had gone to find shelter for our mother and baby sisters and brothers (the fact that we had a big family would add another touch of truth, for all good Germans had lots of children for the Führer). We would say that when we returned our family had gone.

There would be questions, of course. Our papers were with Mother who had them in a bag with all our valuables. . . . We

189

would use our own first names, Ilse and Gerda; they sounded good and German. Our last name would be—Kügler. We would be asked if we belonged to the BDM? Yes, of course, we were in the Hitler Youth. I memorized a chapter number. Our father was in the Wehrmacht. His serial number? I thought myself very clever to devise a foolproof way not to forget a complicated serial number: Ilse's house number, mine, and the year the war started—569419391! It sounded impressive, and would be easy to remember. Our father, we would say, was fighting on the Russian front.

I felt that by walking straight into the lion's den we would overcome the first suspicion. Besides, I thought, the police now had too many problems to stage a big investigation. In my mind I tried to prepare as complete and simple a plan as possible. I knew they might question Ilse and me separately—our stories had to check. I had staged many dramatic performances in Bolkenhain; this would be my greatest coup. I was painfully aware that I held Ilse's life as well as my own in my hands.

Then I told Suse and Liesel. They thought the idea sound, and said that they would drop from the column a couple of days later, and cook up a similar story.

All night I rehearsed with Ilse.

"Ilse, remember," I repeated, "we cannot be afraid of the police. They are our friends, Germans as we are."

It had now been two days since we had seen the Silesian peasant women. If we escaped the next day, stayed in the woods that night, and went to the police on the fourth day, we surely ought to be safe. In the barn we kissed Suse and Liesel good-by, for we intended to escape in the late afternoon. I was excited all day. As if in answer to my wishes, we did not have our rest break until around four in the afternoon. Shadows were already long on the snow.

"Perfect," I whispered to Ilse. "When the SS is not looking, we will crawl into the woods."

I glanced at Suse, our eyes met. Liesel bit her lip, as she always did in moments of emotion. I lifted one eyebrow, signal-

190

ing Ilse to get behind a tree. She looked at me, her eyes big and frightened. Then she caught my hand.

"Gerda, not now!" she whispered. "Please, not now! I am afraid."

Until then I had not been afraid; excitement had buried my fear. Only when Ilse showed her fear did my doubts come to the surface. What if our plan did not go well? Until that moment I had discounted that possibility. I knew that we just had to escape. But now I hesitated. The decision was not mine alone: Ilse's life was as dear to me as my own. I looked at her again.

"We must go," I wanted to whisper. Instead I heard my voice saying: "Maybe tonight."

"All assemble!" the voices of the SS rang out.

For some moments we stood ready. Then we heard screams and frightened begging from the forest. Three SS men had rounded up fourteen girls in the forest. Now they lined them up in front of us. The commandant took out his pistol. The girls screamed. The commandant fired again and again and the girls fell, one on top of the other.

I closed my eyes and held Ilse's hand tightly. We marched on. At that moment I vowed that I would never try to escape, never take our lives into my hands, never step off the path that was leading us to death.

A week passed, two, perhaps three. We lost count of time. About every second day there would be warm soup, if one were lucky enough to be among the first in line, cold soup when one was among the last. At times there wasn't enough to go around.

We usually slept in barns. One night we rested in a bombed-out church listening to artillery fire both from the East and farther away from the West. We felt ourselves lucky if we found a few grains of wheat or oats in the barns.

Everywhere we left some dead. Some we buried, others we simply left. Hundreds of girls had frozen feet, bloody and full of pus. I saw one girl break off her toes as though they were brittle wood.

Waking one night in a barn, I felt the girl next to me leaning too heavily on my legs. I protested. She did not move. My legs ached, I felt crushed under the weight. I tried to push her—and found she was dead. I remembered her from Bolkenhain. She had worked at the loom next to mine. I don't remember her name, but I do remember the way she stooped over the loom to repair a thread—the way she smiled when our eyes met.

One girl spotted a milk can leaning against a tree. She ran out of line to see if there were any milk in it. An SS man grabbed her by the neck, forced her to her knees. I saw her turn, petrified, when he took the rifle from his shoulder.

"Mercy! Mercy!" she pleaded.

She threw her arms up as he fired. Was it in prayer or desperation? And as he turned to go, the SS man kicked her aside.

I watched it all in horror and wished that I were dead.

There were planes roaring above us; we heard machine guns in the distance. The front lines were not far, yet they weren't close enough. How fortunate the soldiers were, to be able to carry guns! I had dreams about stealing a gun from an SS man during the night and shooting them all. But those were only dreams—I didn't even know how to fire a gun.

Why did we march? Why did we let them slaughter us? Why did we not try to fight back? What difference would it have made if they had killed some of us? We were dying anyway, and they would kill the survivors sooner or later in any case.

Our group shrank to a quarter of its original size. Why should I hope? I thought. Why should I be free, and the others dead? Why should I think that I would be a privileged one? But these thoughts were dangerous. I had to hope. I had to go on to the end. If Papa, Mama, and Arthur survive, they will wait for me, hoping and praying. I must not disappoint them.

"Be strong," Arthur had whispered, almost six years before.

"Be strong," Mama had called over the mass of voices as I left Bielitz.

The snow melted and it became mild. It could almost have

192

been spring. For miles and miles now we saw road signs pointing to Dresden. A big, beautiful city—I remembered it from my history books. We must have marched about two hundred and fifty kilometers since Grünberg. The SS evidently wanted to reach the city before nightfall. It was getting dark, and big trucks were constantly coming toward us, forcing us off the road, and slowing our march.

As we approached the outskirts of Dresden we heard air-raid sirens blowing warnings, and soon hundreds of planes roared through the skies.

We stood on a bridge over the Elbe as the SS watched us from the banks. They probably felt the bridge was a likely target and this would be an easy way to get rid of us.

It was as if the world were coming to an end. Giant bombers roared over us. Heaven and earth shook. Houses collapsed like dominoes. People screamed and some jumped in flames into the icy river. Germany was being destroyed.

I was not afraid for my life, I felt triumphant watching Dresden being destroyed. And yet I had a painful feeling of detachment and utter loneliness. I don't remember how long the attack lasted, how we finally got off the bridge, I only remember the triumph and the loneliness.

And so passed another night.

The mild weather held for a few days, and we marched on. One afternoon as we passed through Freiberg the windows of a pretty house were open, and someone inside was playing the piano. Soft music floated in the air. As we came closer, our steps drowned out the music; only after we passed the house did I begin to hear it again.

In my mind I wrote a story to go with the music. It was about someone who tended a plant all his life, and it never blossomed. Only after the person died did the flower bloom.

I looked at Ilse. She was crying without a sound—the way Mama cried when we took Papa to the station for the last time.

Chapter 13

It grew colder again, crushing our timid hopes that perhaps nature would be kind and spare us. It was stormy and snow fell constantly. We marched on and on. During the day I wished for the night, and during the icy, fearful night I wished for a new day.

As if in a nightmare we walked through bomb-damaged cities. I remembered Chemnitz vaguely from my geography lessons and because my Uncle Leo from Turkey had purchased textile machinery there on one of his visits. Now Chemnitz was rubble, some buildings still smoking. I can still see an old woman with a black shawl collecting wood in a basket.

We marched through Zwickau, Reichenbach, Plauen. On and on with the snow falling, the wind howling about us, and the all-pervading hunger gnawing within us. We were two hundred and fifty kilometers or more beyond Dresden, more than five hundred from Grünberg. There were perhaps no more than four hundred girls left. It must have been around the twentieth of March; we had been marching for almost two months. Now we came to another camp, Helmbrechts. It wasn't a death camp; we saw with relief that there were people there, and no furnaces.

The SS guards departed and a new commandant took over. The previous commandant left his girl friend at Helmbrechts. Her golden days were over.

We were put into an empty barracks with a dirt floor. I looked at the electrified wire along the fence and again I had that terrible feeling of being trapped. I thought that our chances of survival were much better out in the open, no matter what the circumstances.

Before we entered the barracks we stood in the freezing

courtyard and undressed down to our shoes. Our clothes were bundled up and taken away. We were given a strange assortment of clothing, still wet, that had been dipped in a solution said to kill vermin. I was given a pair of heavy slacks and a thin organdy blouse. Ilse received just a long navy-blue coat.

The camp consisted of perhaps a dozen barracks. We were housed in one large one. There were Ukrainian women in some of the others, but they had roll call at different hours and we rarely saw them. The whole camp was encircled by fences topped with electrified wire. Beyond the fences stretched snow-covered plains as far as the eye could see. There were no homes or buildings.

We all had diarrhea now. At night a wooden barrel was put near the door for the use of perhaps four hundred girls. We were told that it must not overflow. . . . We had to run all night, stand in line, and plead for our turn. When the SS women came in the morning, they beat us, calling us every filthy word in their vocabulary.

Our food was meager. Hungry and without anything to do, the girls began to speak of food, exchanging recipes for the richest pastries. It was terrible to listen to. I tried to tell myself that the gnawing pain in my belly was just like a broken leg, I had to stand the pain, and in time it would get better.

It was in Helmbrechts that I met Lilli. She was from Hungary. She and her husband—she had no idea where he was— were university professors. I noticed her one morning as we stood at attention for a long time waiting for a kettle of yellowish, tasteless, lukewarm liquid—our "coffee."

It was one of those mornings of many deaths. It was strange: some days hardly anyone died, other days we lost many. Some would fall muttering a few words, but for the most part they fell silently to the frozen ground. Then a creaking wheelbarrow would come and the bodies would be thrown into it.

That morning, as I watched the loaded barrow being pushed away, I thought: It will make more trips today.

When I lifted my eyes I met the sad gray eyes of one of the Hungarian girls. Strange as it seems, even under those unspeakable circumstances there were still prejudices. The Hungarians were not popular with us, nor we with them.

"Are you thinking the same thing?" asked the Hungarian girl in beautiful German.

"Probably," I answered.

"It won't be long until our turn comes," she said matter-of-factly.

"Maybe it never will," I replied.

"You are silly!" she exclaimed. "Do not tell me that you still hope."

"I do, and you do too!" I snapped back. "If you did not, why wait? There it is." I pointed to the charged wire that ringed the camp.

She smiled wanly and walked away.

That afternoon we heard artillery fire again. We had not heard it since we had arrived at Helmbrechts. The door of our barracks was locked. I was restless and as I walked about I saw the girl with the gray eyes sitting on the dirt floor killing lice.

"Come, keep me company," she said.

I could see the angry glances of our girls as I sat down. They didn't like to see anyone fraternizing with Hungarians.

"Well, well," someone said sarcastically, "the end of the war will come when even the Poles and the Magyars get together!"

We burst out laughing, and that laugh sealed our friendship.

The days, except for the hunger, were not so bad, but we dreaded the nights. Without bunks or blankets, we had nothing but the earthen floor to lie on. Shivering, our bones aching, we huddled in groups and we waited for the dawn.

One night, somebody shook me out of a sound sleep. It was Tusia, the giraffe-necked girl I had been friendly with in Bolkenhain. I hadn't talked to her in a long time. In a way, I felt guilty about it. I quickly get interested in people but just as quickly avoid them when they expect to be my only friends. I am sure that I hurt many people in that way. It was the case with Tusia. I respected her deeply—her wisdom fascinated me and she never bored me—but she did irritate me.

"Come on," Tusia whispered now.

I followed her to her sleeping place, near the door and the barrel. A terrible stench was all around.

"What is it?" I asked.

"I want to talk to you."

"Yes, about what?"

"Just talk."

"Did you have to wake me for that?" I was vastly annoyed.

"Gerda," she whispered again, her hand fumbling in the darkness for mine. "Gerda, do you remember, once you said that we would be free for our birthday?"

Tusia and I were both born on May 8. Yes, I remembered.

"Will we be free?" she whispered eagerly.

"Yes, of course!" I was short with her.

"You don't seem too convinced."

"Tusia, what do you want me to say in the middle of the night, when you wake me to ask such questions?"

"Such questions?" She sounded hurt. "Are they not important? Don't you see that I have to know right now?"

Then it dawned on me: Tusia had probably lost her mind. I stopped arguing with her. She pressed my hand.

"Come closer," she whispered. I felt her breath on my face. "Gerda, it will be wonderful when we are free. But you know, we have not talked in a long time. I have watched you. I was hurt by you. But still I am grateful to you, you have given me belief in humanity."

"What do you mean?" I asked.

"Your spark has not gone out, it never will. You will hurt people but you will make them happy." Then she said again what she had said in Bolkenhain: "You are going through mud, but your feet are still clean."

She rambled on; I did not interrupt her any more.

"I am tired," she said at last, releasing my hand. I went back to my place beside Ilse, but I could not fall asleep again. The things that Tusia had said were troubling me.

It was later than usual when we were led out of the barracks and given our pieces of bread. The sun had risen. As I turned

197

to go back in the barracks, I recognized a body lying face down in the filthy snow.

"Tusia!" I touched her, thinking she had fainted. Her hand was pointing to an empty tin cup—she was dead.

I wished again that I could cry the deep hurt out of me, but I could not. Ilse tried to say something, but I barked at her to leave me alone.

I am hurting Ilse, I thought. This is what Tusia meant.

I thought about Tusia all that day. What had she meant by my "spark"? Then it came to me: my making others happy —as in Bolkenhain, when I arranged the entertainment. How happy those upturned faces had been—and how few of those girls were still living!

I wonder if I still can do it, I thought.

That night I tried it. I went over to a group of girls and swore them to secrecy. This, I knew, would be the best way to broadcast news. Then I told them that I knew from a sure source that the war was going to be over in a couple of days. It could take a week or so, at the very most. To make my story better, I threw in a few figures about American divisions, tanks, and planes. The Germans were retreating. They wouldn't kill us now; they were too frightened.

Some of the girls were skeptical, others overjoyed, but all in all they seemed glad to accept their lot with the knowledge that there soon would be an end. I told Ilse the same story, of course.

"Who told you all that?" she asked suspiciously.

"I can't tell you," I replied.

Her eyes widened. "Does that mean that you don't trust me?"

"Ilse, the person who gave me this information risked her life. If I tell you who it was, and the secret somehow leaks out, you might give her away, under torture."

"You know I would die before I told!" Ilse cried passionately.

"I know," I acknowledged with great dignity, "and that is why I will not tell you."

"Gerda," she said softly, "promise me, please, that when you are free to tell, I will be the first to know."

I never gave a promise more gladly. In that horrible camp we were behaving like the young girls we had been years before, typical schoolgirls, emotional teen-agers, making vows, telling secrets, swearing lifelong devotion.

"I would rather die than tell" had been a favorite phrase, so often and so lightly used, only now death was really close, and keeping a secret unto death might mean but a matter of a few hours, a few days. . . .

My stories caught on; I knew by the way the girls looked knowingly at me when I passed. I doubt if the Allied High Command knew as much about the progress of American and English troops as I kept reporting.

Girls came to me, to ask questions.

"Are you sure it is so?" they would ask over and over. "You know it would not be fair—"

"Not fair?" I asked myself. Not fair to light a spark of hope, to see a grim mouth smile?

Only Lilli and Suse made no reference to my sensational news. They did not seem glad nor did they say they did not believe me. Once, though, Suse remarked, "Too bad you can't write plays now, Gerda. Your material is so plentiful."

Chapter 14

ONE MORNING WE WERE TOLD THAT WE WERE TO LEAVE HELM-
brechts.

"No, no!" moaned Ilse.

"Are you crazy?" I asked her, full of hope again.

I wanted to be in the open, I feared enclosures. Outside, I
believed we had a chance. I still had my ski boots and by now
the clothes we had arrived in had come back to us, free of
vermin. This we regarded as a big favor.

One girl whispered to me as she dressed: "You were right,
Gerda, they are afraid of us. We have our clothes again."

We assembled for our last roll call in Helmbrechts. No more
than three hundred answered their names. The commandant
made an announcement:

"You will rejoice to hear that the greatest enemy of the
Führer is dead. Franklin Delano Roosevelt has died—as all
the enemies of the Führer will die!"

Roosevelt dead . . . Perhaps it was only a bluff. Later we
learned that the news was true. The day we first heard it was
probably April 13, 1945.

We marched away from Helmbrechts in the rain.

Ilse found a margarine wrapper. We licked it dry, tasting
the fat. Though we got no food that day, Ilse said it did not
matter, we had had the nourishing margarine. We were comforted.

We slept outside that night. It was very cold, and the evidence could be seen in the morning in the many stiff bodies
on the ground. That evening, after another day's march, Ilse
suddenly collapsed.

"Leave me here," she whispered, "I can't go on."

I pulled her to her feet, held her arm around my neck, and
dragged her on.

200

"Leave me," she kept begging. "Leave me in the woods. Some peasant will be kind."

"I will stay with you," I said.

Her voice was strong again. "No, you must go on!"

"I will not go on without you," I said. "You would not go without me, would you?"

She did not answer.

It was almost dark. Somehow we got to a barn for the night. As Ilse's arm dropped from my neck, she fell in a heap. Tonelessly, as if to herself, she said, "I cannot walk."

Horror gripped me. I took off her shoes and rubbed her frozen feet slowly and gently.

"It's no use," Ilse whimpered.

Carefully I put her shoes back on. Then I went to look for Hanka. I had met Hanka in Grünberg while working on the night shift, and from the start, we had taken to each other. Occasionally she was called to help in the kitchen and when she did, she always managed to scrounge extra bits of food for Ilse and me. Thus, Hanka had become an angel to me whose kindness I shall never forget. During the march, Hanka had remained relatively healthy and strong, and because of this, the SS commandant had ordered her to help with the ill. Now I ran to find her, foolishly hoping that she might have a magic solution for Ilse. I told her that Ilse would have to ride in the wagon. It sounded like Ilse's death sentence. Since leaving Helmbrechts, we had had a horse-drawn wagon with us on which the sick and dead were transported until there were enough for a mass grave. Then the dead would be unloaded and the sick shot.

"I am going in the wagon too," I decided.

Hanka tried to argue with me but she soon saw that it was useless. All that night I debated with myself: in the morning should Ilse and I remain in the barn under the straw and take our chances, or go in the wagon? I was afraid to stay behind, I was afraid to go on. It was a terrible decision to have to make.

In the morning I dragged Ilse over to the wagon and lifted her into it. She squeezed my hand and turned away from me.

At that moment I got in too. When Ilse saw me she cried, "No, no! You get off, you can walk."

But I knew that at least for that day we would be together.

Early in the afternoon we crossed the Czechoslovakian frontier. The good Czech people at the first village were waiting to greet us despite the shouting and cursing of the SS. They showered us with food! They threw it into the wagon, they brought sausages for the guards, bread and turnips for us. Could there be so much richness in that poor world!

We ate, and I stuffed away some bread in my coat. And wonder of wonders!—an egg appeared in the wagon. How many years since we had seen an egg! I grabbed it and held it to Ilse's lips.

"You first," she insisted.

I took a sip.

Ilse finished the egg.

"You should be ashamed of yourself!" the others cried.

"But Ilse is sick" I pointed out.

"We are all sick," was their answer.

I placed great confidence in the magic power of that egg. I was sure Ilse would walk again.

That night we stopped in an orchard. The trees needed just a day or so of sunshine to make the buds burst open. A deep longing for home started burning in me. I suppressed it quickly.

The other girls had arrived earlier. Hanka had food, and held it out to me.

"We got a lot," I told her excitedly.

I helped Ilse to lie down. She was very tired. The night was chilly. My diarrhea made me weak. Before I ran to the other end of the orchard to relieve myself I placed my supply of bread beneath Ilse's head.

"Watch the food!" I whispered.

"I will," Ilse answered.

When I came back, Ilse was asleep, the bread gone. I scolded her when she waked. "You could have watched it!" I said in desperation.

"I am sorry, sorry, sorry," she repeated.

"Stop being sorry!" I screamed.

I could not sleep, I was so angry. The security of that piece of bread meant so much. Now it was gone.

Ilse was sleeping again. If we could only escape, I thought. Here the people are kind, they would help us. But now we were in a fenced orchard. And now Ilse couldn't walk. How could we escape? If I had known the night before how close we were to the Czech border we certainly would have stayed in that barn. But how could we have known?

In the morning we rode in the wagon again. Ilse slept most of the time. We got no food that day.

As evening approached we were led to another barn.

That night after most of the girls had gone to sleep, Rita Schanzer, my friend of Bielitz days, whispered to me that she was going to try to get away. She wanted me to join her. But Ilse could not walk at all without help, I could not carry her for any distance. It was ridiculous to think of escape.

Next morning was springlike. I scanned the column but failed to see Rita. Perhaps she had gotten safely away. I hoped so.

In the wagon, Ilse immediately fell asleep. The sunshine warmed our frozen, shriveled skins. It felt strangely bright to our eyes, so long accustomed to darkness.

The beauty of the day made me realize how terribly shabby we were. Filthy and stinking, we rode through the gentle Czech countryside. War seemed impossible here. As we passed beneath blooming trees, their branches brushed across the wagon. I tore off a small branch of blossoms and placed it on Ilse's breast. She woke, smelled it, and smiled. Her eyes looked strange. Her teeth were very yellow. She fell asleep again.

The day wore on. We continued through hilly country. It grew much colder. Toward evening we stopped in a meadow. I was driven away from the wagon by a guard. Stronger girls were called to lift the sick and dead from the wagon. After we had stood roll call I looked for Ilse, but could not find her. Then I discovered one of the Hungarian girls dragging her coat from a pile where four bodies lay.

203

Fury possessed me, and I tore the coat out of her hand. "I will kill you!" I screamed.

Though she did not understand my words, she understood my tone, and she let go of the coat.

Ilse was lying on the wet grass. She only smiled when I put the coat around her. The other three girls were dead. Hanka came and helped me carry Ilse away from the corpses. Setting her down in a quiet place, I covered her with both our coats and crawled under them next to her.

I held her in my arms. With effort she lifted her hand and stroked my hair.

"My poor sister," she whispered. "You will be alone."

I cradled her head to my breast to muffle her words. She fell into a light sleep.

Liesel brought two potatoes. I ate one and kept the other in my bosom for Ilse. When she woke, I gave it to her.

"I am not hungry," she insisted. "Eat it. Please eat."

I was so starved, I ate the potato. Before I finished, Ilse was sleeping again.

A fine drizzle fell, it was wet and cold. Several girls got up and moved around.

"Lie down!" yelled the SS.

"Water," Ilse whispered.

I started for the brook nearby. An SS man shouted at me to stop.

"Water for my sister," I begged.

"Get back, you swine!" He kicked at me with heavy boots.

As he followed me to where Ilse was lying, he stopped to slap a couple of girls who got up from the wet ground. When Ilse heard his heavy steps approach, she said feverishly:

"Hear! They are coming! Our saviors!"

"What do you want, you bitch?" demanded the SS guard.

"Water," Ilse whispered.

He kicked her.

"Why?" Ilse cried faintly. "Why?"

"God, have you no mercy?" I sobbed. I flung myself across her body.

"Gerda," Ilse whispered, "I don't want to die. I am only

204

eighteen. I have something to tell you." Her voice grew stronger. With new energy, she said, "If my parents survive, don't tell them I died like this.

"Promise me one more thing," she continued. "You must try to go on for one more week."

I did not answer.

"One more week, promise me!" she persisted.

"I promise."

"I hope nobody is angry at me. I am angry at no one."

"Ilse, please stop!" I begged tearfully.

"You will be very happy, I know it," she went on. "Remember the cards in Bolkenhain. They told us that I am unlucky, but you—you are a *Sonnenkind*."

In Bolkenhain, long ago, someone had read our fortunes. Yes, I remembered.

"Thank you for everything!" she whispered, grabbing my hand.

It stopped raining. Before she fell asleep she licked the few drops of rain I had caught in my cupped hands. I dozed off too.

After a while, she whispered, "Hold my hand."

I held her hand tightly, and we both fell asleep again. When I woke, it was getting light. Ilse's hand was cold. Her eyes were half-open. She no longer breathed.

I ran over to Suse and Liesel, where they huddled together. "Ilse is dead, Ilse is dead!" I told them frantically.

From somewhere a voice came: "Who is Ilse?" And another: "Why the fuss? We all will be dead soon."

I moved away and sat by myself on the wet grass. The sun rose over the hills in a light golden strip—the beginning of the first day that Ilse would not see. Somewhere in the distance a dog was howling. I was alone, so terribly alone. Oh, why was I always alone?

Ilse was buried near some trees. I could not bear to watch. The girls who dug her grave told about it later.

As I climbed into the sick wagon, Hanka tried to dissuade me. "That is sure death. Ilse could not walk, but you can."

"Just today," I begged. "Tomorrow I will walk."

Later, as the wagon rolled through the little town, a window opened above us and a piece of bread fell right into my lap. I clutched it. A dozen hands stretched toward me, begging. For a minute I wavered. Then I divided the bread carefully among the girls.

Chapter 15

THAT WAS A DAY FULL OF TENSION. ALLIED PLANES WERE CONstantly overhead, strafing the woods and our marching column. Obviously the pilots did not know who was marching, they saw only the green-gray uniforms of the guards.

In the evening when we got to a barn, I saw Liesel. She had been wounded in the leg.

"It's nothing," she said, "it does not even hurt."

The barn doors were closed, but the boards did not fit tightly so that light from the outside streamed in. We had stopped marching earlier than usual, probably because the guards were afraid of the planes.

I tried to talk to Liesel and Suse, but somehow the tie between us was broken. Our group was not the same. With Ilse gone, it seemed that they felt that the three of us who remained couldn't last long. Suse planned to ride in the wagon next day. She declared herself unable to walk any more. Liesel, whose legs were covered with pus-filled scabs, agreed to join her.

When morning came I started to follow Suse and Liesel into the wagon. Hanka pulled me back. "You can walk," she said firmly. "Don't ride again."

Meekly I obeyed, though it seemed to make little difference to me. At first my legs hurt so that I thought I could not continue, but as I marched on they felt better. Again and again I found myself turning to my left for Ilse, to my right for Suse. Girls I did not know were marching on either side of me.

We spent another night in a barn. In the morning at least fifty more girls were dead.

When we filed by to get some soup I heard a group of guards speaking excitedly.

"*Ist es möglich?*" one of them asked, and an SS woman answered hysterically: "*Ja, der Führer ist tot!*"

I felt myself tremble with joy.

"Suse, Suse, did you hear?" I whispered.

"Yes," she answered, "but I am sure that now they will kill us for revenge."

I wanted to say no, but something prevented me. Perhaps, I thought, Suse was right.

We marched on, waiting for something to happen. With Hitler dead, things had to change.

"It is happening now," I kept saying to myself. "This is the end. One or two more days, and it will be over."

But somehow it did not matter so much any more. With Ilse gone I did not care, even though I had promised her that I would not give in.

The third evening after Ilse's death we approached a little town in Czechoslovakia: Volary. It was a Friday, I learned later. My legs were hurting terribly; I felt that I could not go on. The SS woman now in charge told us to stand in a row in a meadow. Those who were no longer fit she ordered to stand apart. I was swaying.

"You cannot walk any more," she barked, pointing at me. "Take off her shoes," she commanded Hanka, who stood beside me.

My shoes—the ski boots that Papa insisted that I wear! The order gave me new determination.

Hanka pushed me behind another girl. "Don't let her see you," she whispered.

In the fading light the SS woman ordered our group into a truck.

"Shall I help you up?" Hanka asked.

There were few seats; the rest of the girls would have to stand jammed together. Girls were begging to get on.

"Not yet, Hanka," I said.

"Then you will have to go in the wagon," she said. "It will be here shortly."

"I am in no hurry now," I replied.

The truck rushed away with one SS man and one SS woman

and perhaps thirty shoeless girls. The rest of us sat in the meadow, waiting for the wagon or for the truck to come back. I looked at the sky. The first stars were out. Occasionally a plane or the sound of artillery broke the silence of the spring evening. An hour passed. Neither the wagon nor truck appeared.

I did not feel cold or hungry, only lonely and sad. I allowed myself the rare luxury of thinking of home—of Papa and Mama and Arthur strolling on a spring night in the garden under the darkening sky. I felt strangely consoled. It grew darker.

When the truck failed to return we were led across the meadow to some barracks adjoining a factory. There were a hundred and twenty of us left. After we were marched in, the doors and windows were barricaded. Soon afterward, from the silence outside, we gathered that our guards had abandoned us.

Much later I learned from one of the girls who survived that an American plane had strafed the truck that did not return. The woman guard was killed. The SS man on the truck shot a number of the girls. The rest jumped off the truck and ran away.

In the silence of our barracks we could hear a ticking. So the Germans were going to destroy us after all! We had waited so many years for the end of the war. How many times, years ago at home, in the ghetto, in Bolkenhain, in Märzdorf, in Landeshut and Grünberg, and while marching all those months, had I dreamed of this moment. And now we were not to survive. . . .

Then it began to rain. It was a spring rain accompanied by loud thunder. The planes stopped roaring, the artillery fire ceased. And still the bomb outside continued to tick.

Then some Czechs came and broke the door open. They urged us to run—the SS men were coming back to shoot us because their bomb had not gone off.

Later we heard many stories about that bomb, but we never learned why it failed to go off. We did not pause to look at it. Those who could, ran. Some of us headed toward the factory and hid there. Two other girls and I crawled into a long, metal cylinder lying on the floor. There we waited.

A couple of hours passed. There was shooting in the distance, and then close by, and again the planes roared overhead; we did not dare to move.

Perhaps, I thought, perhaps we will survive, but what then? I will go home, of course. . . . And for the first time in all those years, the thought of going home did not ring right. No, I could not think of it. Not yet.

There was a loud commotion at the factory door, and we heard heavy boots pound along the concrete floor. A voice shouted in German, "Get out, out, you beasts, out!"

We did not stir.

Shots were fired in our direction. One bullet went through the cylinder, creasing my shoulder and one of the other girls' legs. There was more commotion, and then the Germans departed.

We waited again. There was more firing in the distance.

Much later we heard shouting in Czech. A man and two women entered the factory calling: "If someone is inside, come out. The war is over!"

We crawled out of the cylinder, stiff and numb.

"Look!" said the man, pointing to a window. One of the women took my arm to steady me.

From the window, in the early-morning light, I saw a church on a hill. The white flag of peace waved gently from its steeple. My throat tightened with emotion, and my tears fell on the dusty window sill. I watched how they did not soak into the dust, but remained like round clear crystals, and that was all I could think of in that great hour of my life!

Part Three

Chapter I

WE WENT BACK TO THE BARRACKS WHERE MOST OF THE REST OF
the girls had gathered. We found chaos: crying, and shouts
of joy. The hour had struck at last. Somehow I couldn't grasp
it. There were no golden trumpets to proclaim our freedom.
There were no liberators in sight.

Liesel was lying on the littered floor. She knew we were
free but did not seem elated.

"Where is Suse?" I asked her.

"She went out to get water and hasn't returned. She has been
gone a long time."

I went out to look for Suse. She was not at the pump. I
found her off a way lying in the mud. Her eyes were glassy,
unseeing, but for a moment I did not realize she was dead.

"Suse, we are free!" I called to her. "We are free, the war
is over!"

When I touched her, I knew the truth.

I did not tell Liesel. It was too sad for Liberation Day.

As I look back now, trying to recall my feelings during those
first hours, I actually think that there were none. My mind
was so dull, my nerves so worn from waiting, that only an
emotionless vacuum remained. Like many of the other girls
I just sat and waited for whatever would happen next.

In the afternoon a strange vehicle drove up. In it were two
soldiers in strange uniforms, one of whom spoke German.

The German mayor of the town was with them. He was
trying to tell the two soldiers that he really was not anti-
Semitic. The soldiers were Americans; I knew as soon as I
heard them speak to one another. Arthur had spoken their
language a little.

Tears welled from my eyes as they approached us. The Ger-

213

man-speaking soldier patted me with his clean hand. "Don't cry, my child," he said with compassion, "it is all over now." "We must return to headquarters," said the other one in German. "Can you girls wait until morning? We shall return."

I remember nothing else happening that day. The next thing I remember was waking up, wrapped snugly and warm in a coat which the SS had left behind, waking up with what I thought was a smile, which must have seemed more like a grimace in my pitifully thin face.

The barracks was bathed in sunshine, and I woke up with the knowledge that I was free. I was eager to go outside, to move about freely. Perhaps I would meet the Americans again. I swayed as I started to walk. My skin was hot and dry. As I reached the door, the first thing I saw was that strange vehicle bouncing toward us through the brilliant May sunshine. I was overcome with joy.

I called to the other girls that some Americans were coming. The soldier on the left made a motion to the driver who stopped the vehicle a few feet from where I was standing. The soldier jumped out and walked toward the barracks. He wasn't the one who had come the day before. Shaking my head, I stared at this man who was to me the embodiment of all heroism and liberty. He greeted me. I must tell him from the start, I resolved, so that he has no illusions about us. Perhaps I had acquired a feeling of shame. After all, for six long years the Nazis had tried to demean us.

"May I see the other ladies?" he asked.

"Ladies!" my brain repeated. He probably doesn't know, I thought. I must tell him.

"We are Jews," I said in a small voice.

"So am I," he answered. Was there a catch in his voice, or did I imagine it?

I could have embraced him but I was aware how dirty and repulsive I must be.

"Won't you come with me?" he asked. He held the door open. I didn't understand at first. I looked at him questioningly but not a muscle in his face moved. He wanted me to

214

feel that he had not seen the dirt or the lice. He saw a lady and I shall be forever grateful to him for his graciousness.

"I want you to see a friend of mine," I remember telling the American, and we started to walk toward Liesel. On the dirty, straw-littered floor Lilli was lying, covered with rags. As we tried to reach Liesel, she looked up, her eyes enormous, burning in their sockets. She looked at my companion and her face lit up with a strange fire. I heard her say something in English, and saw how the American bent down closer and answered her. Her hands were shaking as she gently, unbelievingly touched the sleeve of his jacket. In the exchange that followed, I made out the word "happy." I understood that word. Then she sighed, released his hand and, looking at him, shook her head and whispered, "Too late."

We moved on to Liesel. Liesel just smiled, and said nothing. She didn't seem to care much. I looked back at Lilli; her eyes were fixed on the American, a solitary tear ran down her cheek. An ant was crawling over her chin. Shortly afterward, Lilli died.

I heard the American give commands in English. He seemed furious that things weren't moving fast enough. He explained to me in German that a hospital was being set up for us. Then he asked me:

"Is there anything I can do for you in particular?"

"Yes, there is," I said. "If you would be kind enough, and could find the time. You see, I have an uncle in Turkey. Could you write to him, let him know that I am alive, and that I hope he has news from my parents and my brother?"

He took out a notebook, and removed the sunglasses he had been wearing. I saw tears in his eyes. He wore battle gear with a net over his helmet. And as he wrote, I looked at him and couldn't absorb enough of the wonder that he had fought for my freedom.

He snapped his book shut.

"I would like to ask you a question," he said softly. "But please don't answer if you don't want to. We are aware of what has happened. Tell me, were you girls sterilized?"

215

I did not answer at once. I was too full of emotion. Why should he, of all people, who looked to me like a young god, inquire about the deepest treasure that I, who must have looked like an animal to him, carried still within me?

"We were spared," I managed to say.

A few moments later, joined by his companion and the mayor, he drove off. Before I had even asked his name—he vanished!

Within an hour, Red Cross trucks arrived. Litter bearers gently but swiftly loaded the ill. Other soldiers carried girls in their arms like babies, speaking to them soothingly in words the girls did not understand. But the gestures of warmth and help were unmistakable. In a trance I walked to a truck and got in. On the soldiers' sleeves was a red diamond, the insignia of the Fifth U.S. Infantry Division. Their uniforms, their language, their kindness and concern made it true: we were finally free!

The hospital we were taken to was a converted school. Wounded German soldiers had been moved to the third floor so that we could be installed in the first two floors. How strange—in a matter of one day, the world had changed: Germans were put out to make room for us.

We were taken to a room where huge caldrons of water were being heated on a stove. Round wooden tubs stood steaming on the floor.

A woman in a white coat motioned me to undress.

Doing so, I stepped into one of the tubs. The warm water, reaching to my neck, felt strange: it had been at least three years since last I sat in a tub. Bidding me stand, the nurse soaped my body with quick, invigorating pressure. It was pleasantly painful to sit back in the tub again and let the warm water engulf me.

A young peasant girl came in, her cheeks rosy and shining, her colorful peasant skirt reaching to her ankles, her deep-cut blouse revealing her full bosom. I felt slight and thin. When I saw the girl gather up my clothes in a basket, I looked at the nurse with a questioning glance.

"They will be burned," she said.

Only one thought remained. With my wet hand I reached for my ski boots, took the left one and reached under the lining. There was the dirty shapeless package containing the pictures I wanted to save. I pulled the pictures out and laid them on the dry towel beside the tub. And the other packet—the poison I had bought in Grünberg—I gratefully let go to the fire.

I stepped out of the tub; the nurse dried my body and hair. As I stood nude, before a clean blue and white checkered man's shirt was put on me, I realized abruptly that I possessed nothing, not even a stitch of clothing that I could call my own. I owned only the pictures of Papa, Mama, Arthur, and Abek that I had carried for three years.

A blanket was thrown over my shoulders as I was led to a bunk. The sheets were fresh and white. A nurse brought me a drink of milk. Milk!—I hadn't had any in three years. As I drank it something tremendous and uncontrollable broke loose within me. My body shook convulsively. I wanted to stop it but I couldn't. I heard my voice and could do nothing about it.

A nurse hurried up; then a doctor. I heard him say, "No, let her cry it out." Long pent-up emotions finally burst out. I cried for Ilse, for Suse, for other friends, and finally for my family too. Deep in my heart I had known they were dead, but dreams about happy reunions with them had kept me going.

When I opened my eyes a night had passed. A nurse was approaching with a breakfast tray. This is the life of a fairy princess, I thought.

As I lay daydreaming after breakfast there was a sudden commotion. Nurses hurried in.

"Germany has capitulated!" they told us. "The war in Europe is over!"

For me, the war had ended with my liberation. I had not realized that the fighting had continued after that.

I looked out the window. Coming down the hilly, winding road was a company of unarmed and bedraggled German soldiers. As they passed my window, I could see their unshaven faces and hollow cheeks. Proud, handsome American soldiers guarded them.

A doctor and a nurse came in. They stopped at each bed. After asking my name and birthplace, the doctor asked for my date of birth.

"May 8, 1924."

"May 8!" the doctor exclaimed. "Why, today is the eighth."

"Happy birthday!" the nurse chanted.

After they left, I repeated to myself, "It's my birthday, my twenty-first birthday, and Germany capitulated!"

I thought of Tusia, who had so desperately wanted my assurance that we would both be free on this day. I remembered her lying dead in the snow. Why am I here? I wondered. I am no better.

As I lay back on my white clean pillow, lost in thought, I heard someone approach. It was the doctor again. He put something in my hand.

"For your birthday," he said, smiling.

It was a piece of chocolate.

Chapter 2

I DON'T REMEMBER THE DAYS THAT FOLLOWED TOO WELL. THE doctors and nurses spent much time over me; I was given injections and pills continuously. My body was rubbed with oil twice a day, for my skin was flaked and dry. I was weighed—sixty-eight pounds. The nurses joked about being able to circle my thigh with their fingers.

My bed seemed very high up, and the distances enormous. I did not feel like talking to anyone; I was strangely silent for the first time in my life. I noticed that many of the girls began to have visitors. I asked for Liesel several times, but was never told where she was.

Time and again I thought of the American soldier who had been so kind to me. Just before he had driven off he had said that he would see me again. With a chill, I recalled that the fighting had gone on after I had spoken to him; something might have happened to him!

A week passed. One afternoon an American came in and glanced into each bunk. My eyes met his as he approached.

"It's you I'm looking for!" he said.

I must have frowned as I recognized him. Out of his helmet and battle gear, he looked different.

"Don't you remember me?" he asked.

"Oh, yes!" I said quickly, and wanted to add how worried I had been that something might have befallen him, but checked myself.

He carried a parcel under his arm. "These are for you," he said, unwrapping two magazines.

"Do you know what this means?" he asked, pointing to four bold white letters on a red background.

I gazed at the letters: L—I—F—E.

219

He repeated his question. "Do you know what it means? It is a fine word for you to learn. I know no better word of introduction to the English language for you."

I pronounced the word and tasted the strange sound of it.

"Say it again," he urged.

I was only too glad to try.

"That's right, that's what I wanted to see."

"To see what?" I asked.

"You smiled," he said. "I wanted to see you smile."

We talked. He told me that he had been busy with large numbers of prisoners, and that was why he had not come sooner. He said that he was stationed in a neighboring village about sixteen miles away. We talked like old friends. There was so much to ask. He seemed amazed at the limited knowledge I had about the development of the war. His German was excellent, though not fluent. At times he substituted an English word for a German one, but I nearly always knew what he meant.

The nurse came in, bringing my dinner tray, and told him that all visitors had to leave. I would have gladly foregone food if he could have stayed.

He left, and I ate my dinner, realizing that I had again forgotten to ask his name. After eating, until the light grew too poor, I studied the magazines. The pictures of the free world were exciting.

Then, unexpectedly, a voice near me said "Hello" in English. "You're not going to throw me out, are you?"

I was overjoyed to see him. It hadn't occurred to me that he might return in the evening. This time I learned his name.

"Kurt Klein," he said, laughing. "By the way, I wrote the letter to your uncle in Turkey. I hope I can bring you an answer soon."

I told Kurt about the strange sensation I felt every time I saw German soldiers under guard.

"Just hurry up and get well," he said, "and I'll show you how many of them are under guard."

And he told me some of his experiences with the Germans' surprise when they heard about their concentration camps.

"It seems we fought a war against the Nazis, but I haven't met a Nazi yet," he said wryly.

And I was actually able to laugh. He could make me laugh, but I was ashamed to cry in front of him. I told him about Ilse. He seemed to understand. He didn't tell me to forget, to draw a line through the past, for he knew that I couldn't. He didn't ask questions either. He listened to what I had to tell him. He was silent when he knew that there was no answer. He joked about the present, and again and again I found myself laughing.

His daily visits continued. Although we came from different worlds, we understood each other. I did not want pity. I did not want him to like me because of what I had endured. Without knowing why, I sensed that there was something in his past that made him suffer.

A couple of days after his first visit he brought me some lilies-of-the-valley. The subtle fragrance brought back memories of my garden in May. I clutched the flowers without being able to speak. I remembered the roses in Grünberg which we had not been allowed to touch. But here were flowers that bloomed for me.

I kept my eyes downcast for quite a while, not daring to raise them and have them full of tears.

Finally Kurt asked, "Do you like them?"

My answer must have been written on my face. There was a catch in his voice when he spoke.

"I knew you would. They were my mother's favorite flowers."

"Your mother?" I asked haltingly.

Then for the first time Kurt told me about himself. He had been born in Germany. His older sister had gone to America soon after Hitler came to power, Kurt following her a year later. Finally the older brother had left for America. The parents had stayed behind. With their children safe, they waited, hoping that the Nazi regime would collapse. I remembered when Papa and Mama had talked the same way. Kurt went on to tell me how the children's combined efforts had failed to get their parents out of Germany. The Nazis had deported them to Camp de Gurs, in the south of France, in 1941. For a while letters reached them from America, then in July, 1942 a letter had been returned, stamped "Moved—left no forwarding address." Kurt fell silent. I understood so well. Impulsively I caught his hand.

"There is hope still," I said.

"Is there?" His voice was slightly ironical, but there was some concealed hope in it.

I had always felt that his understanding of my feelings had been made deeper by tragedy of his own. I was glad now that I had never given him detailed descriptions of cruelty, that I had really never told him what had happened, though he heard it from others later. Yet the knowledge that I could shield him from pain gave me satisfaction.

The days went on. Physically I felt worse and worse. I tried to conceal it even from the nurses and doctors. In the hours when Kurt was not with me, I read the German books he brought and studied the American magazines. Then I began to observe that most of the girls around me were better, and were allowed to get up. Some girls moved into private homes, and I marveled at their courage and ingenuity. How did they manage?

I continually asked for Liesel, and was finally told that she had died after an amputation. I was alone again! None of my close friends remained.

Again and again, the burning question came back, "What do I do from now on?" Sometimes I woke from sleep, covered with perspiration, feeling as though someone had shaken me and shouted "What now?" into my ear. I fell exhausted into my pillows; sometimes I cried silently or tossed for hours until a nurse mercifully gave me a sleeping pill.

The first possibility that ran through my mind would be to go home. Perhaps Papa and Mama, perhaps Arthur . . . but I knew they would not be there. Then I must go home alone! If nothing else, there would be the house, the garden. Perhaps Niania had saved a few things. And then there was Abek. I really had not thought about him until now, and when I did, I became panicky. Why was I so afraid?

222

Then there was my uncle in Turkey. He would surely make me welcome. Yet he and his wife and children lived in a world so remote from mine that I did not think that I could be happy there in it.

Lastly, if these alternatives failed, I would go to Palestine.

One day after Kurt left, while leafing through a magazine he had just brought, I found an envelope between the pages. It was sealed and had my name on it in pencil in a corner. For a few seconds fear gripped me. Was he being transferred and was this his way of telling me? I tore the envelope open. There was no letter in it, just several bank notes.

I was touched by his thought. God knows I needed money, for I owned nothing, but I felt I could not accept it. When Kurt came the next day I told him that he had forgotten something.

"You are not angry?" he asked. "Please do take it. Consider it a loan, pay it back to me. If I should have to leave unexpectedly I would like to know that you have some means to buy the bare necessities and to get home."

He worried about me! Though I felt deeply grateful, and could have accepted the money from a stranger, I could not receive it from him.

"I can't," I whispered, and he argued no further.

About that time Herr Knebel, the owner of the factory in which we were hiding on Liberation Day, started making daily visits to all the girls in the hospital. When I told him my name and where I came from, he told me that he had known either my father or one of his business associates. The following day his two daughters, young married women whose husbands were in Allied hands, came to visit me. The day after that they came again, and brought me a dress.

It is hard to describe the joy that I felt, and the eagerness with which I looked forward to being able to get up and wear it. I know that I will never feel the same way toward any garment, no matter what its value or beauty, as I felt toward that simple cotton dress!

Everyone in the hospital knew Kurt by now; he was commonly referred to as "Gerda's lieutenant." Everyone joked about us. He was undoubtedly the most faithful visitor to the hospital, although none of the girls really understood our relationship. It was pointed out to me many times that he was a fool if he did not provide the clothing and food which I needed and which he as an American could obtain—and that I was even a greater fool for not asking him.

I shrugged it off for I had the feeling that my real reasons would not be understood. Kurt instinctively knew my needs. By not bringing me clothes, he made me feel that he did not see my pitiful need of them, that I appeared to him as a normal girl briefly confined to a hospital. His gifts of flowers or reading material were appropriate. Thus he helped me to gain confidence in myself as a human being.

One day, checking the thermometer the nurse had given me, I confirmed my suspicion that I had a high fever. Since I was expecting Kurt, and I was afraid that I might not be permitted to have a visitor, I shook the thermometer down and handed it to the nurse when she returned.

Kurt came, and he was ill at ease. Then he told me that he was being transferred to Pfarrkirchen in Bavaria, about three hundred kilometers distant.

He showed me some pictures of himself that had just been taken. I wanted one, but could not overcome my shyness to ask for it. I looked at one in particular many times. Finally he asked me if I wanted it.

"Yes," I admitted, "very much!"

"Why on earth didn't you tell me?"

Then an idea struck me.

"Go out into the corridor and write something on it. I have a surprise for you too," I said.

As he did, I called a nurse who had been particularly kind to me all the time.

"I want to get up, I must get up," I told her.

"The doctor won't let you," she said. "You are not strong enough."

"I have to, I have to!" I was close to tears.

The nurse helped me down from my bed, helped me put on

224

the cotton dress the Knebel girls had given me. Slowly I crept toward the door.

Kurt gasped when he saw me. "This is a surprise indeed!" he said, and he took my arm.

The shape of the corridor seemed queer; the echo of voices, the click of trays, the hurrying nurses bothered me. The sounds were metallic, falling on the stone walls and coming back to my ears with a strange edge to them.

Kurt led me out a side door into what had been the school-yard. We walked slowly, each step causing me pain. I remembered Hans Christian Andersen's tale about the mermaid who was in love with a prince. She had a witch sell her a brew that would change her fins into legs, so that she might for once walk with the prince. She had her wish, but the price was a steep one, for each step she took felt as if she were stepping on knives.

"Kurt, do you remember the Andersen fairy tales?" I asked.

"Some," he answered. "Why?"

At this point I decided that it was best not to tell him, and started to laugh. I changed the subject. I don't remember what we talked about. The time went fast.

Kurt wanted to take me indoors and see me safely to bed before he left. I objected; I did not want to say good-by to him with all the girls around us. The lights would be on inside; I did not want him to see the tears that would start at my thought of being alone again.

He did not argue, but walked me as far as the entrance and gave me the picture. I knew it was up to me to say something. I said it very quickly, afraid that my voice might break.

"I want to thank you for everything you have done, I shall never forget it as long as I live."

Kurt took both my hands and held them.

"All I can say is: I shall see you as soon and as much as I can." Then he turned and walked away quickly.

Once in my bunk I started to cry. I cried because there was nothing to look forward to. Kurt would not come; I might never see him again.

I heard Ida, a simple girl with a shrill voice, call out, "You know, girls, Gerda is crying because her lieutenant left."

Someone else said, "Don't be a fool, Gerda. You knew he would leave sooner or later. Did you think he would take you with him?"

I fumbled in my dress and took out Kurt's picture. On the back it said: "To Gerda, at the start of a new life!"

The inscription was in English but I understood it completely.

The night was never ending. I tossed around, my throat was parched, my temples throbbed furiously. When the night nurse came she felt my hand.

"Why, you are burning!" she exclaimed. After checking my pulse she disappeared, almost instantly returning with a doctor.

I was undressed and wrapped in a cold wet sheet. I lost consciousness.

Days passed. Sometimes I did not really feel ill, though I knew that I must be. My temperature remained high. I slept most of the time, or was semiconscious.

One afternoon I opened my eyes to find a nurse peering at me. "You are awake at last," she said, holding ice water to my lips. How good, how refreshing!

Then I saw Kurt. He was smiling at me. After the nurse left he took my hand. My bony fingers felt at peace in that cool strong hand.

I lay there happy and tired. Kurt's voice was softly teasing.

"What's the idea? The minute I turn my back, you get yourself sick!"

The scolding felt good. I smiled. I learned that I had been sick a week.

"I am quite excited," Kurt said. "Just before I came here today I got a letter from my sister in New York. I am going to become an uncle. They didn't let me know before. I wonder what Barbara will have to say."

"And who is Barbara?" I asked.

"My niece, of course." He pulled a picture out of his pocket. I looked at a little girl with pigtails, in a light dress and sweater, a child about three years of age.

I had learned to associate children with death. Children were not permitted to live, to laugh. This child was standing among trees.

"What is she doing with that flower?" I asked, to mask my emotions.

"That is not a flower, that is a lollipop!"

I did not understand the word. Kurt tried to say it in German, and finally made it clear.

"Let me look at the lollipop again," I said, ashamed to tell him that I wanted to see the child.

Barbara had a special place in Kurt's heart, and he delighted in telling me about her—about a game called "Make like a birdie" which he had taught her: he would hold her in his arms and fly around the room, much to the alarm of his sister.

I could see Kurt holding that child in his arms, laughing and enjoying the game as much as the child did. Another picture sprang to my mind: Abek talking about his little niece —full of love too, yes, but with sadness. I could never picture Abek so fully enjoying and sharing the child's play, laughing with her, being so happy.

Before I could check myself, the words tumbled out. "I wish that I had a little niece or a little baby!"

"You," Kurt said, using for the first time the German *du*, instead of *sie*— "You are just a silly little girl yourself, not much older or bigger than Barbara."

It felt wonderfully good and peaceful to be thought of as a little girl, a silly little girl with no worries or problems. With Kurt's hand still holding mine, I drifted off to a strength-giving sleep.

I felt much better the next morning, although my temperature was still up. I asked for paper and pencil. The nurse brought them to me, and I began to make a drawing of the flowers that Kurt had brought me.

Kurt found me at this project when he called. He had spent the night in Volary, but now had to return to Pfarrkirchen,

227

five hours' ride by jeep. He left around noon, promising to come again as soon as he could get away.

The doctors told me that I had come through both pneumonia and typhus, and that I was now out of danger. However, there seemed to be some complications about my feet. I still had no strength in them, and I knew that beneath the bandages they were not healing properly.

Sometimes the doctor who had most to do with me would find time for a chat. He was Austrian. It was never clear to me if he had been in the German army. We spoke about other things. Once he said he would like to write a medical book about concentration camps, about the body and mind under conditions of extreme duress. He asked me if I would help him. I said of course, rather looking forward to contributing my experiences. He seemed vitally interested in people's minds.

One particular evening he asked me again and again how much I thought a mind could stand. I knew he was driving at something. Then, very subtly, he told me that he had had to operate on a number of girls with frozen limbs. As he spoke, he watched me. I knew he was speaking about me.

"Never!" I shouted.

He had expected resistance: there was sympathy in his eyes, and determination.

I have been told many times in my life that I have an instinctive approach to a situation. It happened at that moment too. From the medical viewpoint, amputation of my feet must have been right or it would not have been proposed. But I had greater faith in my own judgment.

"We don't have to do it right away," the doctor continued, "but I wanted you to have the thought in mind in case there is no improvement."

Before he went home that night, the doctor came again to see me. I hardly recognized him in civilian clothes, having seen him only in white.

"Tomorrow," he said, "we shall try something." His voice was impersonal. "We will bathe your feet alternately in hot

228

water and cold water. It may be very painful. Perhaps you know better."

The treatments started. The hot water was boiling hot; the cold was ice water. At first there was not much sensation. Later the hot and the cold were equally excruciating, but I rejoiced in the pain, for it meant that I had life in my legs, that I would be able to walk.

Kurt came again, bringing me roses. He was glad to see me recovering so fast.

Next day, noting that my temperature was up, my doctor laughed and remarked, "Nothing like being in love to raise one's temperature!"

In love, in love—I tasted the sound of the words and liked them. Yet I knew that it was not that simple, even though I cared deeply for Kurt.

One of the nurses had given me a little mirror, and I began to use it more and more. My hair was by now back to its original black. As I combed it daily, it felt thicker and the natural wave returned to it. My cheeks filled out. The dimples that I used to have reappeared.

"You look different, Gerda," the girls told me. "My, what a man at your bedside can't do."

I hardly recognized myself . . . My sallowness was gone. My eyes looked lively rather than tragic. Involuntarily, I smiled: I looked younger than my twenty-one years.

Kurt had told me that too. He said, "When I first met you, you looked forty. Now you are back to sixteen, that's not fair!"

He laughed and I joined in. I was happy and young and gay when he was with me, and I tried not to think of anything else. I was happy for the moment, that was all that mattered.

In the course of conversation, I learned that his birthday would fall on a Sunday—his day to visit me. The previous Sunday I was allowed to get up and take my first steps alone. I planned to take a walk with Kurt when he came, and as a present I wrote a few short essays for him. I told him in advance about the walk we would be taking.

Starting Wednesday, I practiced hard. I actually had to

learn to walk again. The first steps were difficult and frightening. I felt dizzy and longed for bed, but I walked first to the adjacent bed, then to the window, to the door, then once around the room, twice around the room. Finally, I ventured into the corridor. By Saturday I hesitatingly tried the stairs. Sunday came, and I was ready.

Kurt usually came in the morning. He started from Pfarrkirchen at daybreak to arrive around eleven. But this was a special Sunday: I watched the door each time it opened. Lunch time came, and no sign of Kurt! I watched from the window, my heart beating faster as each jeep approached.

The noon hour passed. Perhaps he could not get away, I thought. I went out into the yard behind the hospital.

I heard another jeep approach. I thought I would stay a while before returning to my room. Although Kurt knew I would be up today, he would be surprised to find my bed empty. I counted to five hundred, then went inside. Kurt was not there. I asked the girl in the bed next to mine. No, Kurt had not been there. I could not stand it.

"I am going for a walk," I stammered.

Across from the hospital was a meadow. I had yearned to walk in it for weeks and so I left the hospital and headed for it.

A group of people approached as I crossed the street. I had the desire to run away, and found myself instinctively panic-stricken about the absence of my Jewish star.

I sat down on a slope under a pine tree, and tried to think of my new freedom, but all my thoughts were of Kurt.

Why did he not come? A new fear gripped me: could he have been sent to Japan? No, this couldn't be—he would have come to say good-by.

Then, all of a sudden, it seemed clear. Today, for the first time, I was to walk. That was all that Kurt wanted to achieve. In his kindness he wanted to help me get well. But once I was well . . . ?

Perhaps the whispers and jokes about us had reached his ears. The girls and nurses were constantly saying that we were in love. I searched my heart and came to the conclusion that I cared deeply for Kurt in a silent, suppressed way.

Why should I not? I asked myself. He was kind, understanding, intelligent, and handsome. There was an aura of heroism about him. He had liberated me. He was for me the incorporation of freedom and understanding: Why should I not love him?

Yet, how did Kurt feel about me? He liked me, I knew that. Why else would he come hundreds of miles to see me? He wanted to help me. But what did he think about me as a girl? That I did not know . . .

I certainly couldn't look pretty to him. I recalled the pictures of beautiful American girls in the magazines he had brought me. Those were the girls he knew. Surely I could never compare with those girls. Besides, he must always remember me the way I looked when he met me, more like an animal than a human being.

He is kind not to come again. It is probably for the best.

Yet the thought that I might never see him again became unbearable. One thing I resolved: if I saw him again, he would never know my feelings for him. I would never be a burden for him. And then I realized that he might be married—or engaged. He had never said.

I returned to the hospital, utterly miserable. I just could not believe that on the first day out of bed I could feel so sad and forlorn. The girls teased me—good-naturedly, but it hurt.

Monday came. The week crept slowly by. Saturday, Sunday. I waited, I hoped, but Kurt didn't come. Nor did he send word.

The Knebels took great interest in me. They invited me for dinner frequently and even asked me to stay in their home. I considered doing so, but since I was not yet discharged from the hospital or strong enough to work for my room and board, I declined.

One day I found Mrs. Von Garnier, one of the daughters, sewing a new dress for me, a really beautiful, silky thing with

231

fine stripes of navy and deep pink. Simple in style, with a tiny white collar, it really looked elegant.

Even the new dress did not give me any joy. Kurt would not see it, and I could not pay for it. It was charity and I hated charity.

I told Mrs. Von Garnier my feelings.

"You must not feel it is charity," she said. "Perhaps you can help us someday."

"Help you? How?"

"Well—" She did not finish. I wondered what was behind her remarks.

The Knebels had a well-stocked library. I borrowed books by the armful, and at the hospital I often read late into the night.

I should have been happy. I was free, not hungry (although most of the time I could have eaten more—food was by no means plentiful yet). I was free of lice, had a clean bed to sleep in, and books to read. Yet—and I would never have believed it possible—I was not happy. For I was sure now that I should not see Kurt again. As the other girls put it, it was time to look for a new boy friend. They were plentiful: a whole American division was stationed in the area.

But I wanted to speak to no one. My thoughts were constantly with Kurt. I worried about his safety. Perhaps he had caught my typhus! I woke up one night with that terrible thought.

I could have inquired about him from the local Military Government but pride prevented me from seeking him out. I knew I had to wait.

The week end was approaching again. In the almost three weeks that I hadn't seen Kurt I had come to hate week ends. On Friday evening a captain from the Military Government brought me Kurt's letter. The captain chatted for a while, and I tried to make polite conversation, but my thought was of the envelope in my hand. Was it good-by? I tore it open. A dry flower fell out. No, that was not good-by.

The letter was dated June 27, 1945. It had taken almost three weeks to reach me. Kurt could not write to me directly:

civilians weren't allowed to receive mail yet. His letter had come through official channels. It was a long letter, starting with the thought that I could not get rid of him easily. The army, he explained, had abruptly transferred him to a distant town near Munich. He teased me about my first walk, wrote gaily about his environment, and about his few days of leave which he had used to visit the Austrian Alps.

The letter continued with the hope that I would write to him through the same channels. There was a postscript: "I picked this Alpine rose for you at twenty-five hundred meters."

I read the letter again and again, relieved that my fears had been unfounded, and that I would have more letters to look forward to. And perhaps, as Kurt had written, I would see him again in the not too distant future.

Chapter 3

THE NEXT DAY, SATURDAY, I SPENT WITH THE KNEBELS. LUNCH was served out in the garden under a sprawling tree. The modest fare seemed luxurious to me, and I enjoyed the sparkling silver and fine china, the beautiful tablecloth, and the floral centerpiece quite as much.

That luncheon was particularly good and I remember it vividly. There were fried potatoes, yogurt, and a big salad. For dessert there were field strawberries and the cream that had been removed from the yogurt. And with Kurt's letter in my pocket, the world looked rosy again . . .

After lunch I took a long sunbath in a deck chair. At first I read, then I tried to think about the future, but pushed the thoughts away—the afternoon was too perfect. After a bit, I fell asleep.

I woke up feeling chilled. The sun was no longer shining. Heavy clouds hung in the sky, and gusts of wind were blowing through the trees. I ran toward the house. As I approached it the first raindrops fell. I had always liked rain, and I watched it now from the library window. Soon the gutters were rushing little rivers. Here and there leaves floated on the streams. I watched them journey.

"Miss Gerda!" Mrs. Von Garnier called. "Your dress is ready. Don't you want to try it on?"

I tried it on before the mirror in her bedroom. The lines were simple and it fitted beautifully. It showed my new tan to advantage and made me appear healthier than I was. I kept the dress on and went back to the library.

It was close to six o'clock when the rain finally stopped, and I decided to go back to the hospital. I was saying good-by to my hosts when their doorbell rang. The maid opened the

234

door—and there stood Kurt! Not even in my dreams had I expected to see him so soon.

His raincoat and helmet were dripping, his uniform looked wet through and through. "I looked for you in the hospital, all over," he said. "God, have you changed! And that dress! Are you still going to talk to me?"

I laughed.

Kurt had traveled for eight hours or more in an open jeep in the pouring rain over partially destroyed roads, and he could stay only until noon the next day, for he had to be back in Munich by night.

The Knebels invited him to dinner and to spend the night. He declined the dinner, but said that he would gladly accept lodgings, since it would be difficult to find others.

We left for the hospital. The air was sweetly scented after the rain. Heavy drops hung on the leaves.

After my supper at the hospital we returned to Herr Knebel's. Only the younger daughter was present. The elder and the father had gone out.

Kurt was shown to his room while I waited in the living room. The windows were open, the evening was slightly chilly, and the fragrance of flowers drifted into the room. The furniture was old, dark, polished mahogany with brown leather upholstery; the room was quiet and orderly. That house had survived the war without change. I touched the big chairs; they felt cool. The fringed velvet portieres were smooth. I had known that room now for two weeks, but somehow I felt its character for the first time that night. I walked over to the open window and drank in the beauty and tranquility of the evening.

Kurt returned. For a few seconds we stood next to each other, not saying a word. He must have guessed that my thoughts were of home.

I felt painfully alone and forlorn in that house which so closely resembled that of my childhood, in a country so much like my own, standing next to a man who was so much like my family. Yet nothing there belonged to me.

Did Kurt sense all my thoughts, did he feel as I did? I

235

felt his arm around my shoulder, shielding me from my lone-liness. His touch electrified me: it was the first affectionate gesture I had received in so many years. I was so starved for affection and protection that the touch of his arm brought tears to my eyes. Kurt pulled me closer and held me, stroking my hair. He did not tell me to stop, he held me tight and let me cry.

Suddenly, I remembered Abek. He had said we would cry when we met again, and understand each other's tears and pain.

I looked up at Kurt, trying to form words with quivering lips. He put his finger to my lips: he did not want me to say what he knew would hurt me. Through my tears I could see that he was smiling, that his eyes looked gently and with understanding into mine. Those gentle eyes, that generous, smiling mouth—where had I seen them before? Long ago, in a dream, in Bolkenhain . . .

I buried my face on his chest, feeling safe and at peace at last.

Kurt walked me back to the hospital. For a long time I could not sleep. I thought once again about going home. If I did, would I see Kurt again? I resolved firmly to make a decision soon. I would talk it over with Kurt in the morning, I promised myself. He would know how to advise me.

Sunday morning we walked through meadows in which the countless buttercups and daisies seemed as fresh and well-scrubbed as the peasants whom we had seen walking to church.

Kurt tried to take pictures of me, but I did not let him. I danced over the grass, jumped just when he was ready to snap. He was annoyed but laughed.

We climbed a little hill and sat under a majestic tree. As we talked I regarded Kurt with wonder and some bewilderment. He was gay and teasing. Was he the same man who held me in his arms the night before? Were those the same lips that had kissed away my tears? Was it only last night? It seemed so remote. Perhaps it had been a dream. Yes, it must have been a dream.

For no reason at all I was afraid that he might try to kiss

236

me now. I sat rigid. Kurt noticed my silence. There was concern in his voice when he asked if I felt well. Then I told him what I had been thinking the night before, about going home.

He became serious at once.

"I would not advise you to go before you hear from your uncle in Turkey. He might have news for you about your family. I should have a reply from him soon. Besides, no matter what you may think, you are in no condition to leave the hospital yet. A journey home is not a matter of getting on a train; it would mean hardship and hitchhiking. There is no transportation yet for civilians."

It was good to hear him speak of such things as hardships —a few weeks ago they would have been dreamlike luxuries. I listened earnestly, glad that he was offering me a reasonable excuse for delay, glad that he did not say what he must know: that I was afraid to go home.

When we returned to the hospital, Kurt's jeep and driver were waiting. I asked Kurt to come to my room for a moment. There I gave him the eight essays that I had written for him.

He read the inscription on the first page of the crudely bound booklet: "To Kurt, a few episodes from my life—Gerda."

"It's your birthday present," I told him.

He caught my hands and exclaimed, "It's the nicest present I ever got or ever will get!"

A few hours after Kurt left, I walked to the cemetery, a quarter-mile or so away. Most of the old graves, with Czech names, were not tended, though some had fresh flowers on them. One corner of the yard had a large number of new graves. After some hunting I came upon Liesel's grave. My knees felt weak, I sat down. Here, near me, was Liesel, who could laugh like silver bells on a sleigh, Liesel, whose dreams I knew, with whom I had played pretend about the future. I could hardly believe that she was there, her supple movements stilled forever.

After a time I went to find Suse's grave. There too I put flowers, whispering her name. The sound was strange in the stillness and again I felt terribly alone. Remembering Ilse buried somewhere under a tree, I knew that I must get away from the dead, away from the past, away from my thoughts. I had a future to face. Would my memories haunt me forever?

I made two decisions as I walked slowly back to the hospital. First, I would find out how well I was. Some of Kurt's words had made me wonder if perhaps I was not aware of something I should know. Second, I would not go home until I could know for sure whether my parents and Arthur would be there.

Along with everyone in the hospital I had added my name to a list to be published in Sosnowitz, in Bielitz, and in all other towns where there had been Jews before the war. After my name was the information that I was looking for Papa, Mama, and Arthur, Abek, his people, and Ilse's family. How long would it be before some news would reach me? Again I must push the days ahead and wait, wait to be certain.

My conference with my doctor was inconclusive. "You are as well as can be expected," he answered. Then he corrected himself: "As well as no one dared to hope for. We will take more X-rays in a couple of days and give you a thorough examination after you are off medication. You say that you would like to occupy your mind and hands. This is a very welcome sign. You may, if you wish, help in the office and lab. I shall show you how to make simple tests, label bottles, distribute medicines. But—you should not work a lot, and you must get as much fresh air and sunshine as possible for your lungs."

"My lungs, doctor?"

"Well, pneumonia and the exposure to TB. The sleeping in the snow did not exactly help."

"I want the truth!" I insisted.

"There is nothing wrong with you as far as I know," he repeated, "but I don't know the whole truth yet myself. If I were you, I would not push my good luck too far."

I let it go at that.

About a week after Kurt had left, another captain from the Military Government came to see me. He came quickly to the point.

"You are leaving for Bavaria tomorrow."

I stared at him.

"You are going to Freising, to Kurt."

A number of questions jumped into my mind, but I only said, "I am not going!"

Exasperated, seeing that he would have to do a lot of explaining, he pulled up a chair. "When Kurt was here last week he came to see me. There has been talk that our division might withdraw from here: we might be replaced or perhaps this zone will belong to the Russians. Kurt made me promise that I would bring you to safety if we should withdraw. We have our orders to leave. I will take you to Bavaria tomorrow."

"How about the other girls?" I asked.

"We have been thinking about that. We are trying to work out an arrangement whereby the girls who are well can, if they wish, go to Bavaria. For those who remain we shall try to maintain the hospital as long as the American occupation is here."

Troubled by this new development, I spoke to a number of girls about the prospect of going to Bavaria. Many were willing to go and I learned that some girls whom I had known in Grünberg were supposed to be in Cham. Cham was in Bavaria and quite close to Volary. The girl who gave me this information said she would join me if I should decide to go there. Her name was Mala Orbach and I had struck up an acquaintance with her as a result of her knowing a boy who was stationed with Kurt. The possibility of finding some of my friends in Cham and of learning about others, perhaps of my family, made my decision easy in the end. I would not go to Kurt, but I would go to Cham and there I would decide what next.

That night I went to bid the Knebels good-by. They were sorry to see me go, and gave me some lovely presents—some underwear and a kerchief—as well as an address of some of

239

their relatives who lived in Bavaria, near the Swiss border. They urged me to try to keep in touch with them.

I spent a sleepless night. In a sense I hated to leave Volary: there were so many pleasant memories here, in spite of the tragic ones.

When I awoke I had an excited feeling of anticipation, of adventure. I also felt buoyant and exhilarated, and deeply touched by the thought that Kurt should care so much about my safety.

When the Military Government captain returned for his answer I informed him that I was going, not to Freising, but to Cham.

That was all right with him.

I sought out my doctor. After giving me a favorable report on my latest X-rays, he handed me my discharge papers from the hospital. With it was an envelope as well.

"What is it?" I asked.

"Your wages," he said.

"My wages?"

"Yes, of course—for working in the lab," he said in a matter-of-fact voice.

I understood and was grateful. I did not have a penny of my own. Later, when I opened the envelope, I found a sum many times over the amount I felt my help had been worth.

I packed the few clothes I had, a prayer book that had been given me, my collection of snapshots, Kurt's letter, a few books, a couple of sheets of stationery, and some pencil stumps. All my worldly goods . . .

For one fleeting moment I wondered what I would do if it turned cold or started to rain—I didn't own a coat or a sweater. But I quickly dismissed the thought: it was the end of July, and the weather was fine. Then I laughed a bit at myself, thinking how I had slept out in the snow not so very long ago.

Chapter 4

Late in the afternoon Mala Orbach and I arrived in Cham by jeep after having driven over bomb-damaged roads. The captain was anxious to get back to Volary—it was not safe to drive after dark—so he left us in the center of town at the headquarters of the Military Government. The American sentry told us where we might find other refugees, but when we went to that address nobody seemed to know about the girls we were seeking. However, they had heard that some girls who had been in a Silesian camp were living on the outskirts of town. Our hopes thus spurred, Mala and I decided to look for them. We were given directions and soon found ourselves in a narrow cobbled street. It was almost dark when we knocked at a modern-looking glass-topped door that seemed rather out of place in such a medieval street. We knocked several times before a woman with curlers in her hair stuck her head through an open window.

"What do you want?" she yelled. We explained our mission.

"Those girls left yesterday!" She closed the window.

"Can we stay here overnight?" I called, but she either did not hear or would not answer us.

We did not know where to go. We were tired; it had been a long, eventful, trying day. It was completely dark now and the town was strange. People were suspicious. Skeletons of bombed-out buildings stood like ghosts against the dark sky. Germany was a haunted country—still hostile in defeat.

We stood alone among the ruins. I longed for the hospital, for a bed to sleep in, for people I knew. Where should we go?

A bell rang the half-hour. That was it: there was a church nearby. We found it easily, its steeple outlined in the moonlight, towering over the beaten city. The heavy wooden church door opened slowly. One light was burning near the altar. We lay down on a bench and used our bundles as pillows.

I woke up feeling cold. The stained-glass windows were lighting with dawn. What a strange twenty-four hours it had been, my first day of real freedom!

I had created a happy world of make-believe around me during the long years of loneliness, a world of beauty and love. It had helped me to survive, this lovely world that was to be mine when the war was over. Now the war was over. . . .

The silence in the church made me realize how alone I still was—in a strange town, where I found refuge in a church at whose altar I did not pray.

"Papa, Mama"—I murmured the words, to hear their sound again—"help me! Help me find my way!"

A ray of sun touched the corner of one of the stained-glass windows.

Kurt—he would understand, and not think my dreams foolish. He would understand the world I created. I would go to him.

We hitchhiked from early morning till afternoon. When Mala and I finally arrived in Freising, near Munich, we went straight to the Military Government building. Just as we started up the broad stone steps, I saw Kurt coming down, hurrying, taking two steps at a time. He embraced us.

"I was just on my way to Cham to get you. The captain told me that he had left you there. Everything is ready. I have a room in Munich for you and Mala and when you are ready to work it will be easier to get a job in Munich than here in Freising." Kurt's jeep halted on the outskirts of Munich near the Perlacher Forest just before nightfall. A few scattered villas bordered its edge and there, set in a lovely garden, was the house in which we were to stay.

An elderly woman opened the door and led us to our room. She informed us that her husband was in the hospital, her only son was probably a prisoner of war since he was with the Wehrmacht, and that the upstairs of the house was already occupied by two women whose home had been destroyed by bombs.

I wanted to talk to Kurt and was glad when Frau Bieber, our landlady, left us alone.

"I must get a job soon," I said. "Do you think I could start looking tomorrow?"

Kurt suggested that I should rest for a while first, but I remained firm and before he left he had promised to take me to the offices of the Civilian Censorship Division, which was hiring people who had been anti-Nazi.

Next afternoon he took us to the offices of the Civilian Censorship Division, where we applied for jobs and were interviewed by a charming and most understanding WAC captain. She said that we would have to take a two-week training course, after which we could start working. The job would pay well and give me the independence I longed for.

Kurt stayed on in Munich that second day and came to see me after dinner. We went walking in the woods behind the house. He was strangely silent and so was I. Then we started to talk about our parents. For the first time since I had known him, he spoke with bitterness of what had happened to them and of his inability to save them. We sat near a pile of broken branches, and he held one in his hands and systematically began to break it. His knuckles were white with the effort, as if he wanted to break something more.

"My brother told me later," he continued, "that after my father had put me on the boat for America he said, 'I have a feeling I shall not see my boy again.'"

I felt my eyes fill with tears. I understood so well what Kurt must feel, remembering Papa's and Mama's reactions when Arthur left. Kurt dropped the branch and took my hand silently. We sat in the dusk in silence. Understanding each other better than if we had spoken a thousand words.

We had started back toward the house without saying a word when several shots echoed through the woods. I stopped, petrified, expecting to hear screams and the ra-ta-ta of more shots, but the forest was silent, no more sound came. My heart beat fast, my temples pounded. I felt tears in my eyes and I started to tremble. Kurt removed his jacket and put it around my shoulders.

"You are dressed much too lightly," he remarked, pretending not to know why I was trembling.

I felt the strength and protection of his arm around me and smiled at him.

Early the next morning I resolved to go back to the forest to get used to being unafraid. It was difficult and I trembled every time the branches rustled. Then I thought I spotted something red beneath the evergreens. Drops of blood! No, no, they were berries. I forced myself to touch them. They were only berries, but I could not make myself eat them.

After my training period, I began working for the Civilian Censorship Division, reading confiscated Nazi mail. I often visited the German Museum, which now housed a multitude of displaced persons. There, too, were the offices of UNRRA, where daily were posted the names of people who had survived and were looking for their kin. I would scan the lists, hoping to find a familiar name. Day after day I would walk away frustrated. Once I met some people from Sosnowitz and they told me that all of Abek's family was gone, and that they had heard that Abek had died. I did not believe them then—I did not want to hear such news—but later it was to be confirmed.

I told Kurt about my visits to the Museum.

"You should not go constantly," he said. "Why do you torture yourself like this?"

I couldn't seem to tell him why.

One Sunday in mid-August I was lying on the grass behind our house, looking up to the cloudless sky. Long, long ago I had known countless such afternoons as this.

Just then Kurt came, shouting, "The war with Japan is over!"

He pulled a bottle from his pocket. "Anisette," he said. "We'll drink to peace."

Ashamed to admit that I had never in my life tasted alcohol, I ran into the house for some glasses. We drank to peace, and drank to peace again.

244

"I am dizzy," I told Kurt, sitting down on the grass.

"So am I," Kurt said.

Somehow, it seemed screamingly funny. I burst into laughter. And then—I was in his arms. With that kiss, I felt as if I could fly through the air with the sheer power of happiness, settle on the clouds, kiss the stars, dance on the moon, and love the whole world.

Several days later Kurt brought me the long-awaited letter from Turkey. I held it for a moment before opening it, exalted and happy in the knowledge that my uncle was alive, that there was at least one member of my family left. When I finally tore it open, I read of my uncle's joy at finding me, of his willingness and eagerness to help me do whatever I wanted. The warm bond of my family's love was about me again. But the information that I had asked for and prayed that he might be able to provide, he couldn't give me. Instead, he asked me about Papa, Mama, Arthur. Now at last I knew that I would never go home again.

A few weeks passed. Then came September 13, a Thursday. As I was coming home from work I saw Kurt. I was surprised, not having expected to see him till Sunday.

"Gerda," he said, after the preliminaries were over, "I am going home."

I managed to say, "I am so glad for you!" and then I felt the tears coming.

"Is this all you have to say to me?" Kurt demanded. "I want you to come to America and be my wife."

He gently took my face in his hands, he looked into my eyes and said, "Don't you understand? I love you. I want to marry you."

I clung to Kurt, speechless with happiness, as words of tenderness poured from his lips.

Later, we discussed practical matters. He had two alternatives. He could stay another year or two in the Occupation Forces and we could be married at once, or he could go home and send for me as soon as the consulates were in operation again. It would be harder on me that way, but I would be out of Germany sooner. Kurt insisted that the decision was to be mine, but I read his hope in his eyes.

"Go home," I whispered.

He nodded. "That way it will be better for our future."

That night in my room I faced my fear of being alone again, my fear of losing Kurt as I had lost everyone else I ever loved. This time there would be a separation—even a long separation—but I knew there would be no loss.

"Kurt!" I called into the night, "Kurt I love you!"

And there, through the night, through the stars, through the sky, through the leaves on the trees, through the magic of life itself, I felt my cry answered. Wherever Kurt was, his thought met mine. I let the joy that rose to my heart take possession of my being. I had reached the summit, as I had dreamed I would in the dark years of slavery, and there, beyond the sphere of human vision, we met and embraced. We would never be alone again.